An Elbit Systems of America Book

Attack the Enemy's Strategy

Lessons from Counterinsurgency Operations

Edited by

**Colonel John Antal, U.S. Army (Retired)
and
PJ Putnam (Fmr. USAF Spec Ops Pilot)**

Published by Historical Explorations, LLC
www.HX-Warfighter.com

© 2009 Historical Explorations, LLC

ISBN: 978-1-934662-18-2

Published in 2009 by Historical Explorations, LLC
www.HXfilms.com

For

Elbit Systems of America
4700 Marine Creek Parkway
PO Box 136969
Fort Worth, Texas 76136-6969

Attack the Enemy's Strategy

Lessons from Counterinsurgency Operations

TABLE OF CONTENTS

Foreword: Brigadier General Steve Roser, USAF

Introduction: General James Mattis, U.S.M.C., Commander, U.S. Joint Forces Command (USJFCOM) and Supreme Allied Commander Transformation for NATO

SYSTEMS OF AMERICA

Elbit Systems of America is a leading provider of high performance products and system solutions focusing on the defense, homeland security, commercial aviation and medical instrumentation markets.

With facilities throughout the United States, Elbit Systems of America is dedicated to supporting those who contribute daily to the safety and security of the United States. Elbit Systems of America, LLC is wholly owned by Elbit Systems Ltd. (NASDAQ: ESLT), a global electronics company engaged in a wide range of programs for innovative defense and commercial applications.

This book is a second book in the Elbit Systems of American Warfighter Series. The Warfighter Series is designed to provide the warfighter with an opportunity to discuss vital issues that pertain to the defense of the United States of America and its Allies. Elbit Systems of America is proud to present the Warfighter Series' warfighters at ESA's expense in appreciation for the dangerous and difficult service our warfighters provide in defense of the Nation.

<u>AUTHORS WANTED!</u>

For more information on the next Warfighter Series and to submit your articles for consideration for publication, contact Colonel John Antal (Ret.), the Warfighter Series' Editor-in-Chief at:

<u>Editor@HX-Warfighter.com</u>

Special thanks to
Malcolm Quon,
soldier and patriot.

Cover Photo: US Army SSG James Warren provides
security from a rooftop during a combined patrol in
the Shula district Baghdad, Iraq, June 18, 2008.
Warren is in 4th Platoon, Bravo Troop, 1st Squadron,
75th Cavalry, 2nd Bde Combat Team, 101st Airborne
Division (US Army photo).

Dedication:

To the *warfighters* – the Soldiers,
Marines, Airmen, and Sailors – who
put themselves in harms' way to
protect and defend the United
States of America.

COUNTERINSURGENCY (COIN) is the comprehensive civilian and military efforts taken to simultaneously defeat and contain insurgency and address its root causes. (JP 3-24).... Counterguerrilla operations, on the other hand, focus on detecting and defeating the armed insurgent or guerrillas, without solving the societies underlying problems. Military efforts alone cannot defeat an insurgency. US COIN operations include supporting a Host Nation's military, paramilitary, political, economic, psychological, and civic actions taken to defeat an insurgency. Ceasing the creation of new insurgents and forcing existing insurgents to end their participation is vital to ending an insurgency. Additionally, COIN operations often include security assistance programs such as foreign military sales programs, the foreign military financing program, and international military training and education programs.... There are five forces, which are shaping the current operational environment – a population explosion, urbanization, globalization, technology and religious fundamentalism. *From Tactics in Counterinsurgency, Final Draft, October 2008, Headquarters, Department of the Army.*

Foreword

By Brigadier General Steve Roser, USAF (Ret.)

Today, there is no more important issue to the warfighter than the topic of irregular warfare and, specifically, counterinsurgency. In Iraq and Afghanistan, the United States military, partnered with coalition forces, is fighting the "long war." The outcome of this struggle will define the future of the Middle East and the rest of the world.

Attack the Enemy's Strategy, Lessons from Counterinsurgency Operations, is the second volume in the Elbit Systems of America Warfighter Series and contains chapters written by some of the foremost warriors, authors and military historians. The purpose of is to provide a forum for warfighters to write, be published and discuss today's important warfighting issues. Elbit Systems of America is proud to sponsor this effort and looks forward to publishing future volumes in years to come.

This book is focused at the tactical level of war where young warriors led by non-commissioned officers, lieutenants, captains, majors, and colonels face the fire each day. The authors of the chapters that follow come from a wide range of backgrounds and levels of experience. All are experts in their own right on the subjects they present. All care deeply that our warfighters "get it right."

I want to thank the Warfighter Series' Editor-in-Chief, Colonel John Antal, US Army (Ret.), and the authors for contributing to this important effort. I specifically wish to thank General James Mattis, United States Marine Corps, for graciously writing the introduction to this book.

Sincerely,

Steve Roser
Brig. Gen., USAF (Ret.)
Elbit Systems of America

INTRODUCTION

Department of Defense Commander
U.S. Joint Forces Command

To our Warriors:

Confronted by America's demonstrated conventional warfighting superiority, many of our enemies have chosen an irregular form of warfare, insurgent war, to pursue their ends. This form of warfare is not new and reflects the fundamental nature of war, well chronicled in history that recognizes a thinking enemy will adapt the character of his warfighting approach in a manner that avoids his adversary's strengths.

We will not win these "wars among the people" by virtue of the nobility of our cause, the number of tanks in our arsenal, or the wealth of our nation. Rather we will require military leaders at every level whose study and appreciation of war will prevail in an environment that rewards initiative over dogma and doctrine.

Leaders in this sort of war will encompass the usual high ranking officer and NCOs, but emphatically must include our junior NCOs and officers. The latter carry a heavy burden on the decentralized counter insurgency battlefield because they lead at the points of greatest danger and friction where tactical actions can have strategic impacts.

This sort of war is hardly a mystery. In our own American history, we have fought as insurgents and against insurgents. We fought well when there was common understanding of what matters and how best to win. And make no mistake about it. In today's battle it is our military's mission to achieve the conditions to win. Figuring out how to win is your challenge, and begins with study that each of us must undertake individually. That is what this anthology is designed to promote.

Counterinsurgency is a type of war that defies template. While there are principles, they must be adapted to the specific circumstances by thinking leaders who can identify the enemy's logic. Self-analysis is always difficult, but in this work you will find authors who are committed to honest assessment. We must further the debate over how best to break an enemy who fights in a manner that negates some of our traditional strengths. But the enemy's efforts also reveal vulnerabilities to those warriors who can grasp them – vulnerabilities that will doom our enemies if we can clearly, relate to historical lessons learned, and act forcefully, ethically, and swiftly against them. This anthology will open eyes, incite arguments, and spark action. This is all to the good, but the reader will also find their appreciation of war's complexity enhanced – and in that personal growth will be one more nail in the coffins of our enemies, and an extension of this experiment in freedom that we call America to pass on to the next generation.

Counterinsurgent leaders in our Army, Navy, Air Force, Coast guard, and Marine Corps are made, not born. We need tough hombres who can think on their feet. We need morally strong leaders who speak up with sound ideas and avoid running the ethical sidelines. We need leaders whose love of their subordinates will provide their charges an emotional shock absorber in the morally bruising combat environment. And we leaders at all levels who will not falter in tough circumstances, but who will constantly reinforce their troop's confidence and fighting faith. Leaders such as these must be at the top of their game physically, morally, and intellectually. This anthology will help guide you there, so when the tests come your way, you will break the enemy, take care of your troops and protect the innocent.

I wish you good reading and good hunting.

Semper Fi,

JAMES N. MATTIS
General, U.S. Marines

US Marines of 1st Platoon, 1st Squad, Foxtrot Company, 2nd Battalion, 7th Marine Regiment patrol a suspected enemy passageway in Now Zad, Afghanistan, Oct. 5, 2008. The Marines conducted the patrol to clear improvised explosive devices (USMC photo).

CHAPTER 1

THE IMPOSSIBLE QUEST:
Searching For a
Counterinsurgency Formula

By Ralph Peters

The problems with the U.S. Army's current manual for coping with insurgents, terrorists, ethnic gangsters, militias and all the others who refuse to "fight fair" begins with the title: It should be plural, COUNTERINSURGENCIES and not COUNTER-INSURGENCY. Unwittingly, the singular noun reveals our psychological weakness: Despite protestations to the contrary within the manual, its drafters, as well as countless politicos, diplomats and other soldiers, want a universally applicable checklist to apply when our forces are sent (usually against their protestations) to fight the new, global Indians given to violent raids on civilization and its encroaching wagon trains.

As so often happens in human affairs, we say the right things ("All insurgencies are different!") but act contrary to our own admonitions. We're further deceived by the fact that insurgencies do display commonalities—although it's the variations that get you into trouble—and by the Western intellectual's determination to resist the mounting, bleeding evidence that the world has changed and refuses to match our comfortable template.

On the first count, *insurgencies involve armed human beings attacking the personnel, facilities and symbols of a government or source of authority against which at least part of the population has a complaint.* But that's about where the dependable similarities end (increasingly, we also see new, non-violent forms of insurgency emerging, such as cyber-resistance, but this essay focuses on the violent actors). Some insurgencies garner broad support, based upon legitimate grievances. Others are eccentric and tout complaints Westerners regard as irrational or impossible of fulfillment. Insurgencies differ based upon

1

local traditions, the psychological impact of religion and myth, the education level of the population, the level of economic development, the degree of urbanization, the impact of resource competition, ethnic rivalries, ideologies and on down a list with hundreds of entries. Many factors can influence a single insurgency in varying proportions and at different stages, with one set of factors more powerful among urban classes and another driving tribal rebellion in the same country, or a subordinate goal becoming the primary goal of an insurrection.

U.S. Army Soldiers attached to the 4th Battalion, 31st Infantry Regiment search for three missing soldiers in the streets of Yusifiyah, Iraq, May 14, 2007 (USAF photo).

Not only must an intervening power acutely judge the many objective and subjective factors in play, but it must also deal with the tyranny of the calendar: The best approach to a given insurgency depends not only on the general environment of the conflict, but on the point at which intervention occurs. If a threat is identified and addressed in its early stages, limited force and few resources may be required; however, if intervention is delayed (as it usually is for the military forces of democratic states), a greater use of violence and a far-greater resource commitment is generally required. At times, the human, ethical, informational and financial costs of confronting an insurgency simply may not be worth paying. In other cases, intervention may be ordered by decision-makers for political, humanitarian or simply mistaken reasons—despite the improbability of success. Sometimes, insurgencies may go ignored because we find them peripheral or even useful.

Compounding the difficulties inherent in counterinsurgency warfare (or operations short of war) is the contemporary lack of resolve among Western political leaders. The iron rule of *every* form of warfare is that those who are unwilling to pay the butcher's bill up front will pay it with compound interest in the end. Or, to use another colloquial analogy, it's never wise to delay the trip to the dentist, since the cavity only gets worse. U.S. hesitation to act decisively in Iraq in the summer and autumn of 2003 is a textbook case of the attempt to postpone pain (in the form of bloodshed and uncomfortable headlines) resulting in a profound deterioration of an initially promising situation. To cite only one example from the period, in the summer of 2003, when he stood behind the assassination of leading clerics well-disposed toward the Coalition, U.S. authorities refused to eliminate Moqtada al-Sadr, a young demagogue with weak religious credentials and a limited following: In 2003, al Sadr had a gang, but a year later he had a militia numbering in the tens of thousands. Unwilling to take a limited amount of pain up front in the form of a few days or a week of localized rioting, the U.S. authorities "made" Moqtada al-Sadr, allowing him to portray himself as a patriot resisting foreign aggression and defending both his faith and the impoverished. Predictably, it wasn't long before al-Sadr's Mehdi Army was fighting pitched battles with U.S. forces, and we got far higher casualties on both sides, more destruction and alienation, and far worse headlines than would have been the case had we acted decisively and promptly. Allowing al-Sadr to create himself as a champion of oppressed Shi'a Muslims was a phenomenally stupid decision on the U.S. part, and it is the sort likely to be repeated in future conflicts: We do not lack capability, but want the resolve to do what must be done.

3

U.S. Army Soldiers from 2nd Battalion, 503rd Infantry Regiment, 173rd Airborne Brigade Combat Team, Afghan National Army soldiers, and members of the Afghan Border Patrol prepare to conduct training on how to enter and exit a CH-47 helicopter in preparation for operations in Afghanistan in early 2008 (US Army photo).

Part of this is squeamishness in the face of the global media, but much is the result of the degeneration of our understanding of the realities of all forms of warfare, thanks to a witch's brew of think-tank nonsense (usually concocted by those who never served in uniform), defense contractor promises that technology will solve all of our battlefield problems--if we just keep buying--and the hidden penalty of ending the draft (ending conscription was great for our military, but terrible for our country, since it has resulted in a population in which ever fewer citizens or legislators have a sense of military realities). Our leaders persuaded themselves that war could be waged on the cheap, in terms of blood, numbers, time and commitment—the lie that even now will not go away.

The "New" Insurgencies

If all of this were not sufficiently complicated, the second factor mentioned above, our unwillingness to see the changed world as it is, rather than as we wish it to be, devastates our efforts to defeat contemporary insurgencies.

Fatally, the counterinsurgency field manual cherry-picked the historical examples it cites in order to support pre-determined arguments (counterinsurgency may sometimes seem like eating soup with a knife, but equally often it resembles eating manure with a pitchfork—and I'm putting it politely). But the world refuses to be simplified and restricted to fit our favored models. In the manual, every major discussion and nearly every brief mention of an insurgency is drawn from the 20th century—and even then the case studies are carefully chosen. The authors gave us familiar, reassuring examples as their favorites—Malaya in the 1950s, the more-promising U.S. efforts in Vietnam, and so forth. There is, however, no acknowledgment of how bloody Malaya actually was, nor any mention of an even more-successful British counterinsurgency effort in the same decade, the suppression of Mau Mau. Why? Because Malaya fit the drafters' case, but Kenya didn't. After realizing it wasn't a police matter, the British broke Mau Mau through the use of concentrations camps (almost 200,000 inmates), kangaroo courts (which hanged almost 2,000 blacks), and a relentless military pursuit that tracked Mau Mau bands into the mountains and killed their members until the last survivors surrendered. It was as persuasive a counterinsurgency success as one could ask—perhaps the most complete defeat of insurgents in the 20th century--but it revealed counterinsurgency's dark side, wasn't politically correct, and, thus, was inadmissible. But when reality is inadmissible in military circles, we're headed for trouble.

Similarly, the French army *won* the Battle of Algiers (France left Algeria because of a loss of political will, not because it was driven out). But the methods, including large numbers of extra-legal arrests, widespread torture and summary executions, are not acceptable even for our analytical discussions. In other words, we can't talk about what works, if what works in nasty. Yet, we should be investigating *why* such methods worked when others didn't, in order to help us develop less vicious alternatives to reach the same end. Actions may be forbidden—with good reason--but nothing should be taboo when it comes to attempting to *understand* a phenomenon such as insurgencies.

None of this should be taken as a recommendation that the U.S. adopt torture or kangaroo courts as routine counterinsurgency tools. The point is that we must be willing to examine historical examples honestly and inclusively, to analyze and discuss even the most repugnant case studies. Otherwise, we're just playing pretend.

The manual's selective examples are even more troubling in the sense that none of them—not one—is relevant to the insurgencies we increasingly face at the opening of the 21st-century. Each cherished example cited is an *ideological* insurgency. Yet, today we face no ideological opponents in Iraq or Afghanistan, but insurgents motivated by religion and/or a quest for ethnic supremacy. Such insurgencies are as different from ideological rebellions or ideological terrorism as cancer is from influenza. The difference can be illustrated simply enough: In Malaya, no villager was born a Maoist or Marxist, but was persuaded to become one. Likewise, he could be "un-persuaded," convinced, one way or another, that Mao wasn't going to do right by him in the end—or even keep him alive. By contrast, no Arab can become a Persian and no Kurd can become an Arab. And you are extremely unlikely to persuade anyone to abandon his or her religion.

We live at a unique confluence of historical currents, with the brief 200-year Age of Ideology, of Marxism, Maoism, Nazism, Fascism and all the other isms, finally dead (except in Latin America and a few other backwaters). Humanity is returning, at head-over-heels speed, to its default identities of ethnicity and religion, blood and belief. Given the powerful, often painful—even terrifying--dislocations of globalization, human beings on every continent increasingly ask the fundamental question, "Who am I?" And, increasingly, the answer isn't "I'm a Belgian," or "I'm a Marxist," but "I am a Serb," or "I am a Shi'a." This matters enormously. And this return to the basic-integer motivations for collective violence is aggravated by the repair-the-wounds challenges of the post-colonial era, in which humankind must cope with the fatal imperial legacy of dysfunctional borders, of frontiers that either trigger or exacerbate brutal conflicts (bad borders and "phony" states have been factors in every single conflict in which U.S. forces have been involved since the collapse of the Soviet empire).

This unwillingness on the part of military intellectuals to accept that the terms of conflict are now wildly different reflects the prejudices of society at large—especially the refusal of our educated elites to accept that, contrary to the lyrics of the pop songs of their youth, the world is *not* a nice place farther down the geopolitical food chain; human impulses do not run toward a global Age of Aquarius; and, worse, humans are skilled and willing killers. (One might easily make the case that warfare is what human collectives do best.)

The Real Lessons of History

If we lift the restrictions on acceptable-for-analysis examples from the 3,000-year-plus history of insurgencies, we find that (1) insurgencies overwhelmingly have been sparked and fueled by religious or ethnic rivalries—or both simultaneously; (2) insurgencies overwhelmingly have failed when confronted by a determined, robust state or other authority; and (3) insurgencies of blood and belief almost always had to be put down with extensive, exemplary bloodshed. This is not a comforting lesson, but its ugliness does not mean we can simply disregard the legacy of three millennia. At present, we are more concerned with good geopolitical manners than with what works.

Not only are we unwilling to speak of "killing" (I made myself unwelcome at West Point by using that word), but we adamantly refuse to take religion seriously as a strategic factor or inspiration to violence. For thousands of years men have slain others or willingly gone to their deaths for their gods, but we believe we can wish it all away—because discussing religion might offend someone or, worse, reveal truths we are unprepared to accept. Our Islamist enemies tell us openly what they believe and what they are willing—even anxious—to die for, yet their open protestations do not fit our mental framework, so we

7

dismiss their deepest beliefs as nonsense or irrelevant or feigned. In Washington, D.C., I've been told countless times that the violence in the Middle East has nothing to do with religion, that faith's just a con that terrorist leaders exploit, that everything's just about specific grievances. Yet, no one can explain the complete absence of Western, atheist suicide bombers. After all, Muslims in backcountry Yemen aren't the only human beings with grievances.

First Lt. Blake Faller, with Battery B, 1st Battalion, 9th Field Artillery, 2nd Brigade Combat Team, 3rd Infantry Division, assesses the eight-foot rocket that was dug up with a weapons cache in Madyriah Iraq on Nov. 30, 2007. The rocket was of unknown origin (US Army photo).

Certainly, many factors figure into the violence we face in today's world. But we're arguing that the little stuff is the big stuff and that the big stuff (religion, ethnic hatred) isn't really there at all. The notion that we in the West are rational creatures is nonsense. We believe in more fairy tales than does al Qaeda, with its fantasies of a global caliphate. Human beings believe what they want to believe—or what they need to believe. We may be richer, more powerful and far better-educated in the academic sense than the average tribesman in the Afghan mountains, but I'm not convinced we have a better grip on why men kill each other (or, for that matter, how men feel about killing each other).

Much of the confusion stems from the fact—to which the West is blind—that religion isn't just about an individual's belief.   Religion shapes the social, moral, perceptual and practical environment. Faith is the most-important atmospheric factor at work in human collectives (even the behavior of West Europeans, who have turned from religion, continues to be shaped by a thousand years and more of religious heritage—not least, their taste for self-righteousness). We're baffled by case studies of suicide bombers who "weren't at all religious" in their day-to-day lives, but forget our own Judeo-Christian tradition of lightning-flash conversion (on that road to Damascus).   We cannot fathom the claim of a suicide-bomber's mother that she's proud of her son's horrific deed and happy in his sacrifice. But her world is not ours. Shaped by profoundly different faiths, different societies honor different forms of sacrifice (although the West, too, has had its violent saints and martyrs in the past).

Even Washington "experts" and bureaucrats who go to church or synagogue each week have been educated to a secular world-view. Americans in the hinterlands may still experience the ecstasies and intensities of faith, but religion among our governing elite is polite, superficial and tepid. Raw faith makes Washington nervous. And no one who has failed to experience at least a glimpse of the transformative, captivating power of…call it revelation, or grace, or what you will…can begin to grasp the enthusiasm of the suicide bomber on the way not just to a crowded marketplace, but to paradise.

Turning Gold into Lead

Perhaps the first step in retooling our minds and our military for effective counterinsurgency warfare is to humble ourselves. We're just not as smart as we think we are, and it's high time we faced it. If you examine the historical records, you will find that astrologers in Prague at the beginning of the 17th-century did a better job of predicting the future than did late-20th-century analysts and theorists in Washington. While I don't recommend resorting to the zodiac for foreign-policy advice, it should tell us something about our own post-modern superstitions ("Everyone wants peace" may be the worst) that we've failed so miserably to recognize a future that was perfectly willing to show us its bared backside. I can attest from first-hand experience that our enemies weren't trying to hide their intentions—they were shouting them. We just refused to believe them. We thought they were nuts, when, in fact, they were deadly.

I've discussed the faith factor at length here both because it's critical and because it's a perfect example of our intellectual evasiveness—indeed, of our intellectual cowardice. If we want to defeat 21st-century insurgents, we have to face 21st-century reality. We must accept the world's complexity and stop trying to simplify it, to boil it all down to a checklist. As we often hear (but seldom see), defeating insurgencies demands a great deal of cultural and historical understanding—not to make the enemy feel good, but to make it easier to defeat him. We must make the case that this infernally complex form of warfare rarely yields quick results and doesn't yield clear manifestations of victory along the way. Counterinsurgency successes may only be fully clear twenty or even fifty years after the event. At times, success will elude us. At other times, our efforts will be to buy time for developments elsewhere to come to fruition (as our engagement in Vietnam gave Thailand, Malaysia, Singapore and Indonesia the space to develop beyond any vulnerability to Communism. Some apparent wins will turn out to be defeats, and vice versa. Results will rarely be clean.

In the Middle Ages, philosophers and alchemists (often one and the same) wasted centuries of effort trying to find the "hidden" formula to turn lead or other base materials into gold. We, too, long for a miraculous formula, that seductive check-list, that will make counterinsurgency warfare easier. But it just doesn't exist. Every situation will be unique in surprising ways—all we can hope to do is to minimize our surprise through realistic assessments and intellectual honesty. And when we try to do things on the cheap, we risk turning gold into lead. The correct question is never "How little can we get away with doing?" but "How much might it really take?" A light "footprint" on the ground is fine, if that's what's appropriate to a given situation. But we cannot insist that a light footprint is always going to be the answer. Some counterinsurgency campaigns may be largely a matter of aid and friendly persuasion—but others may require a great deal of killing. Security for the population is generally a base-line requirement, but security can mean different things in different circumstances: At times it will be warding off the gunmen, at other times making sure the rice arrives on time—or even protecting people from their own corrupt government. There simply is no one-size-fits-all approach.

Fights We Don't Want, but Can't Avoid

In summation, there are no perfect or easy answers as to how to do counterinsurgency operations. *Faux* Zen mantras and sound-bites certainly don't help, but only obscure the complexity. At times, a handful of Special Forces A-teams may be able to help a client-state stop an insurgency when it's still in its formative stages. Other cases may require full-blown military engagement and an occupation (and, contrary to the hopes of our military, we aren't going to be done with occupations forever after we leave Baghdad). At times, we may just need to strike key targets to persuade insurgents not to cross certain lines. And we may also find ourselves on the side of the insurgents in more instances than one.

Culture, languages, faith, the physical environment, the level of corruption, popular expectations, ethnic diversity, historical legacies, the availability of armaments, societal resilience, the availability of state resources, traditions of governance, our own reasons for becoming involved—all these factors and still others may differ from one counterinsurgency effort to another. No matter how well we prepare, some developments will always surprise us. Goals may even change in the course of our engagement (as they have in Iraq). Allies and enemies may jump sides (again, as in Iraq). In the end, the best we can do is to train hard, study history honestly, formulate flexible, non-prescriptive doctrine—and keep our minds and eyes open. We will never quite know what we're getting into, and the leader who thinks he knows all he needs to know is going to fail.

We *can* get counterinsurgency operations right. We've succeeded many times in the past, from the Great Plains to the Chiricahua Mountains, and from Central America to the Philippines. Sometimes we managed to end confrontations with treaties, sometimes it took Gatling Guns. But the crucial difference between then and now is that, in the past, we were determined to win, whatever it took. Strength of will is the most important quality in counterinsurgency operations, as in all other forms of warfare. The last man standing wins. ▪

CHAPTER 2

WAR AGAINST A VAPOR

By Bevin Alexander

Between the years 1863 and 1937, four military leaders created modern guerrilla warfare. They were the Confederate partisan raider John Singleton Mosby, the Boer General Christiaan de Wet, the English officer T.E. Lawrence of Arabia, and the Chinese Communist leader Mao Zedong.

When applied correctly, guerrilla warfare can overcome the most powerful conventional armies. It has done so time after time in the past, and is doing so today. Guerrilla warfare has become the *standard* or *dominant* type of combat. Conventional or orthodox warfare has virtually ceased to exist.

Guerrilla or partisan warfare goes back far beyond recorded history. There is solid evidence that raids, ambushes, and surprise attacks on settlements constituted a major component of tribal warfare back into the Stone Age. The great Chinese strategist Sun Tzu summarized guerrilla doctrine around 400 B.C. in the single most profound statement ever written about warfare: "The way to avoid what is strong is to strike what is weak." When the enemy prepares to defend in many places, Sun Tzu wrote, "those I have to fight in any one place will be few." As water seeks the easiest path to the sea, so armies should avoid obstacles and seek avenues of least resistance.

The four pioneers who brought guerrilla war up to modern times followed Sun Tzu's injunctions faithfully, although it is doubtful if any except Mao had ever heard of the Chinese sage. Their methods were also virtually identical to each other's, despite the fact that each operated in different periods, in different environments, in different parts of world, and under different military circumstances.

The deception that Mao Zedong used to draw an enemy into a trap and destroy him was not limited to the tortuous Wuyi Mountains of southeastern China where he carried it out in the early 1930s, but can be applied in any cul-de-sac that an enemy force could be induced to walk into. The techniques that Christiaan De Wet worked out to surround an isolated enemy unit and force its surrender on the South African veldt could just as well be used to force the surrender of an enemy unit caught in a clearing in a Southeast Asia jungle, or on an empty Middle Eastern plain. These similarities and continuities show that the methods these four men developed were not limited to their own times and their own wars, but can be used everywhere.

Afghan commandos conduct a cordon and search of a compound during operation Commando Fury in Tagab Valley, Nov. 13, 2007. The commandos are assigned to Afghanistan's elite fighting force unit, the 3rd Company, 1st Commando Kandak.

Despite its success, guerrilla warfare has been extremely slow to gain widespread recognition. A major acknowledgment took place on October 10, 2007, when Secretary of Defense Robert M. Gates told the Association of the United States Army that guerrilla or unconventional wars like those being fought in Iraq and Afghanistan "will remain the mainstay of the contemporary battlefield for some time." The defense secretary warned the Army not to retreat into "the more familiar task" of preparing for conventional combat, as it did after the Vietnam War.

Secretary Gates was commenting on the fact that, although the U.S. Army in 2008 was placing great emphasis on the battalion (800 to 1,000 men) as its primary "maneuver force," the military was still largely structured around large combat formations like divisions (15,000 men) or brigades (3,000 to 5,000 men), operating with rigid command hierarchies, and fielding heavily armored vehicles, tanks, massive field artillery, rockets, attack helicopters, and bombers.

Guerrilla forces are polar opposites. They have flexible organizations, flexible command hierarchies, and most outfits number in the dozens of men; they move stealthily, usually at night, by private auto or on foot; and their weapons are largely those that can be held in the hand, or they are explosives that can be carried in cars or hidden as "improvised explosive devices" (IEDs) alongside roads.

They don't fit into the U.S. Army's orthodox combat doctrine "to find, fix, fight, and finish the enemy." This doctrine didn't work in the Vietnam War, and it's not working today. Powerful American elements might "find" a guerrilla force, but they can seldom "fix" it and even more seldom can they "fight" and "finish" it. Guerrillas, when they encounter a superior force, retreat or fade into the environment. Guerrillas do not engage in stand-up fights. Their strength lies at the other extreme: they attack targets that are either weakly defended or not defended at all. Once they have hit, they disappear. They hold no territory. As Mao Zedong wrote, "The tactics of defense have no place in guerrilla warfare."

Guerrillas can strike fast and hard with small forces against vulnerable enemy targets, and then get away. In contrast, conventional armies are locked into defense of their lines of communication and supply, bases, airfields, ports, garrisons, outposts, and occupied cities. If an orthodox army's supply line is cut, its means of subsistence are lost. The traditional army will go to any lengths to protect its supplies and depots. This forces armies to disperse and gives guerrillas innumerable targets at which they can strike. It is not necessary actually to destroy these targets. Merely the threat of attack keeps the enemy army divided and largely inactive.

Guerrillas thus have the initiative. They can select when, where, and how to attack. The side that holds the initiative has liberty of action, and can dictate events.

Standard, conventional military organizations are unsuited to challenge this sort of enemy, and conventional training likewise is unsatisfactory. U.S. Army Special Forces troops patrol northern Iraq, alongside nearby Albanian soldiers (US Army photo March 4, 2005).

Standard, conventional military organizations are unsuited to challenge this sort of enemy, and conventional training likewise is unsatisfactory. Orthodox training is designed to teach troops to fight an enemy with similar weapons and similar stand-up fighting practices. Accordingly, the hunt for al Qaeda and the Taliban in Afghanistan fell largely to Army, Navy, and Air Force Special Operations units organized around small cooperating teams that function on the rule of fast approaches and equally fast retreats. These are the methods used by guerrillas. Indeed, Special Ops forces are modeled on guerrilla formations, not traditional military structures. Ordinary military units, whether Marine or Army, are unsuited for dealing with guerrillas. They can hold a position, but they are tied by their heavy equipment and motorized vehicles to roads and to large supply depots in their rear. By comparison with both Special Ops forces and guerrillas, they are immobile, inflexible, and ineffective.

Even the most efficient Special Operations forces cannot prevail over guerrillas over time, however. At best they can slow the gains of guerrillas, or divert their force into political channels. As Secretary Gates said in his speech, success will be less a matter of imposing one's will and more a function of shaping behavior of friends, adversaries, and most importantly, the people in between.

Guerrillas, *when they have strong leadership, are deployed in their own country, and have the support of many of their own people,* are superior to invading armies, and they can stand against oppressive native forces. Any military force that invades another country, however weak this country may be, can be overcome, and any great internal movement can succeed. This was proved in China in the civil war 1928-49, in the Vietnam wars 1945-75, in Afghanistan against the Soviet Union in the 1980s, in Somalia in 1993, and is being proved in Iraq and Afghanistan today.

Guerrilla warfare goes back to the Stone Age, but the modern system began to form in 1863-65 during the American Civil War under the inspiration of a brilliant Confederate officer, John Singleton Mosby, who operated in northern Virginia behind Union lines. The system reached a theoretical culmination in 1937 when the Chinese Communist leader Mao Zedong published a small book, *Guerrilla Warfare* that incorporated most of the received wisdom about this kind of war.

Although Mao cited Sun Tzu for his inspiration, his book actually dealt largely with his own experiences over ten years in China. And, though he made no reference to the work of the three pioneers who had gone before him, what Mao taught was wholly consistent with what they had practiced. For example, Mao's method of striking at isolated outposts and forts was identical to what John Singleton Mosby had shown in the American Civil War. The advice Mao gave for countries attacked by stronger powers—to abandon conventional warfare and adopt guerrilla warfare—was arrived at by the two Boer republics of the Transvaal and the Orange Free State in 1900. Mao's concentration on recruiting untrained, unlettered Chinese peasants for his army, and then giving them almost complete information as to their tactical objective and how they were to gain it, was preceded by Lawrence of Arabia with equally untrained, unlettered Bedouin tribesmen in 1917-18.

The teachings of Mosby, De Wet, Lawrence, and Mao form a body of knowledge that defines a method of war that can be carried out successfully by any weak nation or movement. Mao's short, easily read book especially became the inspiration for insurgent groups in colonies of European imperial powers after World War II. In all of the colonial revolts, the local patriots were greatly inferior to the colonial armies, and—to challenge them—they all turned to guerrilla warfare.

But the vast rise in this form of warfare was largely ignored by orthodox military leaders in the West and in the Soviet Union. Not until the Communists used Mao's theories to drive the United States out of Vietnam between 1965 and 1975 did military thinkers begin to recognize that guerrilla warfare can be superior to conventional methods. Even so, the top military leadership turned the U.S. military back to conventional warfare after Vietnam, as Secretary Gates noted in his speech. This failure of the military leadership to accept changing reality led to the massive inability of the U.S. military to respond adequately after 9/11.

Although the experience of Vietnam was still fresh, military leaders did not see that the invasion of Afghanistan and Iraq would set off guerrilla wars. In Afghanistan our military and political leaders expected to eliminate the Taliban and al Qaeda, install a friendly government in Kabul, and bring about a lasting peace. In Iraq, they thought that the public would welcome the invaders who toppled the dictator Saddam Hussein, that the politically dominant Sunnis would accept their reduced station, that a government incorporating all disparate elements would be set up in Baghdad, that these elements would work out their differences with democratic give and take, and that peace would prevail. The military did not expect a Taliban and al Qaeda revival in Afghanistan, or an insurgency by the Sunnis in Iraq, along with al Qaeda elements that came in to exploit the chaos.

Yet the Vietnam War had laid down an axiom—where a superior military force invades a resisting country, the hostile population will respond with a guerrilla uprising. It's the only means the people have to resist, and it's effective.

Since most military training and organization are still aimed at fighting a conventional enemy, not the guerrilla forces that troops will actually confront, massive restructuring of the military is needed. The model for change will most likely be Special Ops forces. These forces represent only a small fraction of military personnel, and Special Ops requires intensive training and high skills. The question must therefore arise as to whether the U.S. military needs to be bigger or whether it needs to be better trained, more structured to fight the enemy it will in fact face, and composed of more capable, more intelligent persons.

All these changes will require public understanding, which is gravely lacking. Not many members of the public realize that powerful countries will almost certainly fail when they occupy hostile weaker countries. Consequently, threats by powerful states to occupy weaker states will increasingly be seen as empty. This gives weaker states far more freedom than in the past. Powerful states will still be able to strike from a distance by air at uncooperative weaker states, however (this is the final U.S. option to keep Iran from getting the A-bomb, for example). But "over-the-horizon" belligerence may not always be effective, and may engender more hate than acquiescence. The world has scarcely touched on the implications of these new realities.

Unconventional forces are the only enemy we are likely to encounter in the foreseeable future, and we must restructure our military to reflect this fact.

The progression to the new form of modern war was foreshadowed by the thoughts and actions of Mosby, De Wet, Lawrence, and Mao. These four men—responding to the challenges they faced in their own times—saw how to use the power of guerrillas to win. In doing this, they became the primary intellectual forces who created modern partisan warfare. What they thought is being taught in every class on guerrilla warfare today.

John Singleton Mosby (December 6, 1833 – May 30, 1916) also known as the "Gray Ghost of the Confederacy," was a regular Confederate cavalry battalion commander in the American Civil War (NARA photo).

John Singleton Mosby, then a Captain serving under the Confederate cavalry commander J.E.B. Stuart, described how he read the bombastic order from Union general John Pope to his troops in July 1862: "I hear constantly of taking strong positions and holding them, of lines of retreat and bases of supplies. Let us dismiss such ideas....Let us study the probable lines of retreat of our opponents and leave our own to take care of themselves. Let us look before us and not behind."

Mosby responded: "When I read what Pope said about looking only to his front and letting his rear take care of itself, I saw that the opportunity for which I had longed had come. He had opened a promising field for partisan warfare and had invited, or rather dared, anybody to take advantage of it. So I asked Stuart for a dozen men to make the harvest where the laborers were few, and do for Pope what he would not do for himself, take care of his rear and communications for him."

This was a great intellectual breakthrough. Mosby saw in a flash that John Pope's call for his troops to forget their rear offered the Confederates a way to avoid Union strength—the powerful Federal main army—and to strike at its weaknesses—its rear bases, supply depots, lines of communication, and occupied towns.

Mosby used only a few partisans in his surprise strikes on Union bases, railroads, isolated units, and other vulnerable or unprotected Union facilities. He struck so fast and so unexpectedly that he gained the name of the Gray Ghost. In case of danger, his partisan soldiers could disappear into the friendly civilian population. Mosby's guerrilla methods forced many thousands of Union troops to guard bases, railroads, and supply depots, and to engage in the many fruitless "search-and-destroy" missions that the Union army undertook over two years.

All of these Union soldiers were unavailable to fight in the colossal battles against the Confederate Army of Northern Virginia under Robert E. Lee. Mosby's efforts were a minor part of the Confederate effort because Lee was interested only in stand-up battles between his conventional army and the conventional Union army. Although Mosby's force was small and received only modest support, it nevertheless contributed greatly to the defense of the South during the period of heavy battle from early 1863 to war's end more than two years later.

The lessons of the Gray Ghost were carried forward after the Civil War by Mosby's memoirs and by numerous analyses by former Union and Confederate officers about the operations in northern Virginia.

When the British invaded the two small Boer or Dutch republics of Transvaal and the Orange Free State in South Africa in 1899, the Boers attempted at first to challenge the heavily armed British army with conventional or stand-up warfare. They failed miserably, since the Boers were not trained in modern methods and had only a few modern weapons. As a result, they lost most of their army, and suffered the occupation of both of their republics by British troops by 1900.

Instead of surrendering, the Boer commander Christiaan de Wet, followed by other Dutch leaders, discovered that numerous small-to-moderate-sized British forces were operating alone and isolated out in the open terrain of the South African veldt, and that they could be surrounded by quickly assembled superior Boer forces and obliged to surrender. After several of these ambushes, the Boer commanders, under the inspiration of De Wet, restructured resistance to be entirely guerrilla. The Boer generals employed as the basic fighting element their standard unit the "commando", made up of all men in a voting district, thus consisting largely of neighbors and friends. These Dutch commandos, totaling never more than 15,000 men, struck, like Mosby had done 35 years before, at isolated enemy bases, isolated units, and the railway lines bringing up supplies. They exploited natural Boer advantages—dedicated leaders, almost universal horsemanship of the Boer population, wide knowledge of the countryside, and strong support from the Boer population.

Their unexpected surprise strikes, then quick disappearances into the environment, paralyzed the British army of a quarter of a million men, and led the British to approve a face-saving treaty in 1902 that required the Boers to recognize the British sovereign, but gave the Boers everything they wanted—effective independence, recognition of their Dutch language, and continued control of the black population (a condition that lasted until 1994).

A decade and a half later, T.E. Lawrence, a British officer who had graduated with a history degree from Oxford in 1910 and who spoke Arabic, was assigned to induce the Arabs to help the British in their war against the Turks in World War I. The Arabs had revolted against Turkish overlordship in 1916. The British command in Cairo wanted the Bedouin tribes that formed the heart of the revolt to put together conventional military units with conventional weapons such as cannons, and to attack the Turkish garrison of 25,000 men at the Islamic holy city of Medina in the Hejaz region along the Red Sea.

T.E. Lawrence (Lawrence of Arabia), 1888-1935. Lawrence described the Bedouin guerillas as "a vapor, blowing where he listed," while conventional armies were "like plants, immobile, firm-rooted, nourished through long stems to the head."

23

Lawrence drew on his knowledge of the Bedouins, how their tribes were organized, and what were their weaknesses and their strengths. He also analyzed the Turkish situation. Lawrence concluded that the Turks would remain in Medina until the last because their possession of this holy city gave credibility to their claim of leadership of Islam, and their claim of supremacy over the Arabs.

Lawrence realized that the Bedouin tribal structure made it impossible for the tribesmen to accept military discipline. Even in the unlikely event that the British supplied them with modern weapons, they lacked the military leaders who could direct a conventional campaign against the well-armed Turks at Medina.

If the Arabs had come "like an army with banners," Lawrence wrote, the Turks would have defended Arabia by a trench line. "But suppose," he went on "we were an influence, an idea, a thing intangible, invulnerable, without front or back, drifting about like a gas?" In comparison with the Bedouin who "might be a vapor, blowing where he listed," conventional armies, Lawrence wrote, are "like plants, immobile, firm-rooted, nourished through long stems to the head."

Lawrence saw that the single railway running down from Damascus was the "long stem" that nourished the Turks, because it brought the food, ammunition, and other supplies the army required. Lawrence saw that the Bedouins, "blowing where they listed," with light arms and few more skills than they already possessed as desert mounted men, could break the railway, disappear rapidly into the desert, and reappear at some other place, repeatedly. As had happened in South Africa, this would create a military stalemate that the occupying power over time could not endure. The Turks would be forced to use all of their power to keep the railway operating, and would be useless in the great battle shaping up under the British commander Sir Edmund Allenby to seize Palestine and drive the Turks out of the war.

"We had nothing material to lose, so our best line was to defend nothing and to shoot nothing," Lawrence wrote. "Our cards were speed and time, not hitting power. The invention of bully [canned] beef had profited us more than the invention of gunpowder, but gave us strategic rather than tactical strength, since in Arabia range was more than force, space greater than the power of armies."

Lawrence set his program in motion, although the British command continued to want the Arabs to organize into "proper military units under proper command of officers." Lawrence's methods were at the opposite extreme. "Our tactics should be tip and run, not pushes, but strokes," he wrote. "We should never try to improve an advantage. We should use the smallest force in the quickest time at the farthest place." Lawrence kept his men deliberately ignorant of the mechanism of the Hotchkiss and Lewis light machine guns they used. "Ours were battles of minutes," Lawrence wrote, "fought at eighteen miles an hour [the speed of a racing camel]. If a gun jammed, the gunner must throw it aside and go in with his rifle."

Continued strikes by Lawrence's teams repeatedly broke the railroad and in effect turned the Turkish garrison at Medina into prisoners of war, who were obliged to provide their own upkeep. This contributed vastly to Allenby's offensive in Palestine that forced the Turks to sue for peace on October 31, 1918.

A decade after the end of World War I, China's Nationalist leader, Chiang Kai-shek, severed his alliance with the Communists and began killing all the Reds he could find. This forced the Communists into hiding. Mao Zedong emerged as the most successful leader, forming a small "Soviet republic" in the largely inaccessible Wuji Mountains of southeastern China. There he embarked on a program of giving land to the peasants and protecting them from exploitation and high interest rates from the gentry. This generated support from the vast majority of the population, since 80 percent of the people were peasants. Mao created a new kind of guerrilla army in the Wuyi Mountains. It was a partially democratic force without military ranks. Leaders led by example and they told their soldiers in detail what their objective was and why it was important to secure it, a practice virtually unheard of in conventional armies of the day.

Chiang Kai-shek recognized the danger that Mao's Soviet republic presented. He launched numerous "bandit-suppression" campaigns to destroy it. Mao did not challenge these Nationalist forces head-to-head, but withdrew deep into the mountains, pulling the Nationalists after him. There he struck with overwhelming force at units that had become isolated by moving too slowly or too fast, or that had been enticed into an ambush. In some cases the Reds completely annihilated a unit. Mao later said: "Injuring all of a man's fingers is not as effective as chopping off one of them."

These tactics were wondrously effective. In 1934, however, the Communist leadership—following Marxist doctrine that city workers or the proletariat must bring about the revolution (though they made up only 1 percent of the Chinese population)—rejected Mao's emphasis on the peasant and demanded head-on assaults against the latest Nationalist penetration. They lost badly.

Mao Tse-Tung, leader of China's Communists, addresses some of his followers on December 6, 1944 (NARA photo).

The surviving Communists were forced to flee, commencing the Long March. Deceptive moves by the Red commanders kept the fleeing force alive and out of the clutches of Chiang Kai-shek, whose armies pressed on all sides. During this march, Mao took over leadership from the failed doctrinaire Communists trained in Moscow, and led the 6,000 surviving Communists to safety in Yenan province in northern China a year later in 1935. There, he patched up a shaky cease-fire with Chiang in order to fight the Japanese, who were threatening to invade China.

In the years after Mao issued *Guerrilla Warfare* in 1937, the doctrines of partisan warfare he outlined were taken up by the Vietnamese Communists in their war against the French from 1945 to 1954, and against the Americans from 1965 until 1972. These doctrines also were followed by Muslim guerrillas in the war against the Soviet Union in Afghanistan in the 1980s and by opponents of the intervention into Somalia in 1993. They were used by terrorists before 9/11, have been used by them since 9/11. They are being followed by insurgents in Iraq and Afghanistan today. Western and Soviet military leaders were unwilling to accept that these doctrines were effective, continued to try to fight them with conventional armies, and continually lost.

Guerrilla war and terrorism are both built on the maxim to exploit an enemy's weakness, while nullifying his strength. Though they share the same principle, international terrorism differs from guerrilla war in a deep-seated way. The difference is the key to the war against terrorism. International terrorism has one great strength: it makes sneak attacks on unsuspecting people, and thus is difficult to prevent. But it also has one profound weakness: it operates as clandestine cells in an alien environment, and thus can be isolated.

Guerrilla warfare is the most successful of all forms of conflict, but it is decisive only in lands into which a foreign army has invaded or where many of the people oppose the reigning power, as was the case in Nationalist China in the 1920s and 1930s.

Guerrillas and terrorists can operate successfully only where at least a significant portion of the population is friendly and supportive. They cannot succeed where the population is hostile. In hostile lands they can make unanticipated strikes, such as the terrorists carried out on 9/11. But—because the great bulk of the population does not support terrorists and will report suspicious persons or activities—terrorist cells in the United States and in Europe can be weeded out by traditional police and detective techniques, such as informers, careful observation, and infiltration of suspicious groups.

On the other hand, the West can only lose in places like Iraq, Afghanistan, Somalia, and other lands where the people are opposed to the West and where they support partisan movements. By using counterinsurgency methods (which are essentially the same as guerrilla techniques), we may be able to minimize the effects of partisan activities for a time in countries where many of the people are hostile to us. But we cannot eliminate them. Instead, we should substitute diplomatic and other methods to win over or defeat opposing movements.

We can, however, reduce to a low degree the danger from clandestine cells that have sprung up in Western Europe and where some have carried out attacks (Madrid, London, and Glasgow). These cells, unlike the wide movements in the Middle East, have only limited support. Though a cell here and there may occasionally be able to pull off a strike, all cells ultimately can be rendered ineffective or can be destroyed.

In the open societies of the West, there can be no total safety, for most potential targets are not protected at all. But, because our people are overwhelmingly opposed to terrorists, we are immune from widespread and repeated assaults, such as those taking place in Iraq and Afghanistan today. Assaults in the West must be desperate, isolated, individual strikes carried out by clandestine cells. These isolated groups cannot conduct a sustained campaign.

U.S. Army Gen. David H. Petraeus, the commander of U.S. CENTCOM, speaks to Marines with 2nd Battalion, 7th Marine Regiment at Camp Barber, Afghanistan, Nov. 7, 2008. 2nd Battalion 7th Marine Regiment, based out of Marine Air Ground Combat Center (US Army photo November 7, 2008).

The West's military forces must be largely reorganized and redirected toward quelling terrorist strikes. There is little chance that modern societies any longer can resort to war between themselves. The old Cold War axiom of MAD (mutually assured destruction) in the presence of nuclear weapons still exists, and it has nullified any military action between nuclear-armed states.

For the foreseeable future, warfare is going to be built around countering guerrillas, partisans, or terrorists.

(This article was previously published in the
***Armchair General Magazine* and reprinted with permission.)**

CHAPTER 3

A LONG HARD SLOG:
CAMPAIGNING IN IRAQ

By Major General Daniel Bolger, U.S. Army

"Us. . . and them, and, after all,
we're only ordinary men.
Me . . . and you,
God only knows it's not what we would choose to do."[1]

Something had gone wrong, badly wrong. That much was grimly obvious from the moment the reaction force arrived on the scene. Strewn along the rocky slope, scattered here and there, interspersed with smashed weapons and discarded gear, the stripped, hacked corpses lay rigid in the glare of day. Not a single enemy body could be seen among them.

Finding the enemy—wasn't that always the problem? Patrol after patrol, day after day, seeing plenty of the sullen locals but rarely a glimpse of the hostiles. The opposition wore no uniforms, stood no ground, and knew no doctrine. Yet clearly, they had created this ambush, and done so with ruthless effectiveness.

The American bodies and ground told the story. It had begun as these skirmishes always began, with a sighting. Then came a quick, aggressive mounted maneuver, chasing after a few enemies fleeing across the stony ridge. To grab this running foe, to fix him and hold on, drew in the Americans. Close combat always went to the U.S. Army. So on they came. Upon cresting the ridge, the Soldiers apparently dismounted and opened fire. Discarded golden cartridges glittered in the sun around every dead man. There had been plenty of shooting, all right.

---

[1] The epigraph comes from the song "Us and Them," Pink Floyd, *Dark Side of the Moon* (New York City, NY: Capitol Records, 1973), track 6.

What happened then? Who could say? But it must have been horrific. An enemy who never appeared in numbers evidently did so this time. An opponent who typically shot poorly clearly shot well enough. And trained Americans who went into every firefight expecting to win must have felt gut-wrenching spasms, if they had time to feel anything at all. They figured out too late that this time, on this ugly field, no Americans would get out alive.

So now it came to this. Watchful, wary, the security elements took up over-watching positions to protect the dreadful site. Designated teams began to move among the dead, beginning the sad efforts of recovery. At the direction of the commander, another Soldier wrote down what he saw, a litany of woe recorded with dispassionate care by someone who had seen it all before, and would see it again: "Eyes torn out and laid on the rocks; noses cut off; ears cut off; chins hewn off; teeth chopped out; joints of fingers cut off; brains taken out and placed on rocks, with members of the body; entrails taken out and exposed; hands cut off; feet cut off; arms taken out from socket; private parts severed."

It had been a bad day, that 21st of December 1866 outside Fort Phil Kearny in the Wyoming Territory.[2] For the Troopers in dirty shirt blue, and the Plains Indians they fought, there would be others, many others. They all bled into a long, long series of campaigns that finally crawled to an ignominious end in 1890-91 in the snows, gunfire, and heartbreak of Wounded Knee.[3] Today, the U.S. Army flag bears fourteen

---

[2] Evan S. Connell, *Son of the Morning Star* (New York City, NY: North Point Press, 1984), 131-32. The aftermath of the battle described is now known the Fetterman Massacre. Captain William Fetterman and seventy-nine others were ambushed and killed by a war party of Ogallala Sioux that may have included Crazy Horse. The report quoted was prepared by Colonel Henry Carrington, commander of the 18th Infantry Regiment. The site of the engagement was within a hundred miles of the Little Big Horn battlefield where Lieutenant Colonel George A. Custer and about half of the 7th Cavalry Regiment met their demise on 25 June 1876.

[3] Robert Wooster, *Nelson A. Miles and the Twilight of the Frontier Army* (Lincoln, NE: University of Nebraska Press, 1995), 185-86. The major

campaign streamers from the Indian Wars. We count them as victories. Not one came easily.

In Iraq

So it goes in Iraq. Following the rapid overthrow of Saddam Hussein's conventional forces and government in March and April of 2003, and then a period of shadowboxing and confusion for all parties, the anti-American insurgency sputtered to life. By spring of 2004, the intensity picked up. There have been ups and downs, to include calm periods after the 2005 election series and the 2007 "surge" operations.[4] But as with the American Plains Indians from 1865-91, the hostile factions in Iraq were never really defeated, merely regrouping.

This kind of war, in T.R. Fehrenbach's oh so apt phrasing, is not the kind of great crusade that energizes our countrymen and marks a generation.[5] It is not the American Revolution of 1775-83, which enlisted much of the populace and had no time for those faint hearts that the intense pamphleteer Thomas Paine tarred as "summer soldier" and "sunshine patriot"

---

engagements at Wounded Knee happened on 28-29 December 1890, with smaller skirmishes on 30 December and then 3 and 7 January 1891.

[4] There are two U.S. Army official histories of the Iraq Campaign. For the initial period of fighting through 1 May 2003, see Col. Gregory A. Fontenot, U.S. Army, Ret, Lt. Col. E.J. Degen, U.S. Army, and Lt.Col. David Tohn, U.S. Army and the Operation Iraqi Freedom Study Group, *On Point: The United States Army in Operation Iraqi Freedom* (Fort Leavenworth, KS: Combat Studies Institute Press, 2008). For the next period, see Dr. Donald P. Wright, Col. Timothy E. Reese, U.S. Army, and the Contemporary Study Team, *On Point II: Transition to the New Campaign* (Fort Leavenworth, KS: Combat Studies Institute Press, 2008). Together, these volumes take the record through 30 January 2005. Additional volumes are expected, with the next already in preparation.

[5] T.R. Fehrenbach, *This Kind of War* (New York City, NY: The Macmillan Co., 1963). Fehrenbach's book is a general military history, a personal account of his own experiences, and a rumination on the character of the 1950-53 limited war in Korea. See 91-93 for the author's views on total versus limited war in the American experience.

types.[6] The present conflict is not the Civil War of 1861-65, the continental struggle over slavery which left a generation north and south "touched with fire," in the memorable words of former Union Army officer and Supreme Court Justice Oliver Wendell Holmes, Jr.[7] Nor is our present clash like the massive, popular American participation in World War II of 1941-45, the "Good War" against Nazi Germany and Imperialist Japan. Even social skeptic Studs Terkel labeled it thus.[8] No, the Iraq war was not a crusade, though al Qaeda propagandists often enjoy naming it that way for their own ends.

The Iraq campaign has not been "a splendid little war," either, to evoke John Hays' memorable paean to the Spanish-American War.[9] If they can't have a once a century crusade, Americans certainly rally enthusiastically to quick, decisive wars, whether they be the 1846-48 Mexican War, the triumph over Spain in 1898, the short American portion of World War I in 1917-18 , or the smashing liberation of Kuwait in 1991. Long

---

[6] Thomas Paine used these famous terms in the opening sentence of the first edition of his series *The American Crisis*. (Philadelphia, PA: Styner and Cist, 1776-77), 19 December 1776, 1.

[7] This idea of Oliver Wendell Holmes, Jr. is often quoted, most notably in the epigraph of Eric Bergerud, *Touched with Fire: The Land War in the South Pacific* (New York City, NY: Vioking Press, 1996), ix.

[8] Louis "Studs" Terkel, *The "Good War:" An Oral History of World War Two* (New York City, NY: Random House, 1984). Terkel put the quotations in place to be ironic. A relentless critic of conventional views, he tried to depict the horrors and tragedies that befell American participants in World War II. Even so, the bulk of the book underscores the worthy and critical nature of the American cause in the Second World War. The final irony might be that Terkel himself missed just how good (just and righteous, and hence worthwhile) the war was perceived to be.

[8] Secretary of State John Hay's characterization is quoted in many sources. See, for example, Robert G. Athearn, et al., *The American Heritage New Illustrated History of the United States,* 16 vols. (New York City, NY: Dell Publishing Co., Inc., 1963), *Volume 12: A World Power*, 1010.

[9] *Ibid.*

before Nazi German news organs dubbed the shattering *panzer* and *Stuka* tactics of 1939-41 as *blitzkrieg* (lightning war), our citizens had shown strong support for such rapid victories. That preference marked our professional Armed Forces as we entered the current Global War on Terrorism in 2001. The initial attacks into Afghanistan in 2001 and Iraq in 2003 followed this confident script with signal success, and consequent strong domestic American applause.

Soldiers from the 39th Brigade Combat Team, an Army National Guard unit attached to the 1st Cavalry Division lead a convoy of vehicles head out to investigate a suspected terrorist near the town of Al Taji, Iraq on August 12, 2004 (U.S. Army photo).

But even a global power does not get to pick its wars. Our enemies also have their say. Along with the epochal crusades and quick wins, America has wallowed through more frustrating interludes: the War of 1812-15, the Indian Wars of 1865-91, the Philippine Insurrection of 1898-1913, the Korean War of 1950-53, the Vietnam War of 1964-75, and many other lesser conflicts. In these wars, some very long indeed, we rely on volunteers in uniform to carry the load.

That is exactly where we stand today. We are moving slowly, painfully along the arc that Secretary of Defense Donald Rumsfeld dubbed "a long, hard slog."[10] That steely man got some things right, other things wrong, and a good many remaining to be determined. But he sure nailed that one.

At War

What is this slog like? As in most wars, the nature of our enemy defines the nature of the fight. Determined to engage and defeat us, the *Wahhabi* Sunni Islamic fanatics of *al Qaeda* (the Base) and the fundamentalist Shia Islamic extremists of *Jaysh al Mahdi* (Army of the Guided One), to identify the two biggest sharks in the school, have chosen tactics that work superbly against our highly trained, technologically enabled force. They have negated much of our airpower and seapower. They have forced us into squad-scale patrol actions among their cultural relatives in the Iraqi populace, people we understand poorly at best. That is an unforgiving formula that would be all too familiar to William Tecumseh Sherman in the Division of the Missouri in 1866, John J. Pershing on Jolo Island in the Philippines in 1911, or Creighton Abrams in embattled South Vietnam in 1971. We have been here before.

Whether Sunni or Shia, this enemy has one goal: to run us out of Iraq. To do that, they must wear us out. It is not in their power to defeat us militarily. While their strategic object is the will of the American populace, the opposition knows that they must engage the targets in front of them. So they go after American Soldiers and Marines, as well as the Airmen, Sailors, Coast Guardsmen, and all the others helping them on the streets of Iraq. Enough carnage among the guys on the ground and the American people may throw in the towel. It has happened enough in recent years: Vietnam 1975, Lebanon 1984, Somalia 1994, and Haiti 1996. That's why the adversary finds it useful to

---

[10] "Rumsfeld's War on Terror Memo," USA Today, 20 May 2005, A2. The memorandum was dated 16 October 2003, but not revealed for some time. The sentence in question reads: "It is pretty clear that the coalition can win in Afghanistan and Iraq in one way or another, but it will be a long, hard slog."

kill our troops, and to keep killing them, all to ensure a steady and demoralizing accumulation of losses.

They do so not just with bullets and improvised explosive devices (IEDs), and not simply with mortar rounds and rocket propelled grenades (RPGs). Rather, our enemies choose to fight us in ways that, over time, do much to erode our willpower. Our foe wants us to see this war as unwinnable.

To do so, the enemy relies on some very effective methods. First, this opponent mixes intentionally and widely with the civil population of Iraq. He wears no uniform. He travels in cars and trucks, and carries on relatively normal economic social and economic activities in between, or in support of, insurgent operations. To find this adversary, American troops and their Iraqi allies must wade through suspicious local neighborhoods. Doing so under arms leads to friction at best, disruption most always, and casualties on all sides at worst. The perils of fighting a non-uniformed enemy are significant.

For the opposition, the lack of uniforms allows freedom of movement and an ability to hide in plain sight that does much to negate American high-technology sensors. Mao Zedong talked about the guerrillas as fish swimming in the sea of the people.[11] Maybe so, but at least you can tell a trout from a bucket of water. With this kind of foe, it's like trying to pick out the traces of Evian from a gallon of tap water. Good luck.

In addition, an ethnically similar enemy moving among his fellows ensures the detention—and sometimes death—of some of the wrong people. Our Iraqi allies in the Army and Police help with sorting this out, but it isn't easy. The hostiles work very, very hard to appear nondescript, to get overlooked. Getting a reliable identification takes a lot of work. When we make a mistake, and drag away the wrong man, it's not hard to predict the results among otherwise undecided civil society.

---

[11] John Shy and Thomas W. Collier, "Revolutionary Warfare," in n Peter Paret, editor, *Makers of Modern Strategy: From Machiavelli to the Nuclear Age* (Princeton, NJ: Princeton University Press, 1986), 842.

Finally, and most damningly, an enemy out of uniform accustoms American Soldiers to killing people in citizen garb. U.S. forces distinguish who to shoot based on activity, but Iraqis can (and do) own their own weapons, so this becomes really tough. It is a very slippery slope. Absent rock-hard discipline and committed leadership, over time, shooting civilians can get much too easy. That's exactly how to lose in a counterinsurgency.

The enemy's failure to wear uniforms grants them tactical advantages that they expand to all manner of behavior. The enemy appears to have adopted the motto of Outback Steakhouse: "No rules, just right." While our forces follow the customary law of war, our opposition knows no restraint. They murder prisoners, often by sawing off heads. They mutilate civilian captives, steal supplies at gunpoint, and take over homes as strongholds. There is no accountability for these outrages, except when the terrorists are killed or captured by Americans or our Iraqi allies. The enemy leadership, such as it is, justifies all as acceptable in this *jihad* (holy war) against the U.S. "occupiers."

War of all times and all types features capricious cruelty unimaginable to those whose only experience comprises books, video games, or movies. Real bodies bloat and stink. There is a lot of blood in a person—a lot more than in any movie scene. Friends don't get another "life." Nothing wraps up neatly in two hours. And you have to go out and do it again, and again, wearing those same ninety pounds of "lightweight" gear. To add to that a foe who delights in inflicting additional injury, who likes to twist every knife he sticks . . . well, it all gets pretty hard to take. Sometimes nineteen year old riflemen and twenty two year old sergeants choose to even up on their own. It's a degenerative and unhealthy by-product of too much death. It's precisely why Soldiers of old wanted some limits on combat, and saw merit in The Hague and Geneva Conventions. Left to his own devices, the average young man under fire won't opt for much of that.

Still, the insurgent terror methods have their limits. The locals of rural Iraq might be strict Muslims, but they have learned to despise *al Qaeda*'s novel medieval variations of *Sharia* law, such as killing people for smoking cigarettes, abusing insufficiently subservient women, or slaughtering *sheikhs* for the inattention of their relatives. Our ability to highlight these crimes played a big role in turning around the Sunni Arab families out in arid Al Anbar Province. Getting that word out has done much to harm the standing of the terrorist elements among the Iraqi people.

That said, our enemies still do it. As Machiavelli warned his prince, it is better to be loved than feared, but plain fear works fine, too.[12] For our Soldiers, it means they are up against an opponent who will torture them if captured, who will desecrate American remains if left behind, and who will slay innocents as it suits their purposes. Bad as that is, when such a vicious enemy surrenders, he gets the same treatment as an *Afrika Korps* riflemen captured at El Guettar, Tunisia in 1943. He may be an "unlawful combatant," a nice distinction for sleek lawyers in Washington, D.C. To our Soldiers, though, he's a detainee and he must be safeguarded and well treated. Interrogations follow careful protocols. Any kind of mayhem is prohibited, and will be punished. It seems like a pretty uneven playing field to the average American PFC.

An enemy that looks like a civilian and fights like a demon is bad enough. But to that we must add the underlying strength that we understand as well as they do. Time favors the opposing side. The longer they can stay active, the longer they can drag this out, the harder it gets for us. The guerrilla enjoys this edge in every insurgency, but it is a hard thing to enjoy, because he must keep bleeding to gain the benefit. Our foe in Iraq appears willing to try it. It's been a long time since 2003. It's longer still because, like most Iraqis, our adversary dates things back to August of 1990. That squats atop eight years of combat against Iran, not to mention the intramural scrums against Saddam, Kurds versus Arab, and more routine blood

---

[12] Niccolo Machaivelli, *The Prince,* W.K. Marriott, translator, 1908, at www.constitution.org/mac/ prince00.html , Chapter XVII.

feuds spiced by earlier versions of IEDs, RPGs, and machine guns.

Our response has been the same as in most of our long wars. We limit exposure. The longest tour in Iraq for a unit is about fifteen months, and that only during the height of the 2006-08 surge period. Most Soldiers serve twelve months, and most Marines go seven. Navy and Coalition Allies (like the British or Polish) serve six. Special Operations Forces and Air Force stints run from four months to a year, depending on the duty. The Iraqi Soldiers and Police, of course, are serving a life sentence—just like the enemy.

Soldiers from the 172nd Stryker Brigade Combat Team prepare to cross an open field during a cordon and search mission in Ur, Iraq on September 22, 2006 (U.S. Army photo).

It is one thing to do a tour. The second gets tougher. The third gets even more onerous. Our sergeants often point out that getting a Soldier to his first firefight is easy. It's the second one, let alone the twentieth or two hundredth, that gets very difficult. Repeated tours take a toll.[13] That we know. How

---

[13] Lt. Col. Dave Grossman, U.S. Army, *On Killing* (New York City, NY: Back Bay Books, 1996), 268.

much, we don't know. Sherman's frontier Regulars held on. Abrams' Vietnam War grunts did not.

Military psychologists tell us that Soldiers have a capacity for only so much violence, and that it varies by individual. Some fold early. Others go well past the norm. Our Special Operations community tries hard to assess and train people in the latter category. Even their tests and evaluations are not perfect. Sooner or later, if you keep dipping into it, the well of courage runs dry.[14]

Like the fuel gauge on your car, you can see the indicators as things wind down. One is a growing malaise, a lack of concern with detail. The French Foreign Legion saw only too much of that in the wastes of Algeria. The tough old *adjutant-chefs* called it *le cafard*, literally "the cockroach," but more colloquially, "the blues" or in its violent manifestation, "going bugf---."[15] Today we dress it up as "post-traumatic stress disorder (PTSD)." This is the kind of thing that happens to you when you shoot too many people dressed as civilians, who follow no rules, and the whole damn thing goes on and on.

If *le cafard* follows this kind of war as night follows day, and I think it does, the guerrillas would be guaranteed victory in every insurgency. Yet that doesn't happen. Why not?

The difference is that *le cafard* can be identified, mitigated and even prevented. I'm not talking about medical intervention. Some cases do require that, and it's needed. Our Army has put a lot of emphasis on identifying and treating PTSD. All wars, and all Soldiers, see post traumatic stress.[16] Whether or not it becomes a disorder depends on many factors, not the least the nature of the conflict. The dirtier the war, the

---

[14] Richard Holmes, *Acts of War: The Behavior of Men in Battle* (New York, NY: The Free Press, 1985), 214-15.

[15] Douglas Porch, *The French Foreign Legion* (New York City, NY: HarperCollins, Publishers, 1991), 426-27.

[16] Grossman, *On Killing*, 281-82.

more you seem to see PTSD. We have seen our share from the Iraq campaign.

But as for most of us in uniform, repeated trips to the pharmacy or worse, the hospital, won't get us to our next battlefield, or keep us there. As Soldiers, we have to meet the challenge of *le cafard*, and the collapse of courage that looms beyond it. If we don't do this, our Army will fail. Our population will give up on us. The bad guys win.

What Is To Be Done

Good armies throughout history, including our own, have cracked the code. The answer reflects a return to fundamentals. It's all about cohesion, training, and leadership.

Cohesion means the ability of a group to hold together under pressure, hardship, and death. It comes from keeping Soldiers together. Familiarity allows the group to endure, drawing on the strength of the collective.[17] It's the old story about four friends able to defeat a lion when eight strangers cannot. In theory, you form a company, a battalion, or a brigade, train them up, send them off to fight, then bring them home together. That sounds easy, but it is not.

For one thing, Soldiering is demanding physically, mentally, and morally. Leaders and Soldiers get hurt at ranges an on field exercises. Some don't measure up. Others get into trouble. If those failures get serious, changes must happen. New people come in to fill holes. The lineup gets dynamic, more so once the unit deploys into combat and battle casualties begin to affect the balance.

In some previous wars, the U.S. Army just let units shrink under this kind of steady attrition. The great Union Army Iron Brigade of the Civil War wasted away after several bloody campaigns. Merrill's Marauders had a similar grinding

---

[17] *Ibid.*, 293.

experience in Burma in World War II.[18] Cohesion was kept, but battle losses reduced these forces to impotence.

In other times, the American Army chose to feed in individual fillers. In Vietnam after the first year or so, each unit consisted of individuals all on one year tours. Platoons lost a man or two a week to tour completion, as well as any lost to combat. If nothing else, it ensured that units got used to turnover. It also led to the bitter observation that the U.S. did not fight eleven years in Vietnam, but the first year eleven times over. This was the opposite of cohesion, aside from any practical small unit teamwork that grew over days out in the jungle.[19]

In the present war, we've chosen to fight as units. We go in and out of Iraq as brigades, separate battalions, and some smaller detachments. Units get only a few replacement Soldiers. Given losses, there is a steady decrease in manning as the tour goes on. But in general, casualty rates in Iraq have not been catastrophic. Over a deployment, a 4,000-Soldier brigade may lose thirty dead and a hundred wounded—bad enough, but leaving cohesion and combat power intact. The Army has ensured that the Soldiers in these units faced tough things together.

Today's cohesive units know each other thanks to training. The American Army trains well on individual and small unit tactics. After the Vietnam War, men like the exacting General William E. DePuy and Lieutenant General Arthur S. "Ace" Collins insisted on practical, common sense training. The Army demands hands-on work, in the field. Tasks are drilled

---

[18] Cmd Sgt. Maj. Robert S. Rush, U.S. Army, Ret., "The Individual Replacement System: Good, Bad, or Indifferent?" presented to the Inter-University Seminar on Armed Forces and Society Annual Conference, Chicago, IL, 26-28 October 2007, 1, 3.

[19] *Ibid.*, 20-21. See also Paddy Griffith, *Forward into Battle* (Chichester, UK: Antony Bird Publications, 1981), 109, 127-28.

repetitively, under increasingly difficult conditions.[20]   Soldiers do a lot of shooting, first aid, radio communications, and land navigation, all critical skills in counterinsurgency patrolling and raids. The Army also insists on physical fitness, very important given the terrain, weather, and loads common in Iraq.

Soldiers from C Co., 2nd Battalion, 502nd Infantry, scan for targets in the desert west of Iskandariyah, during Operation Dragoon, December 17, 2007 (U.S. Army photo).

Good as this unit training became, the Army brought things to an even higher level with the combat training centers at

---

[20] Gen. Paul F. Gorman, U.S. Army, Ret., *The Secret of Future Victories* (Fort Leavenworth, KS: Combat Studies Institute Press, 1992), III-24, III-33.

Fort Irwin, California, Fort Polk, Louisiana, and Hohenfels, Germany. Back in the Cold War, each had a Communist Bloc style opposing force. But today, these facilities recreate the current war. Brigades operate among full scale replications of Iraqi population centers. Hundreds of role players, many speaking Arabic and Kurdish, act as the population. A small number of highly trained American Soldiers portray the *al Qaeda* and *Jaysh al Mahdi* militant hostiles. Two weeks of such exercises wring out everything from squad reconnaissance missions to major heliborne landings.

This training ethos continues in theater. Even the smallest American patrol base typically features a ten meter flat range for shooting practice. Combined training offers the most common mutual effort with Iraqi Army and Police partner units. American units rehearse their raids and battle drills and bring their Iraqi allies with them in these efforts.

How realistic is all of this training? While it cannot ever duplicate the fear and physical danger of combat, it certainly comes close.[21] American Soldiers know what to expect in Iraq. This is especially important because the majority of any American formation (except some of the Special Operations Forces) consists of young troops on their first overseas deployment. The experiences in Iraq can be jarring and awful, but they are neither wholly alien nor unexpected. That reflects a lot of hard work before and during the tour. Conditioning means something.

Leadership drives tough training. It drives tough operations as well. American privates expect to see their sergeants and officers with them on the street. Younger Soldiers benefit from the example of the veterans.

Some might argue that because this is a sergeant's war, the more senior leaders have no business on raids and patrols. If

---

[21] Contemporary U.S. Army unit training is very hard on Soldiers in every respect. In one case at Fort Hood, Texas in 2008, medical experts characterized a new Soldier as suffering from full-blown PTSD. The young rifleman had never been overseas. In the opinion of the doctors, his condition reflected the effects of highly realistic pre-deployment training exercises.

the big guys are military tourists, that's true. We could hardly fault a squad leader who complains about some wandering commander and his entourage hanging around at the back end of a block-to-block fight. Though it definitely beats orbiting overhead in a helicopter as in certain notorious examples from the Vietnam era, it's not real leadership.

Real leadership means sharing the entire experience, from preparation to debrief, not blowing in and out, and certainly not watching it all on a camera feed from a Predator unmanned aircraft. Our Soldiers deal with a lot when they confront an enemy in civil dress, a foe capable of horrific atrocities, and a necessity to do it all again tonight and tomorrow. Being able to look over and see a sergeant major or lieutenant colonel calmly doing his job can settle down a jumpy young rifleman. It works.[22]

Just as important, the presence of leaders keeps violence in bounds. Detainees get treated to standard. Civilians don't get roughed up. Property stays intact. Privates remember their training.

Sherman, who knew about wars great and small, said it best. "No man," he warned, "can properly command an army from the rear, he must be 'at its front'. . . some men think that modern armies can be so regulated that a general can sit in an office and play on his several columns as on the keys of a piano; this is a fearful mistake. The directing mind must be at the very head of the army—must be seen there."[23]

Endurance

Cohesion, training, and leadership, combined with a rotation schedule that allows for a break from combat, allows us

---

[22] For example, see Martha Raddatz, *The Long Road Home* (New York City, NY: Berkley Books, 2008), 320-21. Raddatz' book tells the story of a series of firefights in Sadr City, Iraq on 04-05 April 2004. She records numerous occasions of forward leadership by senior American officers and NCOs.

[23] Gen. William T. Sherman, *Memoirs of General William T. Sherman* (New York City, NY: Da Capo Press, Inc., 1984) U.S. Army, 408.

to keep going. It lets us refill our personal wells of courage. We will have to do it. To win, Iraq demands a long term commitment.

In their day, Sherman's hard-bitten Regulars went for a quarter century. They kept going when the country forgot about them. They kept going when intellectuals back east vilified them. They kept going even when the Congress chose not to pay them.[24] They weren't mercenaries. Neither are we. It's about way more than money.

We fight for America because we fight for our brothers and sisters to our right and left. That's what America looks like when you're in a foreign land with terrorists trying to kill you. We know very well what can happen on that coarse grass just over the hill from Fort Phil Kearny. But we go anyway.

We know the deal. As long as we stay at it, we win. If we quit, we lose. So the long, hard slog goes on . . . and on. ∎

---

[24] Robert Utley, *Frontier Regulars: The United States Army and the Indian, 1866-1891* (New York City, NY: Macmillan Publishing Co., Inc., 1973), 64-66. The Army went without pay for portions of both 1877 and 1879.

CHAPTER 4

THE TIDE TURNS IN AL ANBAR

Major General John Allen,
Colonels John Koenig and Colonel Philip Wasielewski,
U.S. Marine Corps

The struggle continues in Al Anbar province where Iraqi and Coalition Forces continue their promising efforts to bring peace, prosperity, and the rule of law to the province as part of the larger effort in Iraq. While progress in Al Anbar was shouldered in 2007 by increasingly capable Iraqi police and soldiers, their efforts were also joined by growing numbers of legitimate local leaders - elected and hereditary, civil servants, judges, businessmen, and skilled workers – who with the Iraqi citizens of Al Anbar said enough to the violence that consumed their province for several years. There is much to accomplish in Al Anbar before victory can be declared and guaranteed, but tangible success in 2007 and into 2008 has vindicated several years of struggle.

This article is an operational and campaign level explanation of where Iraqis and the Coalition Forces stood by early 2008 in their combined fight to bring peace and normalcy to Al Anbar province. Accounts of Al Anbar to date have been largely local and tactical in nature. The story is multi-faceted and nuanced. It is not a linear story of events because the fight in Iraq, including Al Anbar province, is a particular counterinsurgency struggle involving a fight for a particular people, not territory. Such a struggle requires steady operational vision integrating the guidance and mandates of higher strategy and policy with the tactical facts and opportunities on the ground. Execution of this integrated operational vision further requires operational patience and prudence to comprehend and understand the seemingly slow daily progression of efforts to secure the population against the insurgency in Al Anbar. It also requires agility and energy from key leaders to exploit relevant windows of opportunity. In this manner the Al Anbar campaign achieved a unity of effort to successfully compete against insurgent leadership and convince the population who could govern best and justly.

Al Anbar

Al Anbar province represents one third of the land mass of Iraq but only approximately five percent of its population. The overwhelming majority of its inhabitants are Sunni Moslems belonging to over forty separate tribes that comprise, in the main, the Dulaimi Confederation.

Marines of Alpha Company, 1st Battalion, 23rd Marines, inspect the weapons they found outside of Ar Rutbah, Iraq. The 1st Marine Division is conducting Security and Stabilization Operations (SASO) during Operation Iraqi Freedom in the Al Anbar province of Iraq on January 11, 2005 (USMC photo).

While Anbar's borders reach south to Saudi Arabia and west to Jordan and Syria, its heart is the Euphrates River which courses through the northern half of the province. Ninety percent of the population lives within three miles of the Euphrates, a fertile swath of green through an inhospitable desert. Only two major towns in the province, Rutbah and An Nukhayb, are situated away from this fertile swath of green but these ancient oasis stops for caravans still remain vitally important to the province because they sit astride the lines of communication to Jordan, Syria, and Saudi Arabia respectively. An Nukhayb is also important as a way point for Iraqi pilgrims making the yearly Hajj by road to Saudi Arabia.

There was little fighting in Al Anbar during the Coalition operations which overthrew Saddam Hussein's regime in the spring of 2003. The initial Coalition Forces to enter the province were lightly armed Special Operations Forces units followed by the 3rd Armored Cavalry Regiment. Later in April 2003, elements of the 82nd Airborne Division moved into the province and almost immediately found a nascent resistance coalescing around former regime elements and nationalists. U.S. Marines, who relieved U.S. Army forces in Al Anbar province in March of 2004, prepared to conduct a traditional counterinsurgency campaign focused upon the population and emphasizing non-kinetic operations – a strategy best described by then Major General Mattis as "First, Do No Harm" and "No Better Friend; No Worse Enemy." However, events in 2004 compelled the Marines to conduct intense urban combat operations in Fallujah first in April and then conclusively in November. The success of the November 2004 operations in Fallujah eliminated a major urban haven for the insurgency but it failed to maintain a firm hold on the population elsewhere in the province. The years 2005 and 2006 were deadly ones for Coalition and Iraqi forces in Anbar, a province often described, at best, in the press as "restive" and at worst as the "most dangerous province in Iraq."

From the beginning, the Coalition engaged with tribal leaders to leverage their influence against the insurgency, and worked with local government leaders and civil servants to revive the local economies and urban infrastructures. However progress in 2005 and 2006 was slow against an intense and pervasive insurgent murder and intimidation campaign. Coalition Forces worked with the Albu Mahal tribe in western Al Anbar in 2005 in what was to become a model for later tribal engagements by Coalition Forces. Still, the losses for Iraqis willing to step forward and fight the insurgency were very high in those two years.

The insurgency in Al Anbar was a complex array of disparate elements. Many of these elements were antagonistic to each other and, unlike other past insurgencies from Indochina to El Salvador, there was no common political goal for the insurgency other than the expulsion of Coalition Forces and the murder of Iraqis who did not share their various agendas. Generally, the insurgency in Al Anbar could be divided into two basic factions – nationalists and Salafists or, as they are called by the local population, *Takfiris* - meaning ultra-religious fanatics who see all other Muslims as apostates. The nationalist elements ranged in composition from those Baathists who wanted to see Sunni control reasserted throughout Iraq, to those Iraqis who resented the presence of Coalition Forces on their traditional tribal lands. The Takfiris represented both foreign fighters pledging allegiance to Osama bin Ladin's Al Qaida and indigenous religious extremists espousing the radical Salafist form of Islam. The Takfiris not only opposed Western ideas but also the religious beliefs and traditions of the vast majority of the Sunnis in the province. Both insurgency segments were also ably served by a criminal element that adroitly exploited the street level collapse of law and order; such as Iraqis understood it in the Saddamist era. As long as these elements made common cause in Al Anbar, the fight to bring peace and stability to the province was an uphill one.

Fortunately for the Iraqis and the Coalition, the insurgency possessed some critical flaws. It lacked a coherent, durable, and uplifting vision which sufficiently resonated with the majority of the local Iraqi population to generate and sustain active support. While clear about what they resisted, the insurgents had no message about what they stood for and what better life they could promise after the resistance achieved it ends. Since any insurgency and counterinsurgency centers around the struggle over who can best administer the population, and lacking a strategic vision, the insurgency in Al Anbar descended into nihilistic terror tactics without a strategic aim. As early as 2005 the journalist George Packer had noticed this when he wrote in his book *The Assassins Gate* that, "the insurgency never had a strategy more coherent than fear." Fear was a powerful weapon and tactic for over two years, but the later experiences in Al Anbar showed that the emergence of local leaders willing to face this fear with a message of hope and progress can turn around what, as late as the fall of 2006, seemed to many Iraqi and international observers to be a hopeless military and political situation.

U.S. Marines from Fox Company, 2nd Battalion, 5th Marines, 1st Marine Division, provide security for other Marines from 2/5 during a cordon and search, in Ar Ramadi, Iraq, Al Anbar province on January 21, 2005 (USMC photo).

Hard Fighting

Even for optimists, the fall of 2006 was not an encouraging time in Al Anbar province. Al Qaida of Iraq (AQI) had declared the province's capital Ramadi as the capital of its own self-proclaimed Islamic State of Iraq and even staged a brief parade down one of Ramadi's streets on October 15, 2006 to portray its hold on power. Attacks against Iraqi police and soldiers and Coalition Forces were high, the provincial governor was alone in a besieged provincial government center as his staff of Provincial Directors General had for the most part stopped making the dangerous trek to work. The Provincial Council had ceased meeting in the province and moved to Baghdad because of well founded fears for its safety. Many towns in the province either did not have functioning town councils or had ineffective councils such as in Fallujah where a series of city council leaders were assassinated. The local Iraqi police numbered only approximately 4,600 officers and the two Iraqi Army Divisions in the province were under strength and distrusted as an arm of the Shia dominated central government.

At the same time, however, there were local bright spots. Since late 2005, events in the western reaches of the Euphrates River Valley around Al Qaim had improved considerably as the Albu Mahal tribe and Coalition Forces allied to eject AQI elements. This impeded the movement of AQI support further into Al Anbar and helped generate slow but steady progress down the Euphrates River Valley in areas like Haditha, Baghdadi, and Hit. In Fallujah local security reached the point that the center of the city was turned over to Iraqi Forces in late 2006 with Coalition Forces moving outside the city. South of Fallujah, a major leader returned, Sheikh Khamis of the Albu Issa tribe. In Ramadi, two previous attempts by local leaders to unite against AQI elements, although meeting with brutal assassinations and reprisals by AQI, had set the stage for a powerful indigenous reaction when in July 2006 they overconfidently proclaimed an Islamic State of Iraq with its capital in Ramadi.

In response to the murder by the AQI of his father and uncle, who had cooperated with Coalition Forces, a secondary sheikh in the Albu Risha tribe, Sheikh Abdul Satar Buzaigh al-Rishawi, arose to provide leadership for a grouping of tribes around Ramadi that would ultimately form into the political movement first known as the Al Anbar Awakening (SAI).

Sheikh Satar was a youthful and impassioned figure who worked until his murder in September 2007 to unite the tribes of the Dulaimi Confederation in support of the Coalition Forces. Proclaiming that "Coalition Forces are Friendly Forces" Sheikh Satar took the lead in convincing tribal leaders to oppose AQI and encourage their tribesmen to join the local police and Iraqi Army.

Sheikh Satar's motivation to a large degree was based on his desires to revenge the murders of his kinsmen and not to live under the type of Islam espoused by the AQI. A lesser but also important motivation for him and other local sheikhs was to eject the AQI from its intrusion into tribal businesses. These motivations, voiced explicitly in public, resonated with other tribal and elected leaders, ordinary Iraqis, and even factions within the nationalist insurgency during the second half of 2006 and into 2007. In August 2006, the AQI murdered a well respected tribal figure near Fallujah and, against all religious and tribal mores, left his body in the desert to rot for four days before it was discovered. Another heartless atrocity was the February 2007 beheading of several children of police officials in Ramadi and delivering a box of unspeakably gruesome remains on the front step of a Ramadi hospital. These events were turning points in creating local revulsion against the AQI. As one senior Iraqi figure later noted, "the people originally saw the AQI as romantic figures only to learn that they were just criminals and murders." Thanks to the increasing rejection of AQI by the local population; accelerating improvements around Al Qaim and Fallujah; and Sheikh Satar's courage and public leadership in Ramadi; Iraqi and Coalition Forces in late 2006 and into early 2007 seized an opportunity to initiate a truly effective combined counterinsurgency effort in the province which bore fruit in the summer of 2007 and continues today.

Counterinsurgency, while focused on the population, should not be equated with non-violence or bloodless action. The year 2007 started with hard fighting by Iraqi and Coalition Forces from east of Al Qaim to areas south, east and north of Fallujah. The most dramatic successes occurred in Ramadi and south of Fallujah. Iraqi soldiers and local police, strengthened by new recruits from the tribes, and alongside U.S. Soldiers and Marines, initially under the command of the First Brigade Combat Team (BCT), First Armored Division and then the First BCT, Third Infantry Division, carried out a series of operations that took Ramadi back from AQI - neighborhood by neighborhood. The culmination of this effort in Ramadi was Operation Murfreesboro in February and March 2007 which killed or expelled the last of the AQI insurgents. After the operation, Iraqi soldiers and police and Coalition Forces together established police stations and combat outposts in the recently secured areas of Ramadi to prevent Takfiri insurgents from coming back. Combining Coalition and Iraqi forces, which lived and worked together down to the platoon level to control the same tactical area of operations, echoed the tactics of the successful Marine Combined Action Program (CAP) in Vietnam. The current success in Anbar, like those a generation ago in Vietnam, show that when American and indigenous forces operate together at the lowest possible level for a sustained period of time, they can produce the necessary security and, more importantly, earn the population's trust which is the *sine qua non* counterinsurgent forces need to defeat an insurgency. In Ramadi and in other cities this tactic was reinforced by intense civil-military operations to revitalize or even create local governance and restart normal services and urban facilities.

Similar operations were taking place in and around Fallujah where first the Fifth Marine Regiment and then the Sixth Marine Regiment battled to maintain the hard earned security of the area. Few of the tribes in this area were initially as willing as those in the Ramadi area to rally against the AQI. As mentioned, the Albu Issa leadership saw the merits of working with the Coalition but faced considerable internal factional discord. This was addressed by strong tribal leadership and focused Coalition support to those leaders who rallied to the coalition – first with security assistance and then by restoring critical services – all of which reinforced the legitimacy of the local tribal leader.

In the Western Euphrates River Valley, operations by the Seventh Marine Regiment, continued by the Second Marine

Regiment, began to make progress in former insurgent strongholds especially in Al Qaim, Haditha, Hit, Rawah, and Anah. Security developments in Al Qaim had gained the local elected and tribal leaders the precious time to establish legitimate and effective local governance – so much so that in February 2007 the decision was made to shut down the Coalition Civil-Military Operations Center (CMOC) in Al Qaim in favor of the undeniable effectiveness of the local Al Qaim government. Much remained to be done in Al Qaim, but now it was being accomplished by Iraqi leadership. To the southwest in Rutbah, the 15th Marine Expeditionary Unit dramatically transformed the security situation and, partnered with local leaders and police, took the city back from what had been almost total Takfiri control. This was a local development with operational impact province-wide. If insurgents had maintained control of Rutbah with its strategic position astride the road to Jordan and Syria, an effective insurgent sanctuary would have remained within the province with easy access to an international border and the profitable fuel and trade shipments that traverse it – undermining Coalition gains elsewhere in Al Anbar.

What should be noted here is that the local Iraqi police and soldiers who took part in these operations with their Coalition partners did not and do not operate as tribal or sectarian militias as some reports have suggested. They are organized, uniformed, and disciplined forces that are fully integrated into the Iraqi security system. Coalition Forces in Al Anbar have consistently stressed police professionalism as part of its counterinsurgency strategy because history teaches that a viable, trusted, and non-predatory indigenous police force is essential to the defeat of an insurgency. Not only are the police the most effective means of providing local security to a population but they are also the most effective force to intermingle with that population from which they come and collect the intelligence essential to defeating an insurgency.

The provincial government of Al Anbar and the Coalition Forces worked closely together to get officially sanctioned hiring positions from the Iraqi Ministry of Interior (MOI) in Baghdad so that all police hired in the province would have official standing as well as pay and allowances. Furthermore, once hired, all police recruits attended a training course to begin their professional development. By 2007, all new police recruits attended at least an 80 hour basic policing course or a longer course at the newly created Iraqi Police Training Academy in Habbaniya located between Ramadi and Fallujah. This training academy also conducted recruit training for Iraqi soldiers from the province and is becoming the site for advanced police and army skills training.

Thanks to the cooperation of the Iraqi Ministry of Defense (MOD) which promised that soldiers recruited from the province could spend the first two years of their service in their home province, Iraqi Army recruiting in the province soared. The First and Seventh Iraqi Divisions stationed in Anbar have passed full strength, are heading toward a 120 percent manning level, and are actively operating in the province, mostly in the rural areas as the population centers can now be effectively controlled by the police while the army is better trained and equipped to deal with threats in the province's rural and desert areas. Use of the 1st Iraqi Army Division in the Spring of 2008 outside of Al Anbar testifies to the well founded confidence the Iraqi Government has in the Divisions' proficiency and reliability.

Graduation from Habbaniya is not the end of the effort to professionalize the local security forces but just the beginning. Iraqis and Coalition Force members continue to work hand-in-hand on a daily basis in a relationship called "partnering" which not only describes the Coalition forces embedded in the Iraqi units but also the relationship of the Iraqi unit with a nearby Coalition maneuver unit. The mechanisms for this cooperation are the Police Transition Teams (PTT) and the Military Transition Teams (MTT). Each Iraqi Army Division in the province has an embedded MTT led by a Marine Colonel. There is a Provincial PTT led by a Marine Colonel and other various police training teams usually augmented from within the manpower of the associated Regimental or Brigade Combat Team, or the nearby battalion of Soldiers and Marines working with the local police in the province.

Specialist Jennie Baez, from the 47th Forward Support Battalion, provides security for fellow Soldiers and Marines during an operation in the Al Anbar Province of Iraq (USMC photo, October 11, 2006).

These teams focus on ensuring that the newly hired and trained security forces truly understand their primary mission of protecting the people (as opposed to the Baathist era primary mission of supporting a dictatorship) and how to do that. Police, to include local police chiefs, have been fired or even arrested when they did not understand this crucial difference. An aggressive Iraqi MOI internal affairs organization was becoming active at the end of 2007 and was busily investigating and sacking corrupt police officials and policeman.

From the fall of 2006 to the fall of 2007 the provincial police force in Al Anbar increased from 4,600 to 21,000. A real problem, although from the eyes of the Coalition a desirable problem, has been not having enough hiring positions, training slots, equipment, or even uniforms for all who want to join the police. This infrastructure challenge plagued Coalition logisticians who worked feverishly and ingeniously to overcome Ministry of Interior shortcomings using all means available to clothe, feed, and equip their local partners. Throughout, efforts were coordinated with the Ministry of Interior and, although often frustrating, these efforts were part of the vital requirement to link governance in Al Anbar with the central government.

Increasing Levels of Security

Per counterinsurgency theorist David Galula, as the security situation in an insurgency improves, it should "...afford the political power enough freedom to work safely with the population." In such a manner the insurgency in Anbar would be defeated and the hard earned gains of the Iraqis preserved. Once the local population had security, their interests naturally began to turn to the political, economic and social activities of normal life. Thus began the most crucial part of the campaign in Al Anbar and one of the greatest challenges Coalition Forces face throughout Iraq. While portions of Iraq may look like a scene from Lawrence of Arabia, Iraq is predominantly a modern urban society with sophisticated infrastructure requirements to keep such a society running. Which side in the struggle could administer best and restore normalcy to everyday life was the ultimate test in the battle for the Al Anbar population.

As insurgent attacks began to decline drastically in April 2007, the Coalition Force leadership in Al Anbar decided to shift even more resources and attention to the "non-kinetic fight", specifically in the areas of governance, economics, and rule of law. In April 2007 a new operational concept "Anbar Dawn" was disseminated. Designed to coordinate interagency and provincial Iraqi efforts to improve governance, the economy, and the rule of law throughout the province, it also capitalized upon the arrival of the newly established Embedded Provincial Reconstruction Teams, the reinforcement of the Al Anbar Provincial Reconstruction Team, and the first permanent assignment of USAID personnel to Al Anbar. Part of this strategy was to have Iraqis begin taking the lead in these areas, depend less on the Coalition Forces, and achieve Provincial Iraqi

Control (PIC) as part of the overall counterinsurgency strategy of General Petraeus and Ambassador Crocker.

U.S. Marine Corps Lance Cpl. William Frick, 2nd Battalion, 4th Marines, provides security during a foot patrol through the town of Barwanah, Iraq, Dec. 2, 2006. The 2nd Battalion, 4th Marines, is deployed with Regimental Combat Team 7, 1st Marine Expeditionary Force (Forward), in support of Operation Iraqi Freedom in the Al Anbar Province of Iraq (USMC photo).

In many ways Anbar Dawn offered a very different set of challenges than actual combat operations as it sometimes meant that Marines and Soldiers had to consciously take a step back and let Iraqis work things out rather than take control. Learning "tactical patience" was a key to success since the struggle was becoming less a matter of defeating insurgent formations through kinetic means and more about winning the confidence of the local population within a legitimate local government supported by the central government.

However the entire question of who would form the various local governments and the powers that would reside with the tribal leaders and the provincial government were major issues that had to be addressed at the same time as the non-kinetic efforts of Anbar Dawn were moving forward.

This factor was driven home to the Coalition Force leadership in late April 2007 during a meeting between tribal leaders of the Al Anbar Awakening and the provincial governor and vice chairman of the provincial council. The meeting, often heated, was about who would have how much political control in the province. No conclusive decision was reached and this question would be the central point of much internecine political maneuvering between the two sides. However the Coalition Force leadership noted the "dog that did not bark" during the meeting; at no time during the meeting did either side mention the insurgency. By the spring of 2007 the indigenous elected and hereditary leaders of the province implicitly assessed the insurgency as defeated and were turning their attention from establishing security to politics. Not clear to all at the time, it was in retrospect a major signpost of a return to normalcy in the province. The Coalition sensed this sea change in the Iraqi perception of the security environment, and recognizing there was no near term democratic process to redefine the political landscape, attempted to stay ahead of the post-conflict power sharing conundrum by emphasizing participatory government at all levels. Elections would follow in the indeterminate future when the legislative logjam in Baghdad broke. In the meantime, there needed to be a pressure release mechanism accounting for the new energies being expended in local political organization.

The relationship between the hereditary and elected leaders in the province was often the most difficult one for Coalition Force personnel to understand, but also the most important one to get right for long term success. On the one hand, the Coalition Forces needed the help of the tribal leaders to fragment the insurgency, provide public moral suasion, and contribute drafts for the security forces. On the other hand, the Coalition Forces also had to nurture functioning elected governments that could deliver goods and services, develop a just rule of law, and rebuild the province after several years of fighting.

This was further complicated by the fact that the tribal leadership was mostly rural in nature while members of the provincial government were often the province's urban elites and educated technocrats (although they still retained their own tribal affiliations which further complicated an already complicated situation). In 2005, Sunnis of almost all political stripes had boycotted the national elections - the provincial-wide turnout was less than 4,000 persons. The only party to stand in the elections and therefore win most of the seats for the provincial council was the Iraqi Islamic Party (IIP) – a party that viewed tribal society largely as an historical anachronism and an impediment to modernity. Needless to say, for their part, the tribes generally regarding the IIP with suspicion at best, and at worst as a direct security threat.

As increasing levels of security were achieved in 2007 and attention of the province's leaders shifted to basic politics – who gets what and when – the low election turnout in 2005 led the leadership of the Al Anbar Awakening to question of legitimacy of the IIP dominated provincial council and government. Having sacrificed much in the bid for provincial stability, the SAI believed that it should have a greater say in how reconstruction and other funds were apportioned. However at the same time there were tribal challenges to the political aspirations of the Al Anbar Awakening's leadership. Key tribal leaders around Fallujah and in the Western Euphrates River Valley expressed reluctance to let Sheikh Satar and the Al Anbar Awakening speak for the entire Dulaimi Confederation, and instead viewed them as a local Ramadi based alliance. This too represented a return to historical normalcy among the tribes and at a counter-intuitive level was welcome news if not entirely comprehended by outside observers. As the security situation bought time for the political elements to organize, gain effectiveness, and craft a legitimate way forward, the Coalition Forces served as an honest broker to keep local political differences from erupting into violence and from being exploited by the AQI.

The AQI had proven itself to be an adaptable enemy and no one in the spring of 2007 underestimated the resourcefulness and ferocity of AQI. Caught on the wrong side of the changing security environment, the AQI shifted its tactics and soon a spate of chlorine enhanced vehicle borne IED attacks hit the province to try to re-intimidate the population. Furthermore, as Coalition Forces moved to restore urban areas to gain the acceptance of the province's population, AQI, pushed out of the population centers, sought to exploit its sole remaining advantage, the ability to attack the long and largely unprotected lines of communication in the province - roads, bridges, power lines, and railroad – in order to create the appearance of power and suasion over the lives of the Anbaris regardless of the measures taken by the Coalition and the provincial government.

The two-fold answer to meet these challenges was the earlier mentioned increase in the size of Iraqi security forces in order to have the manpower to control the population centers, patrol the lines of communication, and disrupt AQI cells periodically massing in the desert hinterlands and political efforts to insure tribal politics were stable and could not be exploited by the AQI. Therefore, Coalition Force leadership spent considerable effort convincing tribal leaders who had sought refuge outside of Iraq to take advantage of the new security situation and return to Al Anbar to provide greater unity and vision to the tribal opposition to AQI. By the summer of 2007 many had done so including Sheikh Ali Amer Suleiman, the sheikh of sheikhs of the Dulaimi Confederation, who returned to his house in Ramadi. By the close of 2007, and by the tribes' own reckoning, ninety percent of the relevant sheikhs had returned to Anbar. The return of the tribal leadership allowed the re-establishment of a traditional trilateral balance of power to develop between the sheikhs of the Western Euphrates River Valley, the Ramadi area, and the Fallujah area, which coupled with the presence of the Confederation's respected leader, staunched much infighting and low-level tribal jockeying for power that AQI could have exploited. By the summer of 2007, the Coalition Force leadership in Al Anbar could report to General Petraeus that virtually all tribes in the province were engaging with the Coalition Forces against the insurgency.

With the tribes largely cooperating with the Coalition Forces, this also removed much of the legitimacy for the nationalist elements of the insurgency which essentially ceased operations against Iraqi and Coalition Forces in Al Anbar. At the end of 2007, with AQI essentially defeated in the population centers, there has been no violent resurgence of the nationalist resistance movements. There are many explanations for this but probably the two most likely are the sheer conflict/violence weariness among the population and the generally held and growing view within the nationalist movements that the US in general, and the Coalition Forces in particular, were no longer a threat to Anbar and the Sunni population when compared to the brutality of the AQI, the widely held perceptions of Iranian infiltration throughout Iraq, and perceptions of a hostile sectarian government in Baghdad.

Throughout 2007, the AQI continued sporadic attacks against vital infrastructure targets in an attempt to undermine the ability of the provincial government to provide basic goods and services. The movement of the 13th Marine Expeditionary Unit into a Takfiri haven near Lake Thar Thar furthered the destruction of AQI capacity while other Coalition Forces in the province prevented the re-establishment of new havens. By the summer of 2007 attacks against Iraqi and Coalition forces had come to an all time low and in the former AQI "capital" of Ramadi, days would pass without a single hostile shot being fired allowing Ramadi to hold an organized foot race through its formerly war torn streets.

By December 2007, another example of the improved security situation was the successful execution of Operation Silver Sooners, the transit of over 20,000 Iraqi pilgrims (Shia and Sunni) attending the Hajj in Saudi Arabia via the oasis town of An Nukhayb in southeastern Anbar without the loss or injury to a single pilgrim or the detection of a single enemy act.

Legitimacy

Still, to solidify security gains, a viable provincial government was necessary to rebuild the province. The question of its legitimacy could not be definitively settled until the central government in Baghdad decided on when the next provincial elections could be held. However near term legitimacy and therefore the allegiance of the population could be developed to some degree if the government could demonstrate an ability to get things done by improving the quality of life of Al Anbar's citizens. Therefore, the Coalition Force leadership worked hard to assist the provincial government in reconstruction and infrastructure repair, and revitalizing local city governments and the provincial court system.

In the absence of a democratic process, an election, there needed to be both the appearance and the reality of participatory government. One measure to foster this was a program called "helicopter governance" where Marine aviation ferried provincial leaders throughout the province to engage with local governments and citizens. Provincial Council Chairman Dr. Abdulsalam Mohammed and Provincial Governor Maamoon Sami Rashid traveled tirelessly throughout the province and regularly to Baghdad to lobby the central government for funds and assistance. This effort sought to establish connectivity between the central government and the provincial government and then connect both to the province's cities and towns with the aim of a creating an effective and relevant government for all Anbaris. The provincial council returned to the province and now meets regularly in its renovated chambers in the provincial government center in downtown Ramadi.

One of its main achievements in 2007 was the Iraqi development of a $107,000,000 USD budget for the province from Iraqi reconstruction funds provided by the central government in Baghdad. While funding execution by the central government remains problematic there have been some encouraging signs. For example, the 2007 Iraqi Ministry of Electricity (MOE) budget for Al Anbar province released in the late spring initially only approved two out of over 30 requests for electrical projects in the province. However in July MOE officials traveled to Ramadi to meet with the Governor and discuss what additional projects could be added to the 2007 budget. The MOE officials later explained that when the central government in Baghdad put together the national budget they believed that the security situation in Al Anbar would allow for only two MOE projects to be completed and could not have predicted that the improvement in security by the summer of 2007 would make additional projects practical.

Still, many impediments remain that make governance in the province problematic. One of the greatest impediments is the centralized, socialist, Saddam-era bureaucratic system that still exists in the Iraqi government. This system not only penalizes individual initiative and discourages innovation like all socialist systems but it has proven to be a brake on the speedy processing of reconstruction projects in Al Anbar province.

Another difficulty has been the lack of an effective criminal justice system. While the civil justice system in Al Anbar remained functioning even through the worst of the violence of 2004-2006, the criminal legal system quickly fell apart due to the insurgent murder and intimidation campaign. In many cases, tribal systems of justice replaced any form of felony adjudication. When the police force began to function again in 2007, it almost became a victim of its own success arresting more people than the legal system could process.

The Coalition pursued a two prong remedy to this problem first bringing judges from Baghdad to determine the prosecutorial merit of the cases of the growing detainee populations and, at the same, working with Iraqis to protect judges and renovate the province's judicial infrastructure (courtrooms, jails, judicial offices, etc.) in order to breathe life back into the institution of the provincial criminal justice system. In a solution in place since August 2007, criminal trials take place in the province led by judges from the province itself. Investigative judges are also hard at work reviewing arrest reports, advising the police on proper procedures, and making sure that there is probable cause to hold those arrested in jail until trial.

These successes are first and foremost the result of the efforts and courage of the Iraqis themselves. Where possible and necessary, Coalition Forces have worked with them to assist in removing roadblocks to progress by providing above all security but also advice and, where necessary, funding for infrastructure repairs and materials. The major interface between the Iraqis and the Coalition Forces has been the individual Marines, Soldiers, and Sailors, who have take on the complex task of assisting Al Anbar to rebuild its infrastructure and civil society - with or without the requisite experience. Suffice to say that once home, few veterans who served in Iraq will ever again take for granted the local police and teachers; sewer, water, and electrical workers; garbage men and street cleaners; city hall clerks and managers, and all others who make a modern urban society run. Nor will they take for granted the intangibles of Rule of Law and respect for basic Human Rights that form the basis for personal interaction in a modern society.

While practically all Coalition Force tactical units worked with the population of Al Anbar to assist in either providing security or supporting reconstruction, the main nodes connecting the local population and the Coalition Forces are the civil affairs teams, provincial reconstruction team (PRT), and embedded provincial reconstruction teams (ePRTs).

In 2007, in a break from previous practice, civil affairs units were attached directly to the regiments or brigade combat team operating in Al Anbar. This decision recognized the opportunities now available in the operational environment and proved a positive move as the local commanders now had direct control of these assets and integrated them fully into their plans. Additionally, the success of the PRT/ePRT concept is unmistakable and those who serve in them in Al Anbar, as elsewhere in Iraq and Afghanistan, are major catalysts for change, far out of proportion to their limited numbers.

However, since this program is a success, it is bound to be copied in future conflicts and therefore there are many lessons learned beyond the scope of this article which must be captured and addressed for future coordination of the civil and military sides of a counterinsurgency campaign.

Conclusion

As noted at the beginning of this chapter, the struggle goes on in Al Anbar. However it is a fight led more and more by Iraqis with the Coalition Forces advising and providing additional strength, support, and supervision as needed. New challenges emerge but progress continues – it is a dramatic improvement over what was once seen as a province lost to the AQI.

A UH-1 Huey helicopter with Marine Light Attack Helicopter Squadron 167 lands at a task-force assembly area before a reconnaissance mission in Al Anbar Province, Iraq on May, 1, 2008.

Success did not come cheap. Since the war began, there has been a heavy toll of Coalition Force members killed or wounded in Al Anbar province alongside the even greater casualties of Iraqi security force members. Hundreds of brave Iraqi citizens who stood up to become mayors, council members, judges, and civil servants paid dearly with their lives or those of their families and their tribal members as victims of a horrendous insurgent murder and intimidation campaign. But for every Iraqi who has fallen, several others have stepped forward to take their place. The best example of this spirit was shown in another parade held down Ramadi's main boulevard on October 23, 2007, just 53 weeks after AQI held its parade in the same city.

The parade was led by the sons of Anbar, police and soldiers, who have been the key to defeating AQI and bringing peace and normalcy back the province. To them, and to the fallen, this chapter is dedicated. **HX**

CHAPTER 5

AN OUNCE OF PREVENTION

By Major James Spies, U.S. Army

"A country is not conquered and pacified after military operations have bent all heads by terror; when the first fear is overcome, ferment of revolt will grow among the masses, which the accumulated bitterness caused by brutal action of force will multiply and steadily increase."
General Joseph Simon Gallieni c.1862

There is a recurring theme in US military involvement: A failure to prepare or accommodate for the post conflict reconstruction or destabilization after major combat operations. The question arises then: is there a way to prevent the wave of looting, rioting or civil unrest following combat operations? Is there a way to solve the dilemmas of "Phase IV" and the growth of insurgencies? This article examines the dynamics involved in post conflict planning and provides direction for further development of theory and doctrine. From the Army's first counter-guerrilla manual there is a clear point made that it is best to stop an insurgency early. In a fitting manner this paper seeks to work out how, "An ounce of prevention is worth a pound of cure."

This chapter starts with an examination of why states and the societies within them have such turbulent responses to combat operations. Examining more than the anecdotal recognition that war is violent and it would obviously cause civil unrest. It is necessary to determine when and how civil unrest begins and most importantly how to prevent it. Examples of post conflict planning and operations are drawn from U.S. involvement in Panama, Iraq and the Chinese Civil War.

The invasion of Panama, in Operation Just Cause, provides an excellent example of a rapid, successful, complex operation followed by civil unrest and reconstruction hurdles, despite having individuals and staff sections thinking about solutions and planning for contingencies. Operation Iraqi Freedom (OIF) will be examined in context of post conflict stability operations. OIF and specifically the Special Forces operations in the town of Ar Rutbah provides an example of failing to plan for post conflict operations but implementing effective tactics to stabilize a community. Finally this paper looks to China and the Civil war. Principally the focus is on 1945-1949, a period with major combat ongoing by conventionally organized armies. The Chinese communists managed to employ an operational organization and assigned tasks that minimized the unrest. Using this final case study in contrast to the previous ones I will propose ways to make Full Spectrum Operations work for the Army on the offense.

Formal, conventional warfare seeks to replace the existing regime of a state by defeating its standing military. The defeat of the military provides the victor the ability to coerce the defeated government to comply with directives and dictums by the victor. The premise is at the core of U.S. military dominance. If the US defeats an enemy's military it can control its government. With control of the government secured the control of the
population is established.

This concept has one flaw. The premise rests on this idea that the population will always do as the state says. But individuals don't always conduct themselves as the state directs. The reality is that individuals do not always comply with their current regime. It is only through robust state capacity to implement policies and laws that the social contract is fulfilled.[1] Individual citizens may not desire to pay their taxes, but the state's capacity to collect ensures the social contract is fulfilled.

A mass revolution there is a rapid deflation of the society's normal social controls. In an insurgency there is an erosion of control over society followed by a transition to a sub-

---

[1] Raymond, Millen. "The Hobbesian Notion of Self-Preservation Concerning Social Behavior During an Insurgency." *Parameters*. Carlisle Barracks (March, 2006).

state actor's control. Major combat operations serve a similar function as the revolution. In each of these cases the states capacity to implement policy and rule of law is degraded. A rapid, decisive disruption of normal social controls is exactly what results from conventional offensive operations in populated areas. The leviathan that was the ruling regime is now displaced. Following that is a wake of unrest as individuals find themselves outside the normal constrictions of state control.

In order to better understand the circumstances of the upheaval and social unrest following a major combat operation or invasion it helps to look towards political theory. Specifically in this case it is helpful in understanding how insurgencies grow to look to Samuel Huntington's *Revolution and Political Order.*[2] This chapter explains the difference between western and eastern revolutionary models. His very definition that "A revolution is a rapid, fundamental, and violent domestic change in the dominant values and myths of a society, in its political institutions, social structure, leadership, and government activity and policies," goes as far as disassociating the revolution for the insurgency because of the lack social change.[3] In fact this change in political structure almost always changes the social aspect of a country. Therefore Huntington's argument very much applies to the social upheaval associated with insurgents.[4] Of even greater importance

---

[2] Huntington, Samuel. "Revolution and Political Order." in *Revolutions: Theoretical, Comparative, and Historical Studies.* Harcourt Brace College Publishers (2003) pp 37-45.

[3] *Ibid.*, pp 38.

[4] The insurgent looks towards a fundamental change in the way government conducts itself. If it were possible to change faster the insurgent would. It is a function of the lack of resources that the insurgent must use time, and so as a defining point the use of rapid is applicable in hindsight but nothing more. The core argument of the piece is that the demand for political inclusion and participation is greater than the supply and the society cannot assimilate the new mobilized political entities in a manner that is not turbulent. Out of this disparity between supply and demand the revolution is born. The liberation of individual's perception of political opportunity following an invasion must be similar in effect to the lead lag discrepancy Huntington denotes in his work.

is his description of Eastern Versus Western models of revolution. While Huntington examined the major revolutions of history (China, Russia, French, English) he discovered two distinct patterns by which the revolution developed and resolved itself. In the Western model *the* revolution begins with a violent and rapid collapse of the existing regime. It is as if the regime hits a breaking point where even the elite who prosper by the status quo do not come to the aid of the state and the revolutionary zeal boils over. Violence on the streets and in the government offices leads to a vacuum. The state's capacity to quell violence and restore legitimacy is so profoundly upset that mass revolution ensues. The initiation of the revolution is a demand for change. In the wake of this groups of mobilized citizens organize into respective movements. They assimilate goals and look to gain power and authority where the state has left none. As the competing groups violently and non-violently resolve their differing views of how order should be reestablished there is an eventual outgrowth of new political institutions.

Western Model

Disintegration

New Group Mobilize

Create new Political Institutions

Come to Power

Charles Tilly describes Huntington's model best, "In the Western model, the old political institutions disintegrate and only then do new groups mobilize into politics, create new political institutions, and come to power."[5]   This revolution brings about a rapid, fundamental and violent domestic change. This is what the coalition achieved through its invasion. A rapid and violent change to Iraqi domestic politics was imposed by the very capabilities of the U.S. military. The end result is that the Iraqi state was thrust into a revolutionary cycle.

Huntington outlined two perspectives on revolution. In His argument concerning modernization Samuel Huntington argued that the two revolutionary models differed in their sequence, but not in content.   The difference being the order in which the steps are taken. In the western model of revolution, the first step of the revolution is the collapse of the old regime. The same social, economic and political conditions that existed under the old regime are followed by similar institutions in the new regime. A major shift is seen when the moderates who had initial control of the state following the revolution are pushed from power by more radical forces. Huntington goes on to note that in the western model, the revolution does not come about from the exertions of the revolutionary. As Pettee states, "the revolution, does not begin with the attack of a powerful new force upon the state. It begins simply with a sudden recognition by almost all the passive and the active members that the state no longer exists. Revolutionists enter the limelight, not like a man on horseback, as victorious conspirators appearing in the new forum, but like fearful children, exploring an empty house, not sure that it is empty."[6]

A social vacuum is created that has to be filled. The coalition forces did enter Baghdad closer to riding horses than Petee describes, but the result was the same. From the very rapid victory the coalition forces had control of the country before they were ready to administer rule.

With the collapse of the old regime there is a commonly seen event: rioting. If a new combination of social forces can

---

[5] Tilly, Charles.

[6] Petee, George S. *The Process of Revolution.* Harper and Row (New York, 1938) pp 100-101

secure control rapidly the state machinery and the instruments of control can be utilized to restore order. If elements of coercion by the state are not utilized quickly or dismantled in the case of Iraq, radical groups are left free to mobilize their own coercive systems for attaining control.

Bravo Company, 1st BN, 5th SFG and attachments entering the town of Ar Rutbah during the invasion of Iraq (Photographer: Maj. Spies).

This Eastern model of revolution follows a distinctly different cycle of the same events. In the Eastern model, new groups are mobilized. The small groups of individuals are cultivated into new political institutions that fight for control of the population. The push for control of the population forces the collapse of the state that allows the revolutionaries to come to power. Groups are politicized for change and are combating the state to gain control.

The Western model follows a post-invasion Iraq, while the Eastern model of revolution outlined by Huntington follows a path very much like Maoist insurgency. The rapid collapse of the state that denotes the beginning of Huntington's Western model of revolution looks very much like any post invasion country. A lack of quick action on the part of the occupiers leads to the breakdown of formal and informal social controls.[7] This loss of control leads to the vacuum of power that radical groups use to mobilize individuals into action. In this western model, finally new political entities mobilize and eventually a new order is established. This closely follows how occupying armies attempt to mobilize portions of the public to recreate social control and order once more.

Eastern Model

New Group Mobilize
⬇
Create new Political Institutions
⬇
Disintegration
⬇
Come to Power

From an understanding that a conventional invasion is the equivalent to a western style revolution, where should commanders look to determine tasks to conduct at the local level? In 1995 the Special Operations/ Low Intensity Conflict program of the Naval Postgraduate School produced a thesis that is of critical importance to assisting in this understanding of Full Spectrum Operations. The authors, Bender and Johnson, chose to focus not on why individuals rebel, but rather on the how.[8]

Bender and Johnson work from a contingency theory of conflict. The premise is that the appropriate structure for an

---

[7] *Policing Socisety in Counterinsurgency.* Irregualr Warfare Message of the Month, November 2006. website: http://www.usma.edu/dmi/iw_message.htm, accessed 15 March, 2008.

[8] Bender, William ; Johnson, Craig L. *How Men Rebel. An Organizational Model for Insurgency.* Master's Thesis, Naval Postgraduate School (Monterey, CA 1995) pp 13.

organization is always contingent on a number of both internal and external variable factors that shape the organizations that operate in that environment. There are two environments that organizations operate in: the contextual and the task. The task environment looks at the interaction at the organizational level it, "Represents the system where the organization acquires inputs, takes action and conducts its production and market outputs."[9] It is in this task environment that the insurgent organization takes action to acquire resources, assign and achieve its goals. The contextual environment is the, "Broad socio-political, economic, cultural and demographic environment." The overall viability of the organization is determined by this contextual environment.[10] Contextual environment itself does not cause conflict; it sets the conditions for exploitation and growth by the insurgent organizations.

An Afghan National Army soldier participates in a demonstration to display weaponry and communications capabilities at Camp Joyce, Afghanistan, Feb. 12, 2008 (U.S. Army, Photographer: Specialist Jordan Carter).

---

[9] *Ibid.*, pp 13.

[10] *Ibid.*, pp 11.

These insurgent organizations developed out of associational networks of individuals and small groups. These groups assign leaders and assimilate goals in politically and socially defined openings in society. The understanding of the opening or realization of political opportunity is based on the framework of the individuals. A framework is a term used in Social Movement Theory to define the way a group of individuals within a society collectively assign meaning to the world around them.[11] It was originally developed by Erving Goffman in his theories of symbolic interaction.[12] As these groups of individuals become organized, they begin operating in the task environment where the insurgent organization seeks to achieve its goals. It is important to keep in mind that the two environments have a permeable boundary between them. This means that changes in the contextual environment will affect the framework of the individuals which results in a changed perception of success and failure.

The contextual environment that forms common preference groups within the broader society operate in a market place for organizational support. The market size, "Represents the elements of disenfranchised or disequilibriated society."[13] The insurgent organization seeks to recruit from this pool of disenfranchised individuals. The market therefore represents the demand for political change. With the adoption of movement-countermovement principles the mobilization of one group will naturally see the rise of another. These competing organizations are operating in what is called mobilization space. For most insurgent groups, when they start out they are in a closed space. They operate in an area that the state can bring legal and military assets against them. Most insurgent organizations will adopt a closed structure. This closed structure is used to ensure a small,

---

[11] McAdam, Doug. Comparative Perspectives on Social Movements: Political Opportunities, Mobilizing Structures, and Cultural Framings.

[12] Goffman, Irving. *The Presentation of Self in Everyday Life* Doubleday Books (New York, 1959).

[13] Bender, pp 16.

exclusive, highly committed group can operate clandestinely in a decentralized manner to achieve its goals. This closed structure is less adaptable than open structures, but more secure given the illegal nature of the organization.

In terms of an offensive force moving across a country, as they come to population centers they are entering and existing context environment, but their actions at the task environment rapidly cross into the contextual from the presence and use of force. The longer and or harder combat operations continue the more impact on the contextual environment of framework they will have. There may not be any way to minimize this. There may be no reason to minimize this either. The reality is that the combat operations must continue to achieve success and so what is required is an adaptation of tactics to account for this reality.

The offensive military force has a set of goals that determine how it must act, just as the insurgent does. The key become operating in such a manner that the task environment of the conventional offensive force minimizes the market for the insurgent organization. The fact that formal and informal social controls have been severely disrupted by the conventional force on the offensive means the operational space for the insurgent has grown. Whereas before the invasion there was little space for an insurgency to grow and operate it now has a greater freedom. This means the offensive force must act quickly to minimize the market while simultaneously trying to diminish the space again.

How to go about doing this? If, "Insurgencies succeed or fail based on their ability to develop and sustain a mobilization capacity that attracts and engenders either active or passive support within the population...Its essential mechanism is the 'cause' used to convince recruits to opt out of whatever political process defines legitimate governance and to engage in or support collective political violence."[14] Then the market that

---

[14] Tomes, Robert. "Schlock and Blah: Counter-insurgency Realities in a Rapid Dominance Era." *Small Wars & Insurgencies.* Routledge (London, 01 March 2005) pp 44.

Bender and Johnson talk about becomes a critical factor. A decision has to be made concerning the priorities of short and long cycle decisions. Programs and projects that require more time, but could potentially have high payoff. There is the risk though, that by focusing on the long cycle there will be neglected short cycle decisions that cumulatively would impede progress towards the long term goals. To overcome this, the counterinsurgency force must determine the best way to employ short cycle decisions that align with long term goals. This is equivalent focusing on the task environment with respect towards how it will impact the contextual environment.

It is this task environment determination that Civilian Directed Reconstruction concept becomes critical.[15] To maintain this focus on the short cycle decisions timing becomes critical. The task of providing stability in the wake of the invading force means there is a short time to achieve the interrelated tasks of political and institutional stability, internal security, and economic and social bolstering. These must all be conducted simultaneously, but this of course has a high cost in funding and manpower. Insurgency has many similarities to economic businesses. The market has been discussed. A supply and demand side of the revolution can be seen. And the success of the counterinsurgency force relies on, "Investment at the community level [and] may improve the likelihood of success and sustainability, and consequently more numerous projects at the local level may present tangible results to communities that would be otherwise ignored by more traditional resource-intensive reconstruction projects."[16] To overcome the lack of capacity to absorb reconstruction funds and materials a longer tail is used where local, inexpensive projects are used to increase the number of task markets. Smaller projects reduce the transaction costs associated with reconstruction as it is conducted

---

[15] McNab, Robert. And Mason, Edward. "Reconstruction, the Long Tail and Decentralisation: An Application to Iraq and Afghanistan" *Small Wars & Insurgencies.* Routledge (London, 01 September 2007).

[16] *Ibid.*

currently. This increase in task markets has the collective effect of impacting the task environment.

It becomes critical to ensure that units are decentralized into the smallest unit possible for security and reconstruction. By pushing the authorities for reconstruction funding down to the lowest level the impact at the local level is greater. This is also assured through a judicious approval process for projects. To earn the initial trust of the local population it is first necessary to give them what they want, regardless of what it is you believe they need. Without first gaining trust there is no ability to get any project done. So it becomes necessary to start with small, attainable projects that are chosen by the local council and through the building of trust and influence the local councils can be advised on more pertinent projects than what they may desire immediately.

This process which has been called Civilian Directed Reconstruction has three steps. The first is the identification, selection and employment of local level councils. Relying on ethnographic intelligence unit commanders will have to work with the most appropriate local leadership. In a perfect world this would be a democratically elected body that has representation of all ethnicities in the effected are. The reality is that the local commander will have to do the best they can give the short window of opportunity following the conventional force operations in the area. The second step is the assigning of block grants for reconstruction determined by the council. These grants are intended for the local level and are tied to measurable outcomes. The final step is to audit these grants, determining which projects were successful and assigning new grants based on the success of the previous ones. This entails building a bond with the local council and helping them decide which projects to fund next.

In essence success in the reconstruction is achieved by disaggregating the larger problems into a series of smaller attainable goals. By making the problem solving locally involved individuals become involved in the government process and have by in. The task environment these individuals work in works at modifying the contextual environment. Local projects cannot help but be more responsive to the local consumer. They allow citizens to better control public programs at the local level.

The Company conducting consequence management operations following the establishment of security in the town. Foodstuffs and electricity were the two primary elements of the company's efforts after security of the population was established (Photographer: Major Spies).

Elements of the Combined Joint Special Operations Task Force- West entered into the western desert of Iraq with the mission to prevent theater ballistic missiles from launching against Israel. Responsible for destroying the Iraqi theater ballistic missiles or Scud missiles in the western Iraqi desert, a repeat of the threat from Desert storm, plan 1003V allocated two Special Forces' companies to completing this task. When the combat operations began the western desert of Iraq was flooded with a multinational force that had had as its task a special recon and direct action mission. The hunting to Scuds required high mobility, long range communication and coordination, and had little to do with seizing territory from the enemy. Their mission did not include any reconstruction tasks.

In a testament to the adaptability of the SF the Town of Ar Rutbah, with a population of 25,000 was quickly stabilized following elements of Bravo Company, 1st Battalion, 5th Special Forces Group entering the city. It was after the first two weeks of combat, and the rate of enemy contacts going down elements of B Company encircled the town of Ar Rutbah. On multiple occasions Operational Detachment Alphas (ODAs) had raging fire fights with Iraqi soldiers, but on the day they entered the city the tone was different.[17] Elements of the former regime were gone and the population had a gauged response to this new power entering the city. Many people had been told that the Americans would execute city managers and so were reluctant to go near the U.S. forces as they cleared key structures. ODAs immediately moved towards their pre assigned targets. One of the highest profiles was the Baath headquarters, the nicest structure in town, and the police headquarters. The police headquarters was an old British fort built in 1927. This structure provided a central meeting point for most town activities. After operating around the city for several days they finally entered the city. With dozens of vehicles and aircraft overhead the company seized critical buildings for the control of the town. Former Baathist headquarters and police stations were seized in addition to the military posts in the town.

Within five days the company appointed a new mayor, had police back on the street and began installing social services like electricity and conducting consequence management. Non-Governmental Organizations were brought in to examine possible reconstruction projects and the vetting of the police force was begun.[18] Simultaneous to the teams within the company working on stability and reconstruction, other ODAs were conducting offensive operations to hunt individuals of

---

[17] Robinson, Linda. *Masters of Chaos: The Secret History of Special Forces.* Public Affairs (New York, 2004), pp 220-222.

[18] Ricks, Thomas E. *Fiasco: The American Military Adventure in Iraq.* Penguin Press. (New York, 2006), pp 137.

interest. At the core of what they were doing the company was conducting Full Spectrum Operations.

Ar Rutbah demonstrates that there are forces fully capable of transitioning from Special Recon and Direct Action operations, very offensive operations to Stability, Security, Transition and Reconstruction requirements. In doing this though, there was a loss in the offensive capability. A single unit cannot do Offense, defense and Stability, Security, Transition and Reconstruction at the same time. This fact identifies the requirement for forces that are dedicated to the Stability, Security, Transition and Reconstruction function in the wake of offensive operations. Civil Affairs elements have some of these abilities, but how should they be integrated into the offensive maneuver element?

In the past there has been planning for these contingencies, but poor execution. The invasion of Panama is an excellent example. As of June 1987 the country of panama was becoming more unstable and by the end of the decade the US would be involved in another major combat operation. Anti-Noriega protests were increasing in number and frequency and the "Respect Battalions" put in place by the president were creating an oppressive atmosphere. This sense of impending intervention increased in 1988 with a formal indictment in federal court of Manuel Noriega for drug charges. Increasingly as the pressure went up so did the confrontation with U. S. Troops.[19]

In early 1988 despite the increasing tension there was no plan in place to depose or otherwise force out Noriega. The commander of Southern Command (SOUTHCOM), General Fredrick Woerner, directed contingency plans be created to deal with the possibility of intervention. By early March of 1988 four planning options were created as part of contingency plan Elaborate Maze. Three of these plans were defensive and the

---

[19] *Operation Just Cause: The Incursion into Panama.* Center for Military History. CMH Pub No. 70-85-1.

fourth was offensive looking at direct regime change.[20] The original plan had the ability written in to leave the Panamanian Defense Force in place to provide security. These plans lacked any coverage of restoring civil ordered or essential services. Additionally these plans did not include provisions to support or foster a new government.

The Joint Chiefs of Staff decided it required a more developed plan. The requirement to SOUTHCOM was for an Elaborate Maze to be broken out into phases. The Elaborate Maze plans included 4 phases that lacked the post combat reconstruction and stability issues. The plan called for four phases, three defensive and one offensive. The phases were not synchronized by time or order, but were meant to be employed on an as-needed bases. They could be executed independently or sequentially based on the enemy's actions. The fourth phase was the offense operation that made regime changes the end state. The regime change did not imply a complete dismantling of the government structure, but the ability to selectively oust individuals or groups from the government. This meant the Panamanian Defense Forces could be engaged in combat one day and the remnants engaged the next in an effort to rebuild them for the express purpose of domestic security. The lack of a post conflict reconstruction or security plans the civil affairs planners in SOUTHCOM requested permission to plan a post conflict reconstruction phase. Approval was granted for the new planning and the rotating Civil Affairs (CA) staff began working through the multitude of contingencies. These included loss of basic services, former regime members starting a small insurgency, terrorism and general civil unrest. To rectify this, the Civil Affairs officers on the staff drafted a 5th phase to address post conflict disorder. The plan looked at dealing with a degraded Panamanian government capability, lack of essential services and security. The planners anticipated that the SOUTHCOM commander would assume complete military and civil responsibility for a minimum of thirty days following the

---

[20] Yates, Lawrence. "Panama, 1989-1999: The Diconnect between Combat and Stability Operations."*Military Review*. (May-June 2005) pp 46-51.

invasion. This would give time for the new Panamanian government to stand up its institutions and the SOUTHCOM commander could transition authority in a gradual manner. The CA planners desired to integrate the combat and Civil Military Operations (CMO) more and more as they developed their contingencies. This was opposite from what actually happened. The passing of time and further refinement of the OPORDs (operations order) resulted in a widening divide between the two plans.

Complicating this series of planning and orders process the Prayer Book was restricted to Department of Defense officials only for Operational Security (OPSEC) reasons.[21] The Civil Affairs staff was reservists who rotated every 30 to 90 days. The OPSEC was also extended between OPORD planners so that the different planning cells did not crosstalk. The Civil Affairs planners planned on Civil Affairs units attaching to combat units to conduct simultaneous CMO to manage displaced personnel. The planners for combat operations did not include this and had no provisions to accommodate this necessity.

As events would transpire that would bring the execution of operation Just Cause, there was never time allowed for more coordination between CMO planners the 7th Light Infantry Division and 18th Corps. Additionally the essential premise for the CMO planners that the SOUTHCOM commander would have at a minimum of 30 days as the authority in the country was changed when the President of the United States decided the new president of Panama would be sworn in on the eve of the invasion. The focus on combat operations also meant that the

---

[21] The multiple, independently executable OPORDs that made up Elaborate Maze became complex enough that the JCS directed the single plan be divided into separate OPORDs. The three defensive phases that would include the buildup of U.S. forces were to become Operation Elder Statesman. The combat operations were to become Operation Blue Spoon and the post conflict OPORDer became Krystal Ball which was renamed Blind Logic later when Blue Spoon and Krystal Ball were directly tied together formally in the OPORDer process. Klondike Key was the Non-Combatant Evacuation Operation (NEO) set of OPORDers. The entire series of OPORDers were collectively called *The Prayer Book.*

combat troops never were assigned post conflict roles. With the actual

At 45 minutes past midnight on the 20th of December 1989 the first objectives of operation Just Cause were assaulted and seized. The conventional assaults on the Panamanian Defense forces and other security apparatus within Panama were a resounding success. In the wake of these combat operations some units coped with over 10,000 displaced civilians. Other units had to stop looting in Colon and Panama City. The plans that the Civil Affairs planners painstakingly wrote were not implement as they envisioned. The result was a critical delay execution of security, stability and reconstruction operations. To the credit of the soldiers and commanders on the ground order was restored in Panama, but after 4 days of looting in the major cities. The lag time between the completion of combat operations and the beginning of post combat reconstruction allowed for civil unrest.

Piecing all these concepts together results in the ability to still conduct Rapid Dominance operations along with the ability to emplace methods to discourage insurgent growth. The further development of systems like the Future Combat System will allow the army to move even faster across the conventional battlefield and defeat conventional opponents.[22] This would appear antithetical in requirements to what we have seen in Iraq, Panama and elsewhere.[23] The reality is that as we increase this

---

[22] The Future Combat Systems (Brigade Combat Team) is the cornerstone of Army modernization. Future Combat Systems provides Soldiers and leaders with leading-edge technologies and capabilities allowing them to dominate in asymmetric ground warfare, while allowing the Army to build a force that can sustain itself in remote areas. The FCS program is progressing on time and schedule, using a holistic system of system acquisition approach to get state-of-the-art equipment to our Soldiers now. The FCS program consists of eight new Combat Vehicles, a family of unmanned air and ground vehicles, launch system, and advanced tactical and urban sensors that are all connected by a state-of-the-art network that will help Soldiers share real-time information across the battlefield https://www.fcs.army.mil/program/index.html.

[23] *Tomes.*, pp. 44.

rapid dominance capability the likelihood that we will see a conventional fight will decrease.[24] Our opponents will decide to use more asymmetric means to defeat us, not more symmetric. The Recently published FM 3.0, the foundational document for the army, spends much of its time on explaining how the army should and could conduct Full Spectrum Operations.[25]

Full Spectrum Operations requires that the Army dominate across every possible contingency in a fight at the same time. Offense, defense, stability, reconstruction, counterinsurgency will all be conducted simultaneously. Despite the desire there is no ability to do this today. The debate of military readiness has forced the discussion into two camps. On one side are those who believe the Army in particular has focused too much on counterinsurgency and has lost its conventional edge.[26] Others would notice that there is only one new field manual, FM 3-24, and a single manual does not

---

[24] To quote the NDU paper on the goal of rapid dominance:"The aim of Rapid Dominance is to affect the will, perception, and understanding of the adversary to fit or respond to our strategic policy ends through imposing a regime of Shock and Awe. Clearly, the traditional military aim of destroying, defeating, or neutralizing the adversary's military capability is a fundamental and necessary component of Rapid Dominance. Our intent, however, is to field a range of capabilities to induce sufficient Shock and Awe to render the adversary impotent. This means that physical and psychological effects must be obtained. Rapid Dominance would therefore provide the ability to control, on an immediate basis, the entire region of operational interest and the environment, broadly defined, in and around that area of interest. Beyond achieving decisive force and dominant battlefield awareness, we envisage Rapid Dominance producing a capability that can more effectively and efficiently achieve the stated political or military objectives underwriting the use of force by rendering the adversary completely impotent." Ullman, Harlan and Wade, James. *Shock and Awe: Achieving Rapid Dominance.* NDU Press (Washington, 1996) Chapter 2.

[25] FM 3.0 *Operations.* Department of the Army. February 2008.

[26] Gentile, Gian. "Listen to the Airman." *Military Review.* March-April 2008. pp 114-115.

constitute doctrinal adoption. Both sides have identified the critical requirements of the U.S. military, but neither has worked towards blending two into a new, more comprehensive doctrine. To be truly successful the military has to fight in this blended fashion.

The nature of Full Spectrum Operations is that critical impact is made at the tactical, strategic and operational levels. The irregular and human centric portion of the spectrum of operations requires unit commanders to interface with the average citizens in any country. So how does a conventional force ensure it receives this maximum interface with the average citizen to ensure success? This is in essence asking how we can ensure the task environment is impacting in a way that our short cycle decisions aid our long cycle outcomes.

The answer was shown to us sixty years ago. When Chairman Mao led the Chinese Communist Party a victory over the nationalist forces, he did it with a force that operated across the full spectrum of conflict. From 1946 to 1949 the Red Army went to what Mao named phase three or the strategic offensive. The Army pushed across Manchuria and defeated the nationalist forces of Chiang Kai-shek. More importantly than the offensive military operation is the reconstruction that followed. As the army units would pass through a village a political cadre would be emplaced that immediately began organizing the population.[27]

Mao did not have a preference for guerrilla war of conventional war. He worked with the resources he had available to him. By the end of 1946 he had massive resources at his disposal and was in a position to conduct major offensive operations. By moving into phase three, the strategic offense, where the army conducts an annihilation campaign Mao endorsed the capabilities of the conventional army on the battlefield. The critical point to take away from this is that Mao did not forget the irregular nature of war while conducting conventional operations.

---

[27] Bianco, Lucien. *Origins of the Chinese Revolution 1915-1949.* Stanford University Press (Stanford, 1971) pp 183-190.

In the wake of his conventional army Mao had tens of thousands of students working as political cadre. They organized villages and ran local elections to address local grievances. The organization of the population relied upon the standing grievances of land reform, but moving beyond this they organized village councils and organized the villages to begin reconstruction and maintain civil order at the local level.[28] This concept of immediate civil military liaison hand off, not after but *as* the conventional force moves through the town allows for a form of social control to remain in place and the collective grievances of the population to be addressed rapidly. The primary goal is to maintain civil order and security while not losing too much of the informal social control in place.

The term social control infers the use of proactive means to achieve results. Although social control is exerted in predictive forms, through the development of proactive social controls it can also be seen in its reactive form as well.[29] To understand, and ultimately create and maintain social control both forms are necessary. In both forms, proactive and reactive, social control exerts influence upon the individuals in society. Collectively, this process reproduces combined attitudes, values norms and practices of a society. Informal social controls are prevalent in upward social control. This upward control is the manifestation of the common beliefs and cultural frame of the society's weaker class exerted upon the more powerful. The power elite maintain the ability to modify or adopt formal controls and provide downward social control onto the less powerful sections of a society, but the less powerful have the ability to shape the informal controls, which overtime shifts the perception of formal control.[30]

---

[28] Chassin, Lionel. *The Communist Conquest of China.* Harvard University Press. (Cambridge, 1965) pp 120-150.

[29] Innes, Martin. *Understanding Social Control: Deviance crime and social order.* Open University Press, (England, 2003). pp 6.

[30] Black, D. *The Bahavior of Law.* Academic Press, (New York, 1976).

Mao achieved social control by having a political cadre at the local level immediately, before the social structures deteriorated and chaos started. He took control by using his eastern style of revolution to prevent the vacuum seen in western style revolutions. In operation Just Cause the J5 and planners wrote OPORDs to conduct consequence management and prepare for contingencies such as civil unrest, but they were never able to implement the plan into the combat OPORD Blue Spoon. This led to the disjointed nature of the operation where Civil Military Operations was concerned. The lead-lag of civil security and reconstruction operations was due to the lack of a properly implemented and coordinated plan, not a lack of planning.

In the case of Ar Rutbah, the members of Bravo Company did not have a plan, but had the training and attitude to conduct simultaneous offense, reconstruction and stability operations. The next use of large scale offensive conventional forces will require that the plan include not a phase IV, but an integrated force capable of organizing the local populations in the power vacuum created by the conventional force toppling the higher government. Rapid Dominance operations which are the focus of Army Future Combat System will require a social control apparatus to stabilize and rebuild simultaneous to combat operations, not following.

The Rapid Dominance and the Department of Defense move towards future combat systems in network centric warfare means an increased ability to invade and conduct offensive and defensive operations. What is not integrated is a way to link the Stability, Security, Transition and Reconstruction operations with this rapid dominance. The Civil-Military aspect does not have a reliance on high technology, but on social skills. It becomes necessary to create a new doctrine with the express purpose of linking the high paced conventional maneuver of the future combat system with the slow, methodical irregular warfare that follows. The requirement is to leave forces in place after the initial push through an area. These forces will be required to cope with a multitude of contingencies without the massive resources of the conventional forces.

The conventional offense that socially mimics the western style revolution is best dealt with by implementing an eastern style revolution in its wake. Mao used political cadre to organize villages after his front line units cleared an area of nationalist troops. A similar concept must be employed in a rapid dominance doctrine. An expansion of the original plans for Operation Just Cause required. More than consequence management, a Special Action Force (SAF) would be emplaced with the combined capabilities of Special Forces, Civil Affairs (CA) and Information Operations (IO).[31]

The resulting requirement for SAFs capabilities would equate to every Brigade Combat Team needing a tailored SAF being attached to it for the region they would operate in. The offensive elements of a Brigade Combat Team could minimize its involvement in post conflict Stability, Security, Transition and Reconstruction so that it can continue the offense. The Special Action Force would organize the local population and bring in support. SAFs could become, "The 'hands-on' tool at the operational level."[32]

Planning for these SAFs would require an assessment of the population. The nature of reconstruction and preventing insurgent growth requires tactics tailored for the specific target population and area. There must be an overall plan to co-ordinate the civil and military aspects of the operation and the plans must be thoroughly worked to assess possible contingencies.[33] Post invasion Iraq has proven a prime case study on not addressing these issues. Where theorists like Sir

---

[31] Pushies, Fred J. *U.S. Army Special Forces.* Zenith Imprint (New York, 2001) pp 27; U.S. Army Final Test Report: Engineer Control and Advisory Detachments (1963).

[32] Klapakis, Philip T. *Security Assistance Forces (SAF): A US Military Option For COIN.* Unpublished monograph (1990) pp 2.

[33] Even from the first publication of Counter Guerrilla doctrine there has been this population based requirement. See FM 31-20, Operations Against Guerrilla Forces, October 1951.

Robert Thompson focus on defeating an insurgency by defeating subversion, and ensuring secure base areas: the SAFs that follows the conventional units would focus on establishing secure areas before subversion takes hold.[34]

The offensive operations of the conventional forces would clear population areas of many would-be insurgents. Just as Sir Thompson notes, the guerrilla fighters may not be gone, but they are suppressed.[35] The gestation period for the subversive element of insurgency is short, but dealing with the growth of subversive elements it is possible to undermine the guerrillas. This prevents the insurgent organizations from growing.

This capability is possible with the Army and the Department of Defense. The forces are already in place to take advantage of Rapid Dominance. What is lacking is a force properly organized to be employed at the local level. Through an appropriate development of doctrine within the U.S. Government in approaching future conflicts countries can be stabilized during turbulent military activities.

---

[34] Thompson, Sir Robert. *Defeating Communist Insurgencies: Lessons from Malaya and Vietnam.*

[35] *Ibid.,* pp 48.

Full Spectrum Operations requires that the Army dominate across every possible contingency in a fight at the same time. Offense, defense, stability, reconstruction, counterinsurgency will all be conducted simultaneously. Here, U.S. Army Staff Sgt. Johnson coaches an Afghan National Police officer as he fires a rocket-propelled grenade launcher during a skills assessment mission on a range in Beshud, Afghanistan, Feb. 13, 2008 (US Army photo.)

CHAPTER 6

THE GATES OF FIRE IN MOSUL, IRAQ

By Michael Yon

Combat comes unexpectedly, even in war.

On Monday, while conducting operations in west Mosul, Iraq, a voice came over the radio saying troops from our brother unit, the 3-21, were fighting with the enemy in east Mosul on the opposite side of the Tigris River. Moments later, Staff Sergeant Will Shockley relayed word to us that an American soldier was dead. We began searching for the shooters near one of the bridges on our side of the Tigris, but they got away. Jose L. Ruiz was killed in action.

Although the situation in Mosul is better, our troops still fight here every day. This may not be the war some folks had in mind a few years ago. But once the shooting starts, a plan is just a guess in a party dress.

The only mission I've seen unfold close to what was planned was a B Company raid a few months back. It actually went so close to perfect that we could hardly believe it. The sole glitch occurred when a Stryker hit an IED, but since nobody was hurt, we just continued the mission. In retrospect, it's hard to imagine why I didn't write about it. But times are busy, and, apart from it going nearly perfectly according to plan, it just seemed like any other old raid.

I had been talking with Captain Matt McGrew about the "The Battle for Mosul IV" dispatch, intending to spend the night with him and some Iraqi troops at one of their combat outposts, to glean additional insight, but the on-going battles in Mosul kept getting in the way. On the night before the planned ride-along, the obstacle was a big and sudden push of operations and tasks bundled in a "surge operation." Operation Lancer Fury was launched without notice even to the unit commanders here.

When I'd sat in on the "warning order" (notice of impending operations) for Lancer Fury last week, the plan was so cleverly contrived that the leadership at Deuce Four had to grudgingly acknowledge its excellence, even though the idea had originated from higher-up. In every military unit I have seen, there is a prevailing perception that good ideas trickle down from the top about as often as water flows uphill, so Lancer Fury apparently was a *wunder-plan*.

As a "surge" operation, Lancer Fury is sort of a crocodile hunt, where our people do things to make the crocodiles come out, trying to flush them into predictable directions, or make them take certain actions. And when they do, we nail them. The combat portion of the Surge amounted to a sophisticated "area ambush" that would unfold over the period of about one week.

The top leaders of the Deuce Four: Command Sergeant Major Robert Prosser and Lieutenant Colonel Erik Kurilla making the call to Daniel's Mom outside the hospital.

This Surge is a complicated piece of work, with multidimensional variables and multifarious moving parts. Those parts range literally from boots on our feet to satellites zipping overhead. So, of course, glitches and snags started occurring the first day. Among other things, key gear failed; but overall, the Surge was going well. A few terrorists had already been caught in the first 24 hours.

Thursday night, a revised plan had me following some Deuce Four soldiers on a midnight raid. They had night vision gear, so they moved quickly. I had only moonlight, so I nearly broke my leg keeping up. Sleeking around Mosul under moonlight, we prowled through the pale glow until we came upon a pond near a farmhouse. Recon platoon had already raided one house and snagged some suspects, then crept away in the darkness to another target close by.

Five soldiers from Recon—Holt, Ferguson, Yates, Welch and Ross—were moving through moon-cast shadows when an Iraqi man came out from a farmhouse with an AK-47 rifle hanging by his side. Suddenly encircled by the rifles, lights and lasers of four soldiers, the man was quickly disarmed. A fifth soldier radioed for the interpreter and together they sorted out that he was a farmer who thought the soldiers were thieves skulking around his property. Recon returned the man his rifle, and started making their way back, resolute and silent across the ploughed fields.

During a halt in some trees at the edge of the field, I overheard the voice of Lieutenant Colonel Kurilla, the commander of the Deuce Four battalion, quietly praising one of the soldiers for showing discipline in not shooting the farmer. After loading the other suspects onto Strykers, we returned to base, where I fell, exhausted, at about 3 AM Friday morning.

The Surge continued while I slept.

Alpha Company had deployed during the early hours and was conducting operations around Yarmook Traffic Circle. Sergeant Daniel Lama, who is as much respected as he is liked, was pulling security in an air guard position of his Stryker, when a bullet flew straight at his neck, striking him. As he collapsed into the Stryker, his body clenched in seizure, fingers frozen, arms and legs rigid.

I seldom get letters in Iraq, but waiting for me in the mailroom while I slept was a card. The return address sticker, an American flag on it, was from Jefferson, Pennsylvania. The postage stamp had an American flag waving. The card inside had a picture of an American flag for its cover. The sweet and heartfelt message inside ended with- *Please tell our soldiers we care so much for them. -Dan and Connie Lama.*

I was still asleep when medics brought their son Daniel to the Combat Support Hospital, or "Cash." It's a familiar place for Deuce Four soldiers, who've seen some of the most sustained and intense urban combat of this war, receiving over 150 Purple Hearts in the process.

Bap, bap, bap! on my door. I jumped up and there was Command Sergeant Major Robert Prosser, the top enlisted soldier at Deuce Four. Prosser is always professional, always direct:

"Sergeant Lama's been shot. We're rolling in ten minutes," he said.

"I'll be there in ten," I answered, instantly awake.

Within minutes, I was running out my room, still pulling zips and fastening buttons, when I came sweating into the TOC. Lieutenant Colonel Kurilla was there asking a soldier for the latest report on Sergeant Lama, now in surgery.

When a soldier is killed or wounded, the Department of Army calls the loved ones, and despite their attempts to be sympathetic, the nature of the calls has a way of shocking the families. There is just no easy way to say, "Your son got shot today." And so, according to men here, the calls sound something like this: "We are sorry to inform you that your son has been shot in Mosul. He's stable, but that's all we know at this time."

Lieutenant Colonel Kurilla likes to call before the Army gets a chance, to tell parents and loved ones the true circumstances. Kurilla is direct, but at least people know they are getting an accurate account.

We loaded the Strykers and drove down to the Cash, and there was Chaplain Wilson, who might be the most popular man on base. Everybody loves him. Often when Chaplain Wilson sees me, he will say, "Good morning Michael. How are you today?" But sometimes he asks me, "Are you okay?" and I think, *"Do I look stressed?"*

"Of course I feel okay Chaplain Wilson! Don't I look okay?"

He just laughs, "Yes, Michael, you look fine. Just checking."

But secretly, every time he asks, I feel a notch better.

Chaplain Wilson came out from the hospital smiling and explained that Daniel (Sergeant Lama) was fine. The seizure was just a natural reaction to getting shot in the neck. It was just a flesh wound. As if offering proof, Chaplain Wilson said: "When they rolled Daniel over, the doctor stuck his finger in Daniel's butt to check his prostate, and Daniel said, 'Hey! What are you doing?!'"

Everybody laughed.

I changed the subject by snapping a photo of Command Sergeant Major Prosser while Lieutenant Colonel Kurilla got Mrs. Lama on the Iridium satellite phone. I heard the commander telling this soldier's mother that her son was fine. Daniel just had some soft tissue damage, nothing major. Kurilla told her that he and some other soldiers were at the hospital now with Daniel, who was still too groggy to talk. "Really, Daniel's okay, and don't worry about it when the Army calls you."

We loaded the Strykers and headed downtown.

Some Strykers were scouting for the shooters, while others were working details at Yarmook Traffic Circle. Major Craig Triscari from the 1-17th Infantry from Alaska was with Major Mike Lawrence, "Q," and other soldiers, when he noticed a car with its hood up. The 1-17th will relieve the 1-24th soon, so Triscari has been conducting operations with Deuce Four. The vehicle struck Triscari as odd: it hadn't been there a few minutes earlier.

Automatic weapons fire started coming from at least two places. Bullets were kicking up the dust, and we got a radio call that troops were in contact at Yarmook Traffic Circle. Sitting inside the Stryker with Lieutenant Colonel Kurilla and me were two new faces. A young 2nd Lieutenant who had only been in Iraq three weeks, and hadn't seen any real combat; and a young specialist, who, per chance, is one of the few Deuce Four soldiers who is not a seasoned veteran, though he has seen some combat. Also in the Stryker was "AH," the interpreter, whose courage under fire I had seen before. But the more battle weathered fighters were not there.

Chris Espindola, the Commander's radio operator, a respected and experienced fighter, was down in Baghdad at the Iraqi Criminal Court testifying against two terrorists caught by Deuce Four months earlier. Like the card in the mailroom, the circumstances behind their capture were more germane to the events about to unfold than anyone might have guessed at the time.

Kurilla's reluctance to allow anyone outside Deuce Four ride with his soldiers - including writers - is well known. Partly because of writers, people hearing about Deuce Four in the news might think of Mosul as some kind of thrill ride where everything will end okay after a few hairpin turns. This is not true.

Newcomers, even soldiers, unaccustomed to this level of hostility, can only burden the men with added danger. So Kurilla makes sure they can be trusted by mentoring new officers and having them spend three weeks with him before they are allowed to lead men in this unit.

Some months back, a new lieutenant named Brian Flynn was riding with the Kurilla for his first three weeks, when Kurilla spotted three men walking adjacent to where Major Mark Bieger and his Stryker had been hit with a car bomb a week prior. The three men looked suspicious to Kurilla, whose legendary sense about people is so keen that his soldiers call it the "Deuce Sixth-Sense." His read on people and situations is so uncanny it borders the bizarre.

That day, Kurilla sensed "wrong" and told his soldiers to check the three men. As the Stryker dropped its ramp, one of the terrorists pulled a pistol from under his shirt. Mark Bieger was overwatching from another Stryker and shot the man with the first two bullets, dropping him to his knees.

Lieutenant Flynn was first out of the Stryker, and both he and the airguard CPT Westphal, saw the pistol at the same time and also shot the man. The other suspects started running. But all Kurilla saw was Lieutenant Flynn stepping off the ramp, and then there was a lot of shooting. Kurilla yelled *FLYNNNNNNNNNNN!!!!* and was nearly diving to stop Flynn from shooting, thinking the new lieutenant had lost his mind and was shooting a man just for running from Coalition forces. Soldiers can't just shoot anyone who runs.

Chris Espindola also shot the man. Amazingly, despite being hit by four M4's from multiple directions, the man still lived a few minutes. Soldiers outran and tackled his two associates when they made a run.

During their interrogation on base, both admitted to being Jihadists. One was training to be a sniper, while the other was training for different combat missions. They also admitted that the terrorist who was shot down was their cell leader, who had been training them for three months. They were on a recon of American forces when Kurilla sensed their intent.

The cell leader had a blood-stained "death note" in his pocket stating he was a true Mujahadeen and wanted to die fighting the Americans. He got his wish; and now, Chris Espindola, Kurilla's radio man, was down in Baghdad testifying against the two surviving co-conspirators. Despite their sworn confessions, Kurilla was left with a young radio operator with little trigger-time.

Flynn had now been a platoon leader for six months, but today Kurilla had another 2nd Lieutenant who was being mentored before he became a platoon leader. Our Stryker did not contain the normal fighters that I saw with Lieutenant Colonel Kurilla, but we also had a section (two squads) of infantrymen in Strykers from Alpha Company. This section was led by Staff Sergeant Konkol.

We were searching the area for the source of that automatic weapons fire when Kurilla spotted three men in a black Opel and his sixth sense kicked. When Kurilla keyed in on them, he pointed his rifle at the car and signaled them to get out. The driver tucked his head and gunned the gas. The chase was on.

Strykers are fast, but Opels are faster. We were roaring through little streets and along roads, horn blaring, cars zipping off the sides, the steady chatter of multiple radio channels colliding inside the Stryker. A Kiowa helicopter pilot radioed that he spotted the car. As the chase continued, the Kiowa pilot said, "It's going about 105 mph."

How can the pilot know it's going 105 mph? I thought.

(c) Michael Yon 2005

This Kiowa helicopter shot the Opel.

As if in reply, the pilot radioed that the Opel was outrunning his helicopter. Captain Jeff VanAntwerp came on the radio net saying he was moving his section into position to intercept the Opel.

"Watch out for that kid!" yelled Kurilla over the intercom to our driver as we made a hard turn, managing to avoid hitting the child.

Opels may be faster than Kiowas on straight-a-ways, but when the car made turns, the helicopter quickly caught up. Kurilla ordered the Kiowa to fire a warning shot, then quickly authorized the Kiowa to disable the vehicle.

Kiowas are small, carrying just two people; they fly so low the two flying soldiers are practically infantrymen. The pilot swooped low and the "co-pilot" aimed his rifle at the Opel, firing three shots and blowing out the back window. The Kiowa swooped and banked hard in front of the car, firing three more shots through the front hood, the universal sign for "stop."

The car chase ended, but the men fled on foot up an alley. We approached in the Strykers and I heard Kurilla say on the radio, "Shots fired!" as he ducked for a moment then popped back up in the hatch. Kurilla continued, "Trail section clear the car and clear south to north! I'm going to block the back door on the north side!"

About fifteen seconds later our ramp dropped. We ran into combat.

Folks who haven't done much urban fighting might take issue with the wild chases, and they might say that people should always "stack up" and do things this or that way, but men in Delta Force, SEALs and the like, all know that when chasing wild men into the labyrinth, soldiers enter the land of confusion. If soldiers don't go fast, the bad guys simply get away. Just a few minutes ago, these three guys were going "105 miles per hour," and outrunning a helicopter.

There were shops, alleys, doorways, windows.

The soldiers with Lieutenant Colonel Kurilla were searching fast, weapons at the ready, and they quickly flex-cuffed two men. But these were not the right guys. Meanwhile, Staff Sergeant Konkol's men were clearing toward us, leaving the three bad guys boxed, but free.

Shots were fired behind us but around a corner to the left.

Both the young 2nd Lieutenant and the young Specialist were inside a shop when a close-quarters firefight broke out, and they ran outside. Not knowing how many men they were fighting, they wanted backup. Lieutenant Colonel Kurilla began running in the direction of the shooting. He passed by me and I chased, Kurilla leading the way.

There was a quick and heavy volume of fire. And then Kurilla was shot.

Lieutenant Colonel Erik Kurilla (front right), the moment the bullets strike. The (2nd Lieutenant is front-left; radioman near-left; and the "AH" the interpreter is near-right).

Three bullets reach flesh: One snaps his thigh bone in half.

Kurill's arm and legs are shot. The Commander then rolls into a firing position, just as a bullet strikes the wall beside 2nd Lieutenant's head (left).

Kurilla was running when he was shot, but he didn't seem to miss a stride; he did a crazy judo roll and came up shooting.

Bam, Bam, Bam, Bam! Bullets were hitting all around Kurilla. The young 2nd lieutenant and specialist were the only two soldiers near. Neither soldier had real combat experience. "AH" had no weapon. I had a camera.

Seconds count.

Kurilla, though down and unable to move, was fighting and firing, yelling at the two young soldiers to get in there; but they hesitated. ***Bam, Bam, Bam, Bam!***

Kurilla was in the open, but his judo roll had left him slightly to the side of the shop. I screamed to the young soldiers, *"Throw a grenade in there!"* but they were not attacking.

"Throw a grenade in there!" They did not attack.

"Give me a grenade!" They didn't have grenades.

"Erik! Do you need me to come get you!" I shouted. But he said "No." (Thank God; running in front of the shop might have proved fatal.)

"What's wrong with you!?" I yelled above the shooting.

"I'm hit three times! I'm shot three times!"

Amazingly, he was right. One bullet smashed through his femur, snapping his leg. His other leg was hit and so was an arm.

With his leg mangled, Kurilla pointed and fired his rifle into the doorway, yelling instructions to the soldiers about how to get in there. But they were not attacking. This was *not* the Deuce Four I knew. The other Deuce Four soldiers would have killed every man in that room in about five seconds. But these two soldiers didn't have the combat experience to grasp the power of momentum.

This was happening in seconds. Several times I nearly ran over to Kurilla, but hesitated every time. Kurilla was, after all, still fighting. And I was afraid to run in front of the shop, especially so unarmed.

The Commander fights . . . and fights, as more bullets kick up dust.

And then help arrived in the form of one man: Command Sergeant Major Prosser.

Prosser ran around the corner, passed the two young soldiers, who were crouched low, then he ran past me and right to the shop, where he started firing at the men inside.

A man came forward, trying to shoot Kurilla with a pistol, apparently realizing his only escape was by fighting his way out, or dying in the process. Kurilla was aiming at the doorway waiting for him to come out. Had Prosser not come at that precise moment, who knows what the outcome might have been?

Prosser shot the man at least four times with his M4 rifle. But the American M4 rifles are weak - after Prosser landed three nearly point blank shots in the man's abdomen, splattering a testicle with a fourth, the man just staggered back, regrouped and tried to shoot Prosser.

Then Prosser's M4 went "black" (no more bullets). A shooter inside was also having problems with his pistol, but there was no time to reload. Prosser threw down his empty M4, ran into the shop and tackled the man.

Though I have the photo, I do not remember the moment that Prosser went "black" and ran into the shop. Apparently I turned my head, but kept my finger on the shutter button. When I looked back again, I saw the very bloody leg of Command Sergeant Major Prosser inside the shop. It was not moving. He appeared to be shot down and dead.

I looked back at the two soldiers who were with me outside, and screamed what amounted to *"Attack! Attack!! Attack!!!"* I stood up and was yelling at them. Actually, what I shouted was an unprintable string of curses, while Kurilla was also yelling at them to get in there, his M4 trained on the entrance. But the guys were not attacking.

I saw Prosser's M4 on the ground: *Where did that come from?*

I picked up Prosser's M4. It was empty. I saw only Prosser's bloody leg lying still, just inside the darkened doorway, because most of his body was hidden behind a stack of sheet metal.

"Give me some ammo! Give me a magazine!" I yelled, and the young 2nd Lieutenant handed over a full 30-round magazine. I jacked it in, released the bolt and hit the forward assist. I had only one magazine, so checked that the selector was on semi-automatic.

I ran back to the corner of the shop and looked at Lieutenant Colonel Kurilla who was bleeding, and saw Command Sergeant Major Prosser's extremely bloody leg inside the shop, the rest of him was still obscured from view. I was going to run into the shop and shoot every man with a gun. And I was scared to death.

What I didn't realize was at that same moment four soldiers from Alpha Company 2nd Platoon were arriving on scene, just in time to see me about to go into the store. Staff Sergeant Gregory Konkol, Sergeant Jim Lewis, and specialists Nicholas Devereaux and Christopher Muse where right there, behind me, but I didn't see them.

Reaching around the corner, I fired three shots into the shop. The third bullet pierced a propane canister, which jumped up in the air and began spinning violently. It came straight at my head but somehow missed, flying out of the shop as a high-pressure jet of propane hit me in the face. The goggles saved my eyes. I gulped in deeply.

In the tiniest fraction of a second, somehow my mind actually registered *Propane . . . FIREBALL!* as it bounced on the ground where it spun furiously, creating an explosive cloud of gas and dust, just waiting for someone to fire a weapon.

I scrambled back, got up and ran a few yards, afraid that Kurilla was going to burn up if there was a fire. The soldiers from Alpha Company were heading toward him when Kurilla yelled out that he was okay, but that Command Sergeant Major Prosser was still in the shop. The Alpha Company soldiers ran through the propane and dust cloud and swarmed the shop.

When the bullet hit that canister, Prosser—who I thought might be dead because of all the blood on his leg—was actually fighting hand-to-hand on the ground. Wrapped in a ground fight, Prosser could not pull out his service pistol strapped on his right leg, or get to his knife on his left, because the terrorist—who turned out to be a serious terrorist—had grabbed Prosser's helmet and pulled it over his eyes and twisted it.

Prosser had beaten the terrorist in the head three times with his fist and was gripping his throat, choking him. But Prosser's gloves were slippery with blood so he couldn't hold on well. At the same time, the terrorist was trying to bite Prosser's wrist, but instead he bit onto the face of Prosser's watch. (Prosser wears his watch with the face turned inward.) The terrorist had a mouthful of watch but he somehow also managed to punch Prosser in the face. When I shot the propane canister, Prosser had nearly strangled the guy, but my shots made Prosser think bad guys were coming, so he released the terrorist's throat and snatched out the pistol from his holster, just as Staff Sergeant Konkol, Lewis, Devereaux and Muse swarmed the shop. But the shots and the propane fiasco also had brought the terrorist back to life, so Prosser quickly reholstered his pistol and subdued him by smashing his face into the concrete.

The combat drama was ended, so I started snapping photos again.

Command Sergeant Major Prosser, his leg drenched in the terrorist's blood, as 2nd Platoon Alpha Company arrives.

*Command Sergeant Major Prosser drags the terrorist into the alley
. . . into the light.*

*Command Sergeant Major Prosser flex cuffs Khalid Jasim Nohe and
then stands above the terrorist who bit his watch.*

Sergeant First Class Bowman shields the eyes of his Commander.

When Recon platoon showed up about a minute later, Sergeant First Class Bowman asked Lieutenant Colonel Kurilla to lie down. But Kurilla was ordering people to put out security, and directing action this way and that. When the very experienced medic, Specialist Munoz, put morphine into Kurilla, the commander still kept giving orders, even telling Munoz how to do his job. So Sergeant First Class Bowman told Munoz to give Kurilla another shot of morphine, and finally Kurilla settled down, and stopped giving orders long enough for them to haul him and the terrorist away to the Combat Support Hospital. The same facility where Daniel Lama was recovering from the earlier gunshot wound to the neck.

Combat Support Hospital

The Surge operation continued as we returned to base. The Commander and the terrorist were both being prepped for surgery, when Lieutenant Colonel Kurilla said, "Tell Major Bieger to call my wife so she doesn't get a call from the Army first." But someone gave the Commander a cell phone, and I heard Kurilla talking to his wife, Mary Paige, saying something like, "Honey, there has been a little shooting here. I got hit and there was some minor soft tissue damage." The X-ray on the board nearby showed his femur snapped in half. "I'll be fine. Just some minor stuff."

That poor woman.

The doctors rolled Lieutenant Colonel Kurilla and the terrorist into the operating room and our surgeons operated on both at the same time. The terrorist turned out to be one Khalid Jasim Nohe, who had first been captured by US forces (2-8 FA) on 21 December, the same day a large bomb exploded in the dining facility on this base and killed 22 people.

That December day, Khalid Jasim Nohe and two compatriots tried to evade US soldiers from 2-8 Field Artillery Battalion, but the soldiers managed to stop the fleeing car. Then one of the suspects tried to wrestle a weapon from a soldier before all three were detained. They were armed with a sniper rifle, an AK, pistols, a silencer, explosives and other weapons, and had in their possession photographs of US bases, including a map of this base.

That was in December.

About two weeks ago, word came that Nohe's case had been dismissed by a judge on 7 August. The Coalition was livid. According to American officers, solid cases are continually dismissed without apparent cause. Whatever the reason, the result was that less than two weeks after his release from Abu Ghraib, Nohe was back in Mosul shooting at American soldiers.

Lieutenant Colonel Kurilla repeatedly told me of - and I repeatedly wrote about - terrorists who get released only to cause more trouble. Kurilla talked about it almost daily. Apparently, the vigor of his protests had made him an opponent of some in the Army's Detention Facilities chain of command, but had otherwise not changed the policy. And now Kurilla lay shot and in surgery in the same operating room with one of the catch-and-release-terrorists he and other soldiers had been warning everyone about.

When Kurilla woke in recovery a few hours after surgery, he called Command Sergeant Major Prosser and asked for a *Bible* and the book: *Gates of Fire*. Kurilla gives a copy of *Gates of Fire* to every new officer and orders them to read it. He had given me a copy and told me to read it. In my book, there is a marked passage, which I thought rather flowery. But I have it beside me on the table by the map of Iraq.

> *"I would be the one. The one to go back and speak. A pain beyond all previous now seized me. Sweet life itself, even the desperately sought chance to tell the tale, suddenly seemed unendurable alongside the pain of having to take leave of these whom I had come so to love."[1]*

A short time after Kurilla gave me the book, following the death of one of his soldiers, he said to me, "I want you to write about my men. You are the only one who might understand," the passage registered in my mind.

I asked Command Sergeant Major Prosser if I could go with him to see the Commander. Carrying both books, we drove to the Cash. Major Mark Bieger arrived alongside Kurilla's hospital bed, paying respect. After spending some time with the Commander, Command Sergeant Major Prosser and I drove back to the unit.

The Deuce Four

The truest test of leadership happens when the Commander is no longer there. Kurilla's men were taking down and boxing up his photos of his wife and children, and his Minnesota Vikings flag, when they decided to keep the flag so everyone could autograph it. It wasn't long before there was no room left to sign, but I found a place to scratch. I wanted my name on that flag.

The place suddenly felt hollowed-out.

---

[1] Steven Pressfield, *Gates of Fire: An Epic Novel of the Battle of Thermopylae* (Bantam Press, September 27, 2005).

115

When I came back into the TOC, Major Michael Lawrence - who I often challenge to pull-up contests, and who so far has beat me (barely) every time - looked me square and professionally, in the direct way of a military leader and asked, "Mike, did you pick up a weapon today?"

"I did."

"Did you fire that weapon?"

"I did."

"If you pick up another weapon, you are out of here the next day. Understood?"

"Understand."

"We still have to discuss what happened today."

Writers are not permitted to fight. I asked Sergeant First Class Bowman to look at the photos and hear what happened. Erik Kurilla and Command Sergeant Major Prosser were witness, but I did not want the men of Deuce Four who were not there to think I had picked up a weapon without just cause. I approached Sergeant First Class Bowman specifically, because he is fair, and is respected by the officers and men. Bowman would listen with an open mind. While looking at the photos, Bowman said, "Mike, it's simple. Were you in fear for your life or the lives of others?"

"Thank you Sergeant Bowman," I said.

I walked back to the TOC and on the way, Chaplain Wilson said, "Hello Michael. Are you feeling all right?"

"Yes Chaplain Wilson!" *Why does he always ask that? Do I look stressed?* But suddenly, I felt much better. Chaplain Wilson might be the only man in the universe with a chance of getting me into the chapel of my own free will, but I have resisted so far.

Only a few hours had passed since Daniel Lama and the Commander were shot. It was around 9 PM when I heard Captain Matt McGrew was going to see Kurilla. I asked to come along. We entered the hospital, and saw that Erik Kurilla's bed was beside Daniel Lama's. Kurilla went from asleep to wide awake in about a quarter-second, said "hello" and asked us to sit down. After some conversation, the Commander looked over at the next bed and asked, "How are you doing Sergeant Lama?"

"Great, sir."

"Good," the Commander said, "You are my new PSD."
[Personal Security Detachment: Bodyguard.]

Daniel Lama smiled, got out of bed and I shot a photo of
him reporting for his "new duty."

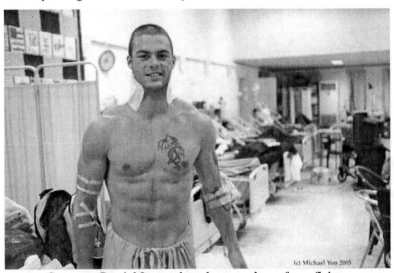

Sergeant Daniel Lama: less than one hour from flying
out of Mosul.

It was near 10 PM when the airplane that would start
their journey back to America landed outside, its engines
rumbling the hospital floor. The terrorist who shot Kurilla, and
who was now a eunuch in a nearby bed, might well have been
the same terrorist who, after being released, shot Lama and
Thompson and others. Kurilla could see Khalid Jasim Nohe, but
made no comment.

As Captain McGrew and I drove through the dusty
darkness back to the Deuce Four, the Commander and Sergeant
Lama, along with other wounded and dead soldiers from around
Iraq, began their journey home.

The next day, Iraqi Army and Police commanders were
in a fury that Lieutenant Colonel Kurilla had been shot. Some
blamed his men, while others blamed the terrorists, although

blame alone could not compete with disbelief. Kurilla had gone on missions every single day for almost a year. Talking with people downtown. Interfacing with shop owners. Conferencing with doctors. Drinking tea with Iraqi citizens in their homes. Meeting proud mothers with new babies. It's important to interact and take the pulse of a city in a war where there is no "behind the lines," no safe areas. It's even dangerous on the bases here.

In order for leaders of Kurilla's rank to know the pulse of the Iraqi people, they must make direct contact. There's a risk in that. But it's men like Kurilla who can make this work. Even and especially in places like Mosul, where it takes a special penchant for fighting. A passion for the cause of freedom. A true and abiding understanding of both its value and its costs. An unwavering conviction that, in the end, we will win.

Make no mistake about Kurilla - he's a warrior, always at the front of the charge. But it's that battle-hardened bravery that makes him the kind of leader that Americans admire and Iraqis respect. Like the soldiers of Deuce Four, Iraqis have seen too much war to believe in fairy tales. They know true warriors bleed.

Iraqi Army and Police officers see many Americans as too soft, especially when it comes to dealing with terrorists. The Iraqis who seethe over the shooting of Kurilla know that the cunning fury of Jihadists is congenital. Three months of air-conditioned reflection will not transform terrorists into citizens.

Over lunch with Chaplain Wilson and our two battalion surgeons, Major Brown and Captain Warr, there was much discussion about the "ethics" of war, and contention about why we afford top-notch medical treatment to terrorists. The treatment terrorists get here is better and more expensive than what many Americans or Europeans can get.

"That's the **difference** between the terrorists and us," Chaplain Wilson kept saying. "Don't you understand? *That's* the difference." HX

CHAPTER 7

BANDITS IN BAGHDAD: CAVALRY TROOP URBAN COUNTER-INSURGENCY OPERATIONS

By: MAJ Klaudius K. Robinson, U.S. Army

An M3 Cavalry Fighting Vehicle from B Troop, 8-10 Cavalry, in Baghdad in 2006.

The deployment of B Troop, 8-10 CAV, 4th ID at the fulcrum of the Battle for Baghdad between December 2005 and December 2006 led to successful counter-insurgency operations in a complex urban environment during a strenuous and polarizing time in the Iraq capital. The lessons learned and techniques applied by Bandit Troop in its Area of Operations (AO) in southwest Baghdad, set the conditions for a de-escalation of violence that was later reinforced by the current surge strategy. This piece is written from a Troop Commander's perspective and will focus mainly on company-level anti-insurgency operations in an urban environment even though the Troop's success is also greatly attributed to the work and support of our higher headquarters commanders and their staffs. The transformation, training, and deployment roadmap of the Troop is an essential preamble in understanding how and why success was achieved.

Bandit Troop, 8-10 Cavalry, just prior to the deployment, was reorganized and transformed from an Air Defense Battery to a Cavalry Troop. This was an extreme undertaking in the sense of transformation, training, and deployment into a combat environment. What made this difficult is that the traditional Modified Table of Organization and Equipment (MTOE) for Cavalry Troops and Squadrons was recently changed to accommodate the new Brigade Combat Team concept. The experienced Scout Non-Commissioned Officers had to learn a new formation and how to fight it. Also, Air Defense Artillery soldiers and NCO's were given the opportunity to transition their careers to become Scouts. Amazingly, the Troop transformed and deployed to Kuwait in just eight months.

In Kuwait, the Troop task organization consisted of two Scout Platoons, each with two Scout Sections consisting of an M2A2 ODS Bradley and two M1114s. The Scout Platoon Sergeant was assigned to another M1114 and the Platoon Leader to an M2A2 ODS and they usually maneuvered separated, one with each section. The Troop also had a Mortar Section consisting of two M1064A3 and the Mortar Section Sergeant's HMMWV and a FIST-V Bradley for the Troop Fire Support Officer. Not organic to the Troop was the maintenance section but upon arrival in Kuwait, they were attached to the Troop. Although not directly in the fight, they proved to be an immense contributor to our successful operations.

While in Kuwait, last minute preparations and the current TTP's utilized in Iraq were discussed among the leadership and soldiers. The Troop knew that this was going to be a year-long deployment and we knew where we were going.

What we didn't know was what would happen when we took over the AO and the sequence of events that led to the huge rift in a section of Baghdad that spilled over to the whole city. As a result of the Samarra Mosque bombing in February 2008, the underlying sectarian rift among the religious sects and ethnic ties began a series of reprisal attacks and extra judicial killings. Most of these happened in the Troop's AO because of the religious fault line running through it between the Shia and the Sunni. In fact, the major EJK activity that led to the Shia and Sunni to the brink of civil war happened in one of our neighborhoods in June 2006. During this time, the Squadron leadership as well as all the Troop Commanders attended the week long Anti-Insurgent Academy started by General George Casey in Iraq. Most of the senior Troop leadership, including me, already completed a previous tour in Iraq at some point. This was a benefit and a curse because of the experience gained but the situation and enemy had changed tremendously since Operation Iraqi Freedom I (OIF I), which is what most of the soldiers based their experiences on during our train-up. The problem with that was the fact that we came into Iraq prepared for a conventional, force on force fight, with little regard on how to manage things after most of the shooting stopped. The reality this time around was a deep insurgent fight with the Iraqi populace as the center piece and the prize. The Academy did what it was intended to do, as far as I was concerned. It changed my mindset as to how I would approach this fight and how I would translate this approach to the leadership of the Troop and more importantly, the Soldiers.

The Troop's arrival in Baghdad began a concerted relief in place effort with the unit(s) there. Briefings were conducted on new equipment as part of the Rapid Fielding Initiative and right/left seat rides were also conducted. Each member of the Troop spent time with their counterpart who had been doing this for the last year. I personally picked the brain of the outgoing company commander. I can't stress how important and critical this piece of the fight is. The relief in place and how it is conducted, sets the tone and stage for how a unit will behave once it takes over the mission. Luckily, the Troop had a great outgoing company and tremendously dedicated leadership to conduct the relief in place with. I saw the benefits of a good relief in place immediately after we took over the mission as the platoons and sections modified what they trained for the past eight months and executed the mission with the lessons learned from the previous unit incorporated into their maneuver. Again, this is an extremely critical piece and needs leadership oversight at all levels to be properly conducted. There can't be a mentality of, "we can do it better, so we won't listen to these guys". There are reasons for why a unit does things a certain way after a year-long deployment and they can't be categorized as right or wrong but rather analyzed for a better understanding of how you will do things.

A mounted patrol in a busy section of Baghdad, 2006.

Initially, the Troop was assigned a sector of southwest Baghdad that incorporated the majority of neighborhoods between the main highway coming in to the city from the south and the Baghdad International Airport. These included the neighborhoods of Aamel, Bayaa, Jihad, Shurta, and Furat which altogether consisted of approximately 800,000 residents. For a one hundred and two man Cavalry Troop, this task appeared daunting and is an extreme example of the principle of Economy of Force. The problem with this AO assignment was that the Squadron itself was falling in on an AO owned by a larger unit. Also, the main effort for the Squadron was the highway connecting the "Green Zone" and Baghdad International Airport, both key pieces of terrain in this fight. As a result, combat power and forces were concentrated on this key piece of terrain with an economy of force mission run elsewhere. The terrain for the Troop was densely populated urban neighborhoods with main, larger streets cutting through the AO. The 360 degree urban environment played a key role in all planning and execution of missions. The AO included a number of religious sites, government institutions, agencies, markets, shops and various other urban related structures making it problematic in understanding the location of all these areas as well as understanding how they all fit into the scheme of the AO composition.

I based my understanding of the anti-insurgent fight mainly on past experiences in OIF I, reading about other anti-insurgency conflicts, and overall general discussions on the subject with my peers. My understanding of the subject was greatly influenced in the month leading up to us assuming control of our AO because of the Insurgent Academy as well as the lessons learned from the unit we took over from. A repeating theme in all this was that small actions, some deemed irrelevant or negligible, may in fact reverberate and cause problems in this type of fight. One Soldier can have a tremendous impact with his actions, good or bad. Therefore, I focused my efforts on this and I attempted to instill this mentality in the leadership of the Troop. It was critical to work together as one, the leadership needed to be in-line with our philosophy and our purpose. The commander's intent took on a whole new meaning and clear direction and guidance was a must in order to ensure that any action(s) by my Soldiers was in line with what I and the leadership were trying to do. I did not want to apologize for the actions of my Soldiers or leaders to the populace in the AO. I wanted to know that what they were doing either originated with me or higher headquarters so that I had no surprises to deal with.

The first piece of this information flow was to understand the anti-insurgent terrain and environment in our assigned AO. The relief in place began the process of every soldier and leader knowing the terrain and continued into the first sixty days after our assumption of the AO. Initially I split the Troop AO among the two platoons and attached the Mortars Section to the Platoon with a slightly bigger piece of terrain. My intent was to focus each platoon on a smaller area in order to have them become familiar with that piece of ground. Both platoons becoming extremely familiar with the whole Troop AO would have been difficult. By doing this, each Platoon became intimately familiar with the locations of key terrain, key people, the intricacies, and happenings in their own smaller piece of the pie.

This was still a fight and I have referred to our operations as such, however, in the anti-insurgent environment, the use of weapons and unrestricted engagement is sometimes detrimental. It is critical to use lethal force only in the right situations and with pin-point accuracy. The Rules of Engagement were clear and were not too restrictive in my opinion. As a Troop, we clarified the ROE into scenarios and discussed them among the leadership and Soldiers. Knowing all types of situations that may arise was an impossible task, but we tried to cover the basics and let our subordinate leaders operate within those guidelines and vignettes. The "cookie cutter" approach does not work and each situation is different, therefore educating everybody on the basics and what should happen is important. This also goes back to me mentioning that everybody needs to be in line with what we are trying to accomplish and how we are going to go about it. With that said, the use of our firepower was always an option if a leader deemed it necessary but it was used only under specific circumstances. I always told the leaders and Soldiers to be very cognizant of pulling the trigger, to not do it unless you absolutely wanted to take a life because there is a lot more that follows an action like that than just the initial act of pulling the trigger. On the other hand, if it fell within the ROE and it was an enemy situation, I also told them to not be afraid to utilize all the firepower at their disposal to kill the enemy and/or protect themselves. This may sound conflicting but it is not because of the use of vignettes and a clearly defined ROE, which we had, made it easier for our leaders and Soldiers to make that call. Once that call was made, however, pin-point fires and overwhelming firepower could and were used to win the engagement, but killing insurgents is not how you win this fight. We've killed scores of numbers of insurgents up to this point in the war, but they still keep coming. I am not advocating that killing the enemy does not help, but sometimes it is detrimental to the cause because in the Iraqi society, revenge killings are a part of life. By killing an insurgent, one may inadvertently create two, three, or more to take his place from his tribe or family. This is just one of the second or third order effects of pulling the trigger and doing so must be a last resort in this type of fight, not everyone is the enemy.

My instructions were to treat every member of the populace as a friend unless given a very good reason not to. We knew that some people in the AO were either actively or passively supporting insurgent activities but we still attempted to get them on our side through dialogue and treating them respectfully. We did not want to fan the flames or add fuel to the fire by doing anything to upset the people. We knew that the enemy was intermingled with the populace in the neighborhoods. I personally knew that some of the local citizens I shook hands with on our patrols were probably involved in activities that were detrimental to our operations, but unless I could prove that through intelligence gathering or catching them in the act, they were treated properly. By doing this, we got close to the enemy. Almost all of our patrols were focused on engaging the populace in discussion and getting to know them on a personal level. The insurgents strived to make us a faceless enemy and they failed in regards to doing that because my leaders and Soldiers were known all over our AO by their names and faces. I personally shared stories and talked with the populace about anything and everything to humanize myself and my Soldiers in their eyes. In doing so, it becomes difficult for a man to wittingly attempt to hurt somebody that he has looked in the eye, shaken hands with, and talked about family matters with. By personifying ourselves we stripped the enemy of making us the "faceless US Soldiers" and making it easier to hurt us on their conscience. The term used in Vietnam by the VC was to grab your enemy "by the belt", in other words, to get close to them to minimize their ability to use stand-off weapons and equalize the fight. We did the same thing in this manner by grabbing the enemy by the belt and negating one aspect of his propaganda.

Thinking about second, third, fourth, etc. order of effects is critical in this fight. As I've mentioned, pulling the trigger has after effects that may be hard to gauge. This also applies to any action that you may do in the AO as well. The thing that a leader in this environment has to accept is that not everything you do will have positive outcomes. Your intentions may be just but after completion of an action the opposite effect is felt in the AO. This is all too true in the insurgent fight and is more of a result of cultural or religious misunderstanding than anything else. Before conducting any type of operation you should always weigh the positive and negative outcomes and if at all possible, do it through the eyes of the insurgent and more importantly the populace. This is a very difficult thing to do, especially during what may be viewed as trivial decisions such as when to go talk to people or patrol composition, but it is necessary. Most of the time you should side with not doing something if it will hurt your efforts with the populace, because the populace is key and the center of gravity in this fight. There were several missions we were told to conduct from higher headquarters that because of our intimate knowledge of the AO and further analysis, would have been detrimental to our cause. Mission accomplishment of a certain task always should be nested within the broader context of getting the population to support you and your cause. Sometimes, lesser missions should be abandoned or modified to fit within the overall objective of winning the people. An open line of communication between subordinates and superiors is key in this environment. I made it clear to my subordinates that if something didn't make sense or didn't fit with what we were collectively trying to accomplish, to let me know about it and we would discuss it. I didn't want to present a command climate in which my subordinates were afraid to bring up issues for discussion because collectively we were smarter. However, once a decision was made, we executed it 100%. During execution it was also necessary to adjust to changing circumstances or things we had not thought of. All of our operations were very fluid and one had to be flexible to changes because the enemy certainly was. As a result, I shared the same relationship with my superiors in that I could at any time open a discussion or dialogue in order to find the best path ahead within the broader mission. This type of information sharing and professional discussion from top to bottom fostered a command climate which was positive and allowed everybody to work toward the same goal.

We also included the local populace in planning our future operations. Minus breaking operations security, we always asked what the people thought of our operations after their conduct and sometimes alluded to future operations to attempt to gauge their response. Sometimes what the local population asks for will make you scratch your head and it will not fit into what you may be trying to do. However, most of the time they know what they are talking about, as strange and foreign as it may seem. Since they are the center of gravity, whenever possible we filled their requests as in the end it made them content and helped our efforts. The most difficult part of this is judging what certain individuals are asking for in terms of selfish/personal gains or gains for their ethnic or religious group so that they leverage power in the AO to their side. This is difficult and we gained our understanding of this through trial and error. The important lesson in this is to learn from the mistakes of obliging the requests of the wrong people or groups. Sometimes, we used these mistakes to our advantage by making the person or group feel ashamed of fooling us or by getting something back in return because of their malicious intent. The whole point of this is to have leverage and initiative with the populace and nowhere else is this more evident than on the local government councils.

In the end, counter insurgency revolves around the people and how you deal with personal relationships. Nowhere is this more evident than with the local government officials and the so called "power-brokers" in an AO. In our urban AO, Sheikhs did not play a major role. Local religious leaders, and more importantly, the militia leaders were the ones calling the shots. As a result, we spoke with these people whenever we could to influence them in a positive way. At times I felt as if I was speaking to the enemy (or at least the leaders) face to face, but I could not prove that. Almost all conversations settled on making deals and it is very important to not promise anything that can't be backed up. The other thing is that everything is not absolute, just because something was promised on their end, does not mean it will occur. Compromise is an essential part of negotiation and whenever possible it should be utilized to get what you want. During our time, we also realized that the enemy militias and organizations were a lot more organized than we initially thought. They have infiltrated into almost every organization be it legitimate or not and they do listen to what you have to say. What you say does get back to them through the people and so there is an underlying dialogue that occurs with the enemy which must be taken advantage of.

Talking to all of these people, the Troop developed an intricate informant network which was one of the most vital pieces to our success. We inherited a very good informant network from the previous unit and we built upon that with our efforts. The previous unit utilized a Company website which was posted on calling cards which were handed out to as many people as possible in the AO. The calling cards also had the Company CO's cellular phone number on them. We used the same methods and made an extensive list of informants which was maintained by the Troop Fire Support Officer. He was also a key part of all local populace and local governing council interaction. His maintenance of the database was extremely important. In this manner, the local populace could easily offer tips and information, which they often did. We received more information in this manner than through the official higher intelligence channels. It also offered the populace a sense of security knowing that US Forces who were directly responsible for their neighborhood could be reached immediately with a phone call or email. There were numerous instances when I knew of an event in the AO the minute it was happening because a local national would call me. This decreased our response times and made us very effective at reacting to events in the AO. The bottom line is we captured a lot of insurgents and prevented a lot of activities from escalating into uncontrollable situations because of this network. This network coupled with our tactics on the ground allowed us to control the situation in a huge AO.

Our small unit tactics were a direct result of mixing past experience, the current threat, terrain and a multitude of other factors. Other units did it differently and our lessons learned are not by any means all encompassing as to how to fight an insurgency, but this is what worked for a Cavalry Troop in an urban environment. First, our patrol composition was basically a scout section which consisted of a M2A2 ODS Bradley and two M1114 HMMWV's. Added to this was usually the platoon leader or platoon sergeant and also the commander. The leadership rotated in and out of the sections because we allowed our section leaders (SSG's) to lead the patrols. The overall composition of a patrol was always one M2A2 ODS and two to three M1114's with at least a Staff Sergeant leading the patrol. Every member of the patrol had at least an M4 (no single M9 bearers) with some M249 SAW's, M240's, and M203s interspersed in the patrol. The wheeled vehicles had a mix of crew served weapons. There was no set pattern and each patrol leader equipped his patrol based on weapon availability and what he wanted. Every patrol had an interpreter and if the commander was with the patrol, there were two interpreters. Twelve was the bare minimum for Soldiers on the patrol but we almost always moved with more for security purposes. It was essential to be able to dismount as many people as possible if needed. It was nice to be prepared for any type of situation in case a raid order came down or we had to get on the ground to do anything. More dismounts was always better. At a minimum, each patrol was able to put a four man stack team on the ground and still leave a driver and gunner with each vehicle. Leader's vehicles in the patrol always had to have two radios, one set for the patrol net and one set to the Squadron net. We almost never operated on a Troop net, there just was no need to. Dismounted communications were extremely important. We were limited with the number of dismount radios, but anything a unit can use to enhance communications between dismounts and between dismounts and vehicles is priceless. All of our dismounted weapons were locked and loaded and our mounted crew served weapons loaded but not locked. If a situation arose, all a gunner had to do was charge his weapon and fire. The dismounts could suppress for a few seconds while this was accomplished and this decreased crew served weapon discharges to zero. We also loaded and unloaded all dismount weapons outside the vehicles. Upon returning from a patrol, we utilized buddy clearing, in that a buddy had to watch you clear your weapon and catch the round out of the weapon when you charged it. After we implemented these measures early in our deployment, we had zero negligent discharges. This may not seem important, but accidentally shooting a local national or more importantly, one of your own Soldiers inside the FOB was extremely unhelpful to our mission. One thing that we learned to avoid very quickly was to just "drive around" and look for trouble. In my experience, there were units that did this and one of the main reasons we didn't was a sense of purpose and direction our junior leaders and Soldiers expected. Units whose leaders did not give clear tasks and purposes for patrols led to Soldiers taking on a mentality of just "driving around waiting to get blown up". A secondary result of giving clear task and purpose is a sense of elation and satisfaction gained by subordinate leaders and Soldiers after they accomplish their mission.

Each patrol leaving the Forward Operating Base had a clear task and purpose based on what we were trying to accomplish in the immediate future as well as more long term commitments. Reconnaissance is a basic Mission Essential Task List (METL) task for a Cavalry Troop, platoon, and section. As a result, we conducted mainly three types of reconnaissance: target reconnaissance, Small Kill Team/Observation Post location identification, and terrain familiarization. Target reconnaissance involved either confirming or denying intelligence on possible targets of future raids. It was essential to involve the Squadron S-2 in this task because he was able to pool together different intelligence sources to help mature a target. Maturing a target meant developing enough evidence against a target so that person could be held and tried for insurgent activities. Our reconnaissance methods were almost always soft in the sense that we did not want to "spook" the target. We would drive by the target's location and take pictures from inside the vehicles or sometimes we would conduct a foot patrol and pretend to be taking pictures with the locals but ensuring that the target's location was in the background. Sometimes we spoke to the target by asking general questions about the security of the neighborhood and were able to identify the person that way. Our informant network also helped us by identifying locations or taking pictures of locations and emailing them to us with detailed descriptions. It was essential to become familiar in utilizing the Iraqi address system of Muhalla's, streets, and house numbers because our informants did not understand the Military Grid Reference System (MGRS). Even a ten digit grid did not tell you what side of the street a location was on or exactly which house it was. So target reconnaissance pictures were vital in identifying target locations. We did the same thing for Small Kill Team (SKT) sites and Observation Posts (OP) locations. We preferred abandoned locations but also had to use family homes. We conducted reconnaissance on these locations by doing mock searches. In other words, pretending to do a random search and at the same time having the leaders assess the location's possible future use as an SKT/OP location. Again, pictures were always taken so that these locations could be passed off to other sections and platoons within the Troop. Lastly was terrain familiarization, which mainly involved checking certain assigned locations within the AO in order to maintain positive local national relationships. By doing this, just like the locals, our Soldiers became familiar with the ground and noticed when something was out of place or didn't look right. This helped tremendously in identifying IED's and other detrimental events in the neighborhoods. Other tasks for our patrols were: raids, populace engagement (talking to the locals), area security (usually an OP), SKT support, and secure movement from one location to another (i.e. moving supplies).

Our tactical movement during these patrols was initially categorized as unconventional but over time it became the norm as we realized the success we gained from it. First, we always led the patrol with an M2A2 Bradley. In Baghdad various types of obstacles were erected all over the streets. These included but were not limited to concrete barriers, c-wire, and various other man-made objects. The obstacles became especially prevalent after the Samarra mosque bombing and the initial wave of reprisal killings as each small neighborhood believed they could keep the other side out by emplacing them. A new type of IED threat also emerged during this time, the Explosively Formed Projectile (EFP) and Shaped Charge (SC). Usually the lead vehicle in a patrol was targeted with these IED's and so a Bradley could "absorb" this type of attack much better than an M1114. Lastly, a lot of things needing the use of dismounts happened in the front of the patrol and it became convenient for the Bradley to carry the dismounts and use them. This included moving obstacles, dealing with locals that flagged us down and so on. Spacing between the vehicles was terrain dependant but usually was 50-100 meters.

The two most important concepts we implemented was slow/deliberate movement and staying off major roads. We found that a lot of units moved quickly, utilizing speed to "get away from the IED." That was more fact than fiction because you can't outrun a blast and getting attacked while driving fast also has secondary consequences in that a driver may lose control of the vehicle and cause unnecessary injuries or damage. By moving slowly, we were able to scan the road ahead, especially with the thermal imaging in the Bradley, and pick out possible IED's. Our IED find rate was pretty good; we didn't unexpectedly run up on a lot of them.

The only time we used major MSR/ASR or other major roads was to get in and out of our AO. Even then, the minute we could move into neighborhood roads we did. It was convenient using the major roads, but it opened us up to attacks and separated us from the populace. By moving from one place to another through the neighborhoods, we negated the enemy's use of IED's as he was very reluctant to attack us in a neighborhood. We had a few occurrences of the enemy trying to do that, but the local nationals in the neighborhood didn't want trouble and so, through our informant network, would inform us of the IED. Even simple movements from one location to another resulted in a patrol through the neighborhood which the locals wanted. Our presence deterred sectarian violence and other criminal activities.

Night operations in Baghdad in 2006. Thermal imagers, night sights, and various other technologically superior devices to helped us own the night.

The other tactic applied by other units was to have their vehicles lit up like a Christmas tree in order to find IED's. The conglomeration of lights on vehicles was actually at times an impressive sight. However, the enemy could see you coming from a mile away. We had thermal imagers, night sights, and various other technologically superior devices to help us own the night. So it was perplexing to see this and we didn't do it, we utilized our equipment to move during the night with no white light. No lights also made it hard for the enemy to target us. There were several instances where an IED or some other attack completely missed the mark, probably as a result of not being able to see us at night. The gunner of each vehicle did have a spotlight and eventually we received green laser pointers, like the ones used during briefings. These were invaluable during night operations. We used these devices, especially the laser pointer to get cars or pedestrians to stop. They were very effective at reducing the escalation of force measures which sometimes led to innocent civilians' vehicles getting shot because they didn't understand that they had to stop or slow down near us. There was also a complicated and in my opinion, too detailed, version of what was called escalation of force. In the true sense of the military, it was a very rigid and complicated set of steps that leaders and Soldiers had to take to mediate a threat. The latter steps in the escalation of force involved warning shots and eventually lethal shots to stop a perceived threat. The problem with this was that 99% of the local nationals in the neighborhoods were not going to attack us. Most of these *escalation of force* incidents occurred as a result of a local national being totally confused as to what a US unit wanted him/her to do, resulting in warning shots and sometimes innocent Iraqi being injured or killed because of unnecessary lethal force. We explained this to our Soldiers and also abolished the use of warning shots in our patrols. The Soldiers became very comfortable knowing that 99.9% of the cars and pedestrians were not suicide bombers. Usually a Vehicle Borne IED (VBIED) or suicide bomber wasn't identified until it was too late. Going through a complex escalation of force and trying to engage the vehicle was not a gunner's best chance of survival. So we taught our soldiers, if they identified this threat and it was too late, to duck down in their vehicles and seek the vehicle's armor protection to absorb the blast. This worked and reduced unnecessary warning shots and we had no engagements of innocent Iraqi vehicles and pedestrians. Our vehicles were also equipped with loudspeakers and it helped for the vehicle commanders to know a little Arabic so they could express commands to local nationals. During our patrols, especially during the first sixty days of assuming the AO, we conducted quick and deliberate movements from anywhere in the AO back to the FOB and the military hospital or aid station. We called these events "CaSH Runs." This allowed every leader and Soldier to know the quickest, most deliberate route back to the FOB or more importantly medical help if anyone was wounded. In most emergency situations, time is critical for the wounded and we were able to get to the military hospital within 15-20 minutes from anywhere in the AO, faster than utilizing a helicopter MEDEVAC.

During our patrols it became necessary to conduct raids on emerging or time sensitive targets. Most of the time we deliberately went after targets after we conducted our reconnaissance and the target became mature. Our raids were extremely soft in nature. The locals were used to seeing our foot patrols and our slow movement, so moving quickly onto an objective would likely alert the enemy to our intentions. But if we visited the same place over and over again to speak to the locals, another visit in the neighborhood to detain an individual with slow movement onto the objective did not spook those individuals. Reconnaissance in identifying the target and location before hand was extremely important. Our raids were always a part of a patrol and the platoon leaders and section leaders became adapt at conducting these missions with a tremendous success rate. Detainee treatment and eventual consequence management was also important. The target, no matter at what level he/she was, was always treated respectfully and handcuffed away from the family and other people in the neighborhood. We also did not want to fall into a pattern as far as time was concerned and so, our raids were conducted during various hours of the day or night.

Our Small Kill Team (SKT) and Observation Post (OP) operations were extremely successful in getting inside the enemy's mind. The psychological impact these operation had on the enemy was tremendous. We attempted to select our SKT and OP sites based on enemy pattern analysis and what we were trying to accomplish. This ranged from anti-IED operations to

135

prevention of sectarian violence. Whatever the mission entailed, the Soldiers participating in the operation were briefed on various vignettes and "what-if" scenarios in order to maintain any possible engagement within the context of the ROE. Our SKT's usually were long duration 24-72 hours and our OP's were short duration, usually part of a 6 hour patrol. Our OP's could turn into an SKT if they witnessed an enemy act. Both were similar in personnel composition. There was a team leader, usually a SSG, and five other team members: a designated marksmen/sniper, radio-telephone operator (RTO), machine gunner, and two security personnel. This was always a deliberately planned operation and required coordination with adjacent units as well as higher HQ. Once a location had been identified through previous reconnaissance, the team inserted usually at night through various means. They were dropped off at a certain location and walked into their SKT location or the vehicles dropped them off right in front of it. The most successful method was utilizing the stay-behind technique. We would conduct random house searches throughout the night or even a few days before the operation in a certain area and then leave the SKT behind in a searched location. We would have numerous Soldiers walk in and out of the location during the search as to confuse anybody who was watching this. The patrol which dropped them off would be assigned a secondary task within our patrol framework and would move away from the SKT location, but the patrols primary task was to support the SKT in case of compromise or enemy action. There was always a mounted patrol supporting the SKT throughout the duration of the operation. At times we had to use locations occupied with local nationals. The local national families were secured in the location and told not to leave, make phone calls, or talk to anyone. They were usually extremely cooperative because we paid them through our commander's funds. The enemy was surprised on many occasions with our swift response to his actions. As a direct result, sectarian violence dropped in some areas of our AO, I believe as a result of several successful engagements our SKT's and OP's had, catching these guys in the act.

During our operations, the most dangerous lapse our Soldiers and leaders could fall into is complacency and forgetting or disregarding the basic fundamentals. Our operational tempo was high but rest and recuperation was always part of the plan. A tired Soldier or leader is prone to making mistakes and in our AO mistakes were sometimes catastrophic. Finding a balance between operations, maintenance, and rest was key in our fight and I would rather pull back on the number of patrols rather than send out tired Soldiers. Along with this comes subsequent training and retraining in basic fundamentals. We incorporated a few retraining periods whenever the leadership felt that we might be slipping in upholding standards or forgetting basic scouting tactics. This involved one on one conversations as well as larger group format meetings at which lessons learned, AAR comments, and doctrine were discussed to refine our efforts. The enemy as well as his actions changed in a number of ways during our deployment and it was essential for us to keep up with the changes as a Troop by disseminating information and sometimes collectively coming up with ways to thwart his efforts.

Bandit Troop's counter insurgency operations in a complex urban environment in Baghdad are only a small snippet of time in the overall Global War on Terror, but the lessons learned are valid and proven. The lessons we learned from a year long deployment led to our success and could be utilized or modified in other counter insurgency environments. Some lessons are very enemy-and-area- oriented, while others are more encompassing of other environments. Either way, there are no "cookie-cutter solutions" and leaders must be smart and adapt to their surrounding in order to be successful. Lessons can be modified and adapted to fit other situations. Leaders and Soldiers can and should use creativity to combat an insurgent foe, as long as it is completely understood that the people are the center of gravity and must be won. **HX**

CHAPTER 8

COUNTER-INSURGENCY: THE ART OF CLEAR, HOLD, AND BUILD

Major Diogo P. F. Tavares, U.S. Army

A force protection patrol in S. Central Ramadi in February 2007.

The warriors who serve today have a more difficult fight; it is a thinking fight at every level from the lowest private to the company commander. Company commanders are at the tip of the spear when it comes to counter-insurgency (COIN), because it is the company commander who leads Soldiers on the ground, who in many cases has to come up with quick, rational decisions in combating terrorism. It is a thinking war, where the enemy blends in well and wears no specific uniform. The man on the corner watching attentively as your patrol walks up the alley can easily be an insurgent who wants to harm you.

As leaders, we ask a great deal from our Soldiers. They are disciplined, professional, hard-charging and have, for the most part, perfected the craft of being a thinking fighter. It is important to understand that we as leaders and Soldiers on the ground, up close and personal with the enemy, are much more than well-trained and lethal weapons; we are killers, ambassadors and trainers in the COIN fight. It is important to understand that a Soldier must be the above in that exact order. We train our Soldiers to kill at a moment's notice, to protect the innocent civilians and most importantly themselves. They are taught about culture and respecting other people and their beliefs. Finally, they train the Iraqi Security Forces, as was in our case, so that they may take the lead.

The COIN fight has been around in various forms for many years. Insurgents are the enemy; who may not align themselves with a country, but with organizations of ideas, theology and just sheer terror. The enemy doesn't wear a uniform, therefore making them harder to be identified. Add in a language barrier, the fact they mix in easily with the population and know the area better than you do and you have a very difficult fight on your hands. While you will be given interpreters, your company may only have one or two. In my situation, I had five platoons conducting missions and with only two interpreters you risk over working them as well. Many of you are thinking, that is what interpreters do. You are correct, however, remember that you also have engagements and add that in there and you could be over-tasking your interpreters. We were blessed with some great interpreters, I still am in touch with them today. Learn some phrases and try to see if you have any IPs or IA that you work with who can also speak English, this can help tremendously.

In COIN it is important to always be a few steps ahead of your enemy. Your Soldiers actions could easily be turned into propaganda by the enemy to sway the local population. It makes this fight comparable with a game of chess; where one must think moves ahead of one's opponent.

Our Soldiers are ambassadors. They learn about a different culture, so that they understand how to be sensitive to certain topics. They try to win over the population so that the population picks them over their enemy. Words that are important when one is an ambassador are trust, relationships, rapport; just to name a few. Before our Soldiers arrive in Iraq, many of the local population may have never interacted with Americans; much of what they know is what they have been told and taught. How does one change their thoughts if they are negative? There are many avenues to accomplish that; the three that worked in Ramadi, Iraq while we were there from February 2007 to April 2008 were clear, hold and build. When doing that, it is important to remember that once they trust our Soldiers, they will come around and develop a friendship. Our Soldiers, while they have to be cognizant of what their actions may result in are always ready at any time to kill the enemy if the need arises. One minute you are handing out candy to kids, the next minute you are killing insurgents. As for our Families back at home, it may be hard to imagine the personality change that our Soldiers go through. My wife refers to it as the "Soldier Switch." The Soldier Switch is the ability to detach one's self from the emotional world and get the mission accomplished. It is a hard transition for anyone outside the military to really comprehend, but it must be done to save lives.

This chapter depicts how one unit was able to accomplish what was once thought of as impossible. Before arriving in Ramadi, Iraq the city had been declared a lost cause by intelligence officers and the CIA opined that Ramadi was the most dangerous city in the world. What Soldiers did changed that in the course of a year. Will this example work everywhere? It may not happen exactly how it is laid out here; but it is possible with hard work, collaboration of the Iraqi population and right attitude it can be accomplished anywhere.

The clear, hold and build method, that is used in this example I will lay out, may have been done multiple times, during various and different occasions. While it is difficult to imagine and hard to describe, the method to success that we encountered in Ramadi was conducted in this order to successfully accomplish the mission; this method was conducted on multiple occasions within the Brigade's Area of Operation (AO). In the example of Ramadi it happened in bite-sized chunks. It happened from neighborhood to neighborhood, ultimately from company area to company area, until battalion areas were clean, followed by the Brigade and in this example in the entire Anbar Province with the Marine Expeditionary Force (MEF).

While conducting these stages there are Lines of Operations or LOOs. These LOOs are security, Iraqi Security Forces (ISF), governance, reconstruction and information operations. In order to understand that principles of clear, hold and build; it is important to understand the LOOs. What exactly are LOOs? They are defined using six terms. Here is how I have interpreted and defined them:

- Security. This is seen as the level of safety and security in which the government and locals can operate and live in, and the ability for economic development.
- Iraqi Security Forces (ISF). One of the biggest keys to success is the use of ISF. I have maintained that the use of these forces will be what gets our forces out of the business of protecting the people of Iraq. This LOO is simply training and preparing the ISF to do what they are established to do; protect, defend and serve.
- Governance. The establishment and legitimization of the local leaders and government to provide guidance and leadership will repair the systems that are lacking in the areas.
- Reconstruction. This is simply rebuilding and economic development. While many buildings and infrastructure have been damaged, this can be a powerful tool. Money can also equal bullets. Local citizens need money to provide for their families and the best way to keep them from getting paid to emplace improvised explosive devices (IEDs) is through reconstruction and economic development, such as local businesses.
- Information Operations (IO). This is simply dissemination of the messages to the people. There are

so many things that can be seen in multiple ways. Accomplishing the other LOOs are what helps to build the IO campaign, quickly discussing the things that go wrong are also important, because the enemy will quickly capitalize on the mistakes. This is what makes this a difficult fight as mentioned previously.

Roger Trinquier, an influential French counter-insurgency expert uses three principles. I believe that they can be translated to three simple words; clear, hold and build. While these three principles that he uses are more detailed; we as Soldiers understand them as three simple words. Next to the words in capital letters are the principles as Trinquier uses them.

CLEAR (separate the guerilla from the population that supports him).

Prior to our arrival in the city the Soldiers of 1st Brigade, 1st Armor Division (1/1AD) moved into the city and swiftly and systematically cleared the areas in downtown Ramadi. The clearing allowed them to capture and kill many insurgents of Al-Qaida in Iraq (AQIZ). Ramadi had long been a safe-haven and headquarters for the group. This was one of the steps in separating the insurgent for the civilian. This led them to hold; they established combat out-posts (COP) within the city. One may wonder why COPs are so effective; this will be explained later in this article. Clearing operations continued long after 1/1AD departed. The 1st Brigade, 3d Infantry Division (1/3ID) replaced them in February when the insurgent activity was still high. 1/1AD started the ground work that has led to the success of the 1/3ID in Ramadi.

After having a good foot-hold in the city of Ramadi, 1/3ID continued to conduct clearing operations; all of these with the offensive mind-set. Soldiers continued to operate interchangeably within the three principles. As one area gets cleaned up and safety and security are developed, we must continue in the momentum forward and push into outlying areas, until you can crush them between two friendly forces. So in this example, while the hold principle is applied, clearing operations continues.

Clearing is nothing more than systematically checking every little nook and cranny. You have to cut the cancer away from the organisms that it needs to survive. The offensive mind set is the best one to have. All of the patrols and operations were conducted with that thought at the forefront of our minds. Go out there and find trouble, then eliminate it.

The LOOs during this period were conducted in the following manner:

- Security. We accomplished this initially through combat operations. The mindset was an offensive one, where we brought the fight to the enemy and it was a defensive-offensive operation. Sounds contradictory, but it is not. What I mean by the term I use is, we have placed our units in a defensive position, the combat out-post (COP), protecting our forces and giving it an ability to be close to where the insurgents operate. The enemy has the ability to easily mix in with the population and therefore the COP allows our forces to be in the heart of it, which will eliminate the capability of the enemy. Thus allowing our units to close with and destroy the enemy in an offensive manner. These offensive operations are patrols that allow us to stir the bee's hive. They are well thought out and many times we place ourselves in our adversary's shoes.

- ISF. The focus has been to use them in every single operation that we have conducted. The use of the Iraqi Army (IA) was very important. In using them we were able to develop their skills in a military form. The Iraqi Police (IP) came next, who better to help find the enemy, then the people who know them best. Iraqi Police are courageous people who are made up of locals. They know the enemy and know where they live and operate. Their intelligence proved beneficial on many occasions. The other success in bringing the IPs second was that while the IA kicked in the doors, the IPs came later and were therefore looked at as the protectors of the people. The IPs were used more during the hold stage, but even while in the hold stage there was still plenty of clearing to be conducted.

- Governance. During our initial clearing operations there was not much in terms of governance going on. The key was to find people who would be interested in leading this city. The second step was to establish city councils and leaders at the tribal level. The tribal leaders are a very important piece of the puzzle. Many of them had fled the area to places like Jordan, Saudi Arabia and Syria, however, the goal was to get them back to Ramadi.
- Reconstruction. There is very little going on in terms of reconstruction. What we did at the initial point was to assess things that would need to be reconstructed upon the start of the build phase.
- Information Operations (IO). When conducting clearing operations, IO is a key in letting the local citizens know what was going on in their city. The most commonly used methods were; flyers with pictures; as many locals are illiterate and loud speakers. Allowing the ISF to put the message out also created a legitimization of those forces.

HOLD (occupy the zones that the guerillas previously operated from, making them dangerous for him and turning the people against the guerilla movement).

1/1AD started this with building COPs in the city. The importance of this is that it shows the people and the insurgents that you are there to stay. It brings a sense of security to the locals and by living among the local population our Soldiers see everything and can note changes. 1/3ID continued in the same fashion and established Joint Security Stations where US Forces, Iraqi Army and Police all lived and worked together sharing information, planning operations and getting to develop bonds of trust.

My company lived on COP FALCON; a well fortified group of buildings. When we replaced 1/1AD we replaced them with more tanks than they had. In my opinion, this was a morale killer for the enemy. The enemy had seen the death and destruction that the tank brought to the area; we were replacing someone with 3 times the number of tanks. The second key to success is having infantry; who can, on foot, patrol and get to locations faster and many times easier than a tank.

Observation and security

In occupying the area, we were able to meet the locals, much like getting to know your neighbors. Our neighbors could be good or bad; the key is separating the bad ones from the good ones. So here again, clearing operations are conducted simultaneously.

Your neighbors get to know you, they develop rapport and trust. When they feel that you will help them and they know that they have our Soldiers and ISF to protect them, they begin to assist you in the process.

One of the things that I feel 1/1AD did extremely well was they used Iraqi Army (IA) Soldiers to help them in the clearing process. Every operation is done jointly. After all, it is their country and they need to learn how to handle it on their own. They later introduced Iraqi Police (IP). What this did was allowed the IA to get the stereotype of being strong handed and the IP of being there to serve and protect the populace.

The LOOs during this period were conducted in the following manner:

- Security. In the hold stage we continued to operate with and offensive mindset. The COPs continue to be the key and it also sends a clear message to the locals, that the Coalition Forces (CF) were there to stay. For the locals that brings a sense of security and safety, which brings them out to give you information. The local population is no different than a U.S. city resident; they want a safe and secure environment for their children and family to be raised in, with good paying jobs and an ability for their children to become educated. The IPs addition in the initial hold stage brought CF better capabilities to succeed.

- Iraqi Security Forces (ISF). We continued to train and use the ISF in all operations. The IPs came at the initial hold stage and their knowledge of the area and the locals was something that the IA, who tended to come from Baghdad could not provide. The feeling among the locals was a great one, I will never forget the day I heard people in the Civil Military Operations Center (CMOC) say that they trusted the IPs and said they were not corrupt as in the previous regime.

- Governance. The success was realized when Sheik Sattar Abu Risha reached out to the CF and developed the Anbar Awakening, a group of tribal sheiks that pledged their support to the CF. This, in my opinion, is the turning point. The city councils begin to develop and the government makes leaps to legitimization.

- Reconstruction. At this stage reconstruction is still difficult, but there were infrastructure reconstruction that helps show the local population that the CF cares about their needs. The projects that we accomplished during our time in the hold process were repairs of pipe leaks in the streets, many of which were sewer lines, fixing and/or adding street lights, electricity, sewage pumps and other efforts. The government began working as they re-established the Director Generals (DG) of departments such as water, electricity, etc.

- Information Operations (IO). Getting the right message out at this point is important. The establishment of the CMOC allowed concerned citizens to raise their problems and to bring information that could be changed into intelligence. Information was analyzed and compared, turned into intelligence allowing for the development of operations. Other things that worked in terms of IO was conducting special projects, such as bringing school supplies to schools, handing out candy to the kids on the streets and bringing the items to the people that they had previously been without.

BUILD (coordinate actions over a wide area for a long enough time that the guerilla is denied access to the population centers that could support him).

The word build is not just synonymous with the actual building of structures; you can build many things. It includes building on the relationships that you have established. Sometimes these relationships take time to build. I share a story with you about our Iraqi counterparts. Our Soldiers quickly developed ties with the IA and IP. My philosophy was to treat them as if they were my own. In all cases they had it just as good as my own Soldiers. I developed great, long-lasting relationships with the leadership of the IA and IP. Today, I still maintain contact with some of the leaders. The most wonderful experience I had was having chai (hot, sweet tea) and the discussions about their culture and country. Many times we shared our vision of where this city could go and how wonderful it could be. I hope someday that a trip to Iraq can be taken, not as a deployment but as an ability to show my Family what great things happened while we were there.

Prior to us being replaced and moving into another part of the city, the IP leadership sat with me and a map. They told me all about the area that my men and I would be heading to. They told me that we were brothers and that we had achieved many great successes in Ramadi as a team. They always felt confident that no matter what the operation was they would be well taken care of should anything happen to them.

We introduce things that the people need and gather information that can be turned into intelligence. We incorporate the civil-military operations (CMO) into the picture. At our COP we established a civil-military operations center (CMOC), which was available twice a week for people to come and talk to military members. This allows us to gather information that can help Soldiers to target and at the same time the ability to know what the locals need.

Our Soldiers didn't just go out with bullets when they patrolled; a key ingredient was sugar. Our Soldiers would hand it out to the locals; this helped to develop a sense of trust between the locals and the military. The other key in CMO is listening. It is so powerful, hence the reason God gave us two ears and one mouth. It is because of our CMOC that we were able to respond to the local populace's needs and when AQIZ could not deliver on their promises, the military did.

The LOOs during this period were conducted in the following manner:

- Security. The security in Ramadi has increased. Today one can walk and drive the streets and conduct daily life using the shops and markets that are open. You see people going about their daily errands and life as it should be. It has been a large contrast to go from daily fighting, where people fear for their lives therefore, staying inside most of the day and go to what Ramadi is today.
- Iraqi Security Forces (ISF). During the build stage, the ISF has almost taken complete control of the city. Today as the build stage continues, small Military/Police Transition Teams (MTT/PTT) have partnered with the IP stations and advisors work with the IA. I had an opportunity to visit with an old IP major of mine who has since become the Police Chief, to see the sense of pride and joy in his eyes is simply amazing. I don't feel that Al-Qaida will ever be able to gain a foothold in Ramadi again.
- Governance. We built and re-established their government, developed relationships with their leaders; the sheiks, imams, etcetera. The development of the Anbar Awakening was another key event in the success of this city. Led by Sheik Sattar, their influence reaches to Baghdad and the prime minister. Sheik Sattar was able to see that a partnership with the US military was the way ahead. He influenced many other sheiks to side with him; they supported IP stations and moved ahead.

- Reconstruction. We conducted many projects; such as electricity and water assessments, cleaning of neighborhoods and rebuilding of actual infrastructure and buildings. We hired many local contractors; this brought jobs to the local area. Instead of AQIZ paying locals to emplace IEDs we paid them to take pride in their city and clean it up.
- Information Operations (IO). Today our IO has been that Ramadi is a great city to live and work. It is truly the "Heart of Anbar" and has become a model for Iraq.

Sheik Sattar was killed just days into Ramadan, but what he started was so strong that it continues to lead this city to greatness.

While it is always difficult to leave your Family behind and deploy for a year, then be extended three more months, my Soldiers got an opportunity to experience all three stages in one deployment, which is something that not many other Soldiers get to experience. My company's leadership was phenomenal, when word that we would be extended an additional three months got out, our Soldiers handled it as true professionals, they simply looked at it as they had a job to be done. I firmly believe that this is all because of the reflection that their leaders made.

We deployed with simple goals:
1. Kill as many insurgents as possible to protect the people of Iraq;
2. Leave Ramadi better than when we arrived;
3. Train Iraqi Forces to replace us; and finally,
4. Bring all my Soldiers home alive.

As a leader you have to set tough goals for yourself and your Soldiers, think of every way to accomplish those goals and just drive the points home over and over again. I don't have all the answers and I don't claim to know everything, but I can say that my Soldiers and I with the help of the ISF and local populace accomplished all four of our goals. Call it luck if you will; but I think that is a lot of luck to have in 15 months. I firmly believe that it is because of the leadership you have above and below you, the way you carry yourself and yes a little luck with the right place at the right time. The final piece of advice that I will leave other leaders with is to also have fun. Allow for time to unwind and escape the reality of combat, when possible. We did this with video games, movies and intramurals back on the main Forward Operating Base (FOB). I also took time out to develop my platoon leaders, giving them responsibilities to make them better leaders, as my battalion commander had done for me.

The end result in Ramadi is a complete change from when we first arrived in February 2007. Our success was a collaboration of all forces and assets available and started as a simple vision that was echoed from the top down. Without everyone believing that the vision could become reality, the success would be more difficult. **HX**

CHAPTER 9

PLATOON OPERATIONS IN IRAQ
LESSONS LEARNED

By 1LT Kyle T. Trottier, 3rd Infantry Division
1st Brigade Combat Team,
2-7 Infantry Battalion

C/2-7Infantry, M1A1 patrolling downtown Ramadi,
February 2007.

First Brigade 3rd Infantry Division developed a model for success in the city of Ramadi defeating Al Qaeda in Iraq on the field of battle and earned the respect and cooperation of the local national population. At the platoon level Soldiers and their leadership need to be aggressive, intelligent, and disciplined. The tactical level leader should implement these three characteristics into every aspect of daily operations in order to make lasting contributions to the security and stability of their area of operations. This chapter discusses my lessons learned concerning platoon leadership, training, discipline, patrolling, and the conduct of counterinsurgency operations.

Leadership

"Leadership is influencing people by providing purpose, direction and motivation while operating to accomplish the mission and improving the organization."[1] Subordinates will replicate and embody the attitude and demeanor of their leadership. Leaders who are aggressive, intelligent, and disciplined will develop highly skilled warriors capable of succeeding in the complex and often undefined realm of counterinsurgency operations. The counterinsurgency fight is difficult because it asks Soldiers and leaders to be highly flexible and adaptable through a full spectrum of operations. The Secretary of the Army Transition Team (SATT) began to emphasize "pentathlete leaders" in 2005. SATT defines leaders as "innovative and adaptive, culturally astute professionals that demonstrate character and integrity." They further expressed a desire for "a leader that is well versed in a range of areas and not just one discipline; leaders who have mastered their military or core career field tasks and have developed skills in the broader, more complex, politico-military arena."[2]

My experience in Iraq taught me that the priorities a leader displays will be followed by those they lead and establish the daily operational tempo for success. The daily life of a soldier must be tempered with maintaining good order and discipline based upon his military training. Some examples of promoting good order and discipline include:

---

[1] U.S. Department of the Army, *Army Leadership,* Field Manual 22-100 (Washington D.C.: U.S. Department of the Army, 31 August 1999), 1-4.

[2] Colonel Robert A. Tipton, Professional Military Education for The "Pentathlete" Of The Future, Strategic Research Project (Carlisle Barracks, U.S. Army War College, 15 March 2006.), 2-5.

- Daily sensitive item checks ensure accountability of all property; enable leaders to inspect the living quarters of Soldiers, and the condition of their equipment.
- The unit leader must ensure thorough pre-combat inspections are completed prior to each mission. Leaders are obligated to check each minute detail of their Soldiers' and their equipment to ensure mission success.
- Every mission, no matter how small, must have a thorough patrol brief from the unit commander. Every Soldier must understand all aspects of the operation, contingency plans, and be familiar with adjacent units when applicable. A thorough back brief is a highly effective tool to ensuring unit comprehension of missions.

Vehicles in a combat zone regularly get abused through rugged terrain and long mission hours. Effective leaders plan maintenance into their patrol schedules in addition to pre and post operations preventative maintenance checks and services (PMCS). Each unit must have a dedicated day for 20 level maintenance and vehicle services to be completed including quality assurance and quality checks (QAQC), and vehicle dispatching. If this is neglected, leaders will fail their Soldiers by not providing them with reliable transportation and may endanger their lives in the event of a vehicle breakdown in hostile locations.

Combat requires leaders with great initiative, who work within the commander's intent, and often with minimal guidance. Leaders must be highly motivated and possess the will to fight and win on the battlefield. It is a platoon leaders' job to create a disciplined environment where subordinate leaders can display these characteristics without destroying the team's capacity to find, fix, and destroy the enemy and while still providing security and a non-threatening front to the civilian population. The fundamentals of leadership, planning, fire and maneuver provided by commission source training and officer basic course will provide a firm platform from which to build a units capacity to fight and win in combat however, the platoon leaders flexibility and adaptive nature will be the decisive element in the counterinsurgency (COIN) environment.

Training

Pre-deployment training is equivalent to the 400m dash track and field event. Units will cram over a year's worth of training into about a six months' time frame including, small arms, wheeled, tank gunneries, shoot house training, battalion and brigade level field problems, and a rotation to the National Training Center (NTC) or Joint Readiness Training Center (JRTC). As well as dozens of other mandatory training classes ranging from combat life saver (CLS) to Arabic language and cultural sensitivity training. The 12 and 15 month deployments of the US Army are marathon races, tests of mental and physical endurance. Over the period of the marathon the skills of the individual and unit which were sharpened during the crash course training period will deteriorate and remedial training is essential in every warrior task and drill to ensure mission success. Physical training (PT), marksmanship, and medical skills are three vital areas to continually focus training efforts while deployed.

Physical training is the corner stone of training success. The modern US warrior will be required to execute a great variety of tasks. My platoon and I executed mounted operations in our M1A1 tanks and M1114 humvees, dismounted patrols, observation post operations (OP), traffic control points (TCP), training the Iraqi Security Forces (ISF), and other missions. Each mission required great strength and agility. The body becomes taxed carrying individual body armor (IBA), ammunition, water, and mission specific equipment no matter the season. Missions can also be extremely long in duration and a person in good physical condition will be better able to stay alert and execute tasks when physically strained. "The benefits to be derived from a good physical fitness program are many. It can reduce the number of soldiers on profile and sick call, invigorate training, and enhance productivity and mental alertness. A good physical fitness program also promotes team cohesion and combat survivability."[3] Additionally, PT is an excellent way for NCOs to develop individual Soldier and unit discipline, when standards are enforced.

Marksmanship is the heart and soul of a Soldier. He must be lethal with all weapons systems and weapons platforms. But, as Robert Tomes stated, "Mistakes made in the process of waging a counterinsurgency war often reinforce an insurgent's propaganda."[4] Hitting a target is the easy part, hitting the right target is the difference between widespread insurgency support and killing the enemy.

While deployed units will have access to more ammunition than they could ever dream of in the US. Leaders need to take advantage of the unique training opportunities around them, sometimes requiring some creativity and ingenuity, in order to keep the warrior skills of their Soldier's sharp. My platoon and I established Joint Security Station (JSS) Arcala 40K east of Ramadi with 65 Iraqi Security Forces (ISF). The JSS was a permanent check point established on Main Supply Route (MSR) Mobile, the primary east-west route between Baghdad, Syria, and Jordan. The purpose of the check point was to prevent the shipment of illegal supplies and materials from Syria and Jordan into Baghdad and the denial of Vehicle Borne Improvised Explosive Devices (VBIED) and illegal materials into the city of Ramadi. We had the perfect combination of miles of unpopulated desert, a huge stock pile of ammunition, supportive chain of command, and creative leaders which enabled us to build a small arms and crew serve range. We built targets out of excess HESCO barriers and other construction material and developed a training plan to shoot small arms and crew serve weapons weekly. For the small arms we would confirm zero then execute various scenarios shooting from the prone, kneeling, and standing positions. We would execute

---

[3] U.S. Department of the Army, *Physical Fitness Training*, Field Manual 21-20 (Washington D.C.: U.S. Department of the Army, 1 October 1998), 6.

[4] Robert R. Tomes, "Relearning Counterinsurgency Warfare," Parameters (Spring 2004): 22.

reflexive fire drills and "stress tests." The "stress test" was designed to provide realistic training for Soldiers by sprinting, crawling, and buddy rushing, or carrying their buddy up to a given point and then firing from a pre-designated position (prone, kneeling, standing). The realistic training not only met the "train as you fight" principle, but also gave great confidence to the individual Soldier and built immense trust and unit cohesion.

On a separate day, once weekly, we would execute crew serve gunnery from both the M1114 and M1A1 platforms. It was a great way to confirm zero of the tank coaxial machine gun and maintain 19K skill sets, as well as building confidence in the gunners on the trucks. Concurrent training must include weekly classes on the rules of engagement (ROE) and escalation of force (EOF). Multi-National Force Iraq (MNFI) has disseminated training slides with their specific ROE/EOF guidelines. It is essential Soldiers have these seared into their memory weekly so they will not hesitate to make a correct decision. It will likely come to the point where they can repeat slides verbatim without reading them, when this happens leaders must get creative in their training to continually instill these values.

Just like the PT plan, marksmanship training must be aggressive, intelligent and disciplined. If executed properly, leaders will find themselves with strong warriors who will not hesitate when called upon to pull triggers, and will do so with great accuracy and lethality. More importantly warriors will be disciplined and intelligent enough to know when not to pull a trigger, which in the counterinsurgency fight may be even more important to winning the trust and respect of the local national population

After PT and marksmanship, medical skills are the next most important Soldier skill to master. The platoon level medic will serve as the primary trainer of medical training and use the Combat Live Saver (CLS) skill set as a basis of training. Every Soldier must be knowledgeable with the Hemorrhage Control Compressing Bandage, nasopharyngeal airway devise, and tourniquet they carry in their medical pouch. After Soldiers have a firm grasp of those basic devises I highly recommend the medic open up the Warrior Aid Liter Kit (WALK), which each vehicle is equipped with, as well as his aid bag and demonstrate the purpose of each medical item in the event the medic is unavailable during an emergency situation. The annual recertification of CLS training the Army requires is not good enough for combat conditions. Monthly recertification at the platoon level, supervised by the medic, will provide Soldiers adequate skill levels and confidence to treat wounds and save lives. A unit full of intelligent warriors, competent in CLS, is a major combat multiplier by increasing the capability of the force to continue operations and accomplish the mission with degraded power.

With intelligent training, leaders will ensure the skills and level of focus of their Soldiers is maintained through the long and strenuous combat deployment. By conducting physical training, marksmanship, and medical training with routine discipline and increasingly more rigorous standards for success Soldiers will not only become aggressive and lethal in the execution of their warrior tasks, but also be intelligent and disciplined in their behavior in order to win the trust and respect of the local national population. An intelligent and disciplined warrior will respect the power he controls and will be judicious with the implementation of that power when properly trained and that training is reiterated regularly. It will enable the unit to deal with the dichotomy of counterinsurgency warfare, "to redress the basic social and political issues of a nation while being shot at."[5]

Patrolling

Patrolling is the bread and butter of a combat platoon. Patrolling requires the warrior to be at his best. As a junior leader it is the culmination of all the school house classes, training mentioned above, and mission planning. This section will discuss the simultaneous role of combat patrols to gather

---

[5] David Kilcullen, "Twenty Eight Articles Fundamentals of Company Level Counter Insurgency," (http://smallwarsjournal.com/reference/counterinsurgency.php) 8.

intelligence while integrating maneuver and information operations, and successful tactics, techniques, and procedures (TTPs) of both dismounted and mounted operations.

Intelligent patrol leaders must understand the motives of their enemy, how they will fight, and the tools they will implement against you. "The insurgent may not seek to *do* or achieve any practical objective, but rather to be a *mujahidin*, earning God's favor (and hope of ultimate victory through his intervention) through the act itself."[6] Another option is, "insurgents act as "strategic spoilers", seeking to discredit and undermine the government by targeting coalition forces."[7] Political power is the major point of contention during an insurgency. Highly skilled and organized men will try in every way possible to discredit US and coalition forces. The high level leaders of insurgent organizations will recruit the "mujahid" who may not fully understand the political details being planned, but are willing to sacrifice themselves for the cause to "earn God's favor." Knowing Al Qaeda in Iraq's (AQI) objectives helped shape U.S. operations to serve multiple purposes. Operations had to be lethal, but disciplined in order to eliminate AQI presence and simultaneously develop positive rapport with the local populace.

In a RAND Corporation essay titled "Rebellion and Authority: An Analytic Essay on Insurgent Conflicts," Leites and Wolfe describe counterinsurgency conflicts. Essentially the insurgent problem can be broken down into two forces: the Rebels (R) and the Authority (A). R always starts with an information advantage over A (because they almost always start small and on the fringe of society). A always starts with a force advantage over R. The COIN fight essentially is the capacity of R to grow fast and thereby overcome its force disadvantage and A's capacity to overcome the information disadvantage and

---

[6] Kilcullen, "Counterinsurgency Redux," (http://smallwarsjournal.com/reference/counterinsurgency.php).

[7] *Ibid.*

bring its force to bear on a comparatively weak insurgency (paraphrase).[8]

Leaders with high levels of situational awareness help the US and Iraqi governments, the "authority," overcome the intelligence disadvantage described above by serving as sensory instruments during combat patrols and submitting patrol debriefs within 24 hours to be assessed by the battalion S2. The gathering of timely and accurate intelligence is critical for US and coalition forces to be successful in their counterinsurgency fight, but so is the protection of the local national population from terrorist violence. In Ramadi, AQI proved to have informants in every neighborhood and any local citizen who aided US forces would soon be captured, tortured, and or executed for their actions. To combat this issue our company would execute large scale intelligence gathering operations where platoons partnered with Iraqi Army (IA) and Iraqi Police (IP) would conduct soft raids under the cover of darkness. We would enter, clear, and secure a house then conduct a thorough search for any contraband or intelligence. We would check all persons against the high value target list (HVT) and all vehicles against the "be on the lookout" list (BOLO). Then we would speak with the elder men of the house to gather all available intelligence and then leave. The tactic proved highly effective.

The company would be able to visit 25 or more households in a night and gather a great amount of intelligence which would be untraceable to a single person and thereby protecting the citizens from AQI harassment. We utilized this opportunity to create and regularly update a data base with pictures, names, ages, occupation, and other information for the occupants of each house. Since personal contact between US forces and Iraqi nationals was minimal at this time, it was a golden opportunity to display our truest intentions to the locals; that we were here for their assistance not to make their lives more miserable. We would distribute sugar, stuffed animals to

---

[8] Leites and Wolfe, *Rebellion and Authority: An Analytic Essay on Insurgent Conflicts*, (RAND Corporation, February 1970, pp. 8-12).

children, and other small goods encouraging the citizens to become active forces for the revival of their city. This combination of maneuver operations and information operations was a highly effective way to defeat the insurgent tactics mentioned above. Through disciplined and respectful treatment of the civilian population we were able to not only being credit to US and coalition forces but also discredit AQI and reduce their ability to recruit mujahid. Operating in this manner took away the information advantage shared by AQI (Rebels) and transferred the initiative to coalition forces in Ramadi and in the process built trust between coalition forces and the civilian population.

Another highly effective, but much more dangerous means of gathering intelligence is the utilization of a dismounted observation post (OP) or small killer team (SKT) normally consisting of sniper teams. The SKT could provide great information covering traffic patterns (vehicular and pedestrian), behavioral patterns of citizens, or can be utilized as part of an ambush at frequently utilized mortar launch sites or locations of multiple improvised explosive devices (IEDs). Incorporating SKT requires serious consideration including planning for the infiltration and exfiltration of these teams and a quick reaction force (QRF) must be ready in the event of them being compromised. Communications is a huge consideration due to the varied reception of urban terrain. SKT leaders must be aggressive and disciplined in their scanning of their sector for possible threats, but must be intelligent and know when they are compromised and need to exfiltrate.

Dismounted and Mounted Patrol Tactics, Techniques, and Procedures

While conducting dismounted operations, I cannot stress the fundamental principles of patrolling enough; "planning, reconnaissance, security, control, common sense."[9] I recommend

---

[9] U.S. Department of the Army, *Ranger Handbook*, Student Handbook 21-76, (Washington D.C: U.S. Department of the Army, 2000), 5-1.

the use of the Ranger Handbook, even if you are not a Ranger, to assist with planning considerations of dismounted patrols. Whether clearing urban terrain in downtown Ramadi, mud hut villages and palm groves along the Euphrates River, or conducting traffic control point (TCP) operations, thorough planning and reconnaissance followed by a solid OPORD is essential. 360 degree security at all times and maintaining a forceful presence will send a strong message through body language that your unit is comprised of disciplined warriors.

Due to the prevalence of suicide bomber vests in the Ramadi area, a regular tactic, technique, and procedure (TTP) was to maintain a 50 meter standoff distance from all local nationals when patrolling congested areas. When stopping by market areas a frequently used TTP was to search the shop owners and their shop prior to talking to them in order to ensure security. While patrolling in the same area over time we were able to become familiar with people, their typical dress, and behaviors and would cease the search in order to build greater trust and rapport with the citizens. In the U.S., competent police departments describe this activity as "Community policing". Our form of community policing led to a greater exchange of information during conversations where Iraqi citizens would regularly voice their likes and dislikes with the current situation and made suggestions for future improvements. This is one example of how a culturally astute leader who has situational awareness and makes fine tune adjustments during a patrol can simultaneous combine the gathering of intelligence and spreading positive information during a maneuver operation. This was a major turning point for the city of Ramadi when Soldiers and citizens had built enough rapport to engage in verbal exchanges in free and open dialogue. Our actions proved to the citizens that choosing the side of the US was more advantageous than AQI because we would listen to them and respect them, even if they criticized our actions, and they would not receive any punishment for openly expressing themselves.

In his article titled "Counterinsurgency Redux" David Kilcullen, states "at the operational level counterinsurgency remains a competition between several sides, each seeking to mobilize the population in its cause. The people remain the prize."[10] The bottom line is that it is not only what a Soldier does, but what he also fails to do that the local national population will observe. The daily actions of a patrol will either serve as a bridge between the local populace and the desired end state of a free and democratic Iraq or will form a wedge further separating the two and making the achievement of the end state even more difficult. If a civilian knows a US patrol will make contact with insurgents in their neighborhood, Kilcullen suggests "far from finding the "presence patrol" reassuring, the population finds them alienating and a source of danger."[11]

Dismounted Patrol

Mounted patrols varied greatly for our unit over our 15 months in Ramadi from kinetic use of tanks to patrolling vast stretches of the main supply route (MSR) in M1114s; but the

---

[10] Kilcullen, "Counterinsurgency Redux," (http://smallwarsjournal.com/reference/counterinsurgency.php).

[11] *Ibid.*

principles of being aggressive, intelligent, and disciplined never changed. The training principles mentioned above become critical for a gunner in a vehicle moving 35kph and has only a few seconds to make a decision. Escalation of force (EOF) must be implemented at all times, but is especially important with mounted operations. Gunners must have day and night signals to alert drivers of a US patrol and for them to pull over to the shoulder of the road. Pen flares are especially effective instruments for this purpose, both day and night. They provide both an auditory and visual signal to civilian traffic and are non-lethal. M1114s throughout the country have been receiving the new gunner protection kits (GPK) with electric turrets and rear view mirrors. There is no excuse for a gunner to stand up unless he is engaging a target (audio, signal, or weapon). This product greatly increases the survivability rate of the gunner in the event of an attack. All vehicles should be equipped with a Chameleon or similar electronic counter measure (ECM) device. The ECM should always be used especially in high density locations. And yes, seat belts must be worn. Leaders must ensure all occupants in their vehicle buckle up, even if it is uncomfortable in all their gear, it will save lives in the event of an IED or vehicle roll over. Mounted patrols should avoid driving against the flow of traffic if at all possible. This has resulted in numerous vehicular accidents and increases the need for escalation of force and may needlessly end in the use of lethal force.

Tactical level leaders in Ramadi demonstrated how to simultaneously gather intelligence while integrating maneuver and information operations into combat patrols. Soldiers in Ramadi proved to be highly flexible and adaptable thru a variety of missions, mounted and dismounted. They maintained a balance of lethality and disciplined respect for the local national population which shaped the battle field and served to be a catalyst for peace, security, and rebuilding in the city of Ramadi.

Mounted Patrol

Integration of Iraqi Security Forces

The training and integration of Iraqi Security Forces (ISF) is without a doubt the most important mission in Iraq. It is through proper training and equipping of the ISF that long term peace and stability will be established, legitimate governments recognized by the people will take power, and the US will be able to reduce its force levels in Iraq. If US trainers are able to teach the aggressive, intelligent, and disciplined philosophy to the ISF, we will be setting them up for future success.

After establishing JSS Arcala my tank platoon of 20 Soldiers assumed responsibility for Company 1, 2d Battalion Provincial Security Force (PSF 2), and approximately 65 Iraqi Soldiers. We received a mixed bag of young and old with various previous work experiences from former military to farmers. In many cases they were desperate men just trying to support their families and the PSF was one of the few good paying jobs. David Kilcullen suggests "in modern counterinsurgency, victory may need to be redefined as the

166

disarming and reintegration of insurgents into society."[12] Without a doubt many of the new ISF used to work with AQI for the same reason they joined our ranks-to make money. Failure was not an option. These men had to succeed in bringing security to their area and be an example of cooperation for a peaceful future.

There are a host of unique challenges when creating a military from scratch from training, procurement of supplies and equipment, to trying to forge an esprit de corps within the unit. The first priority for me was to create a positive rapport with the PSF company commander and battalion commander I would support and mentor. It was essential to reassure them from the beginning they would be able to trust me and that I would treat them as my own Soldiers. I would be firm and fair with all decisions I made and would get them every resource within my ability in order to help them become a ready and relevant security force. Over many cups of chi tea and cigarettes (I am not a smoker but understood that smoking was an Iraqi custom that garnered respect) we came to an understanding of the joint mission we were about to embark upon in mutual cooperation.

At the time we established JSS Arcala in May 2007 "The Surge" of five additional brigade combat teams was moving into Baghdad and in Ramadi 1BCT 3ID was still in the process of "clear, hold, and build" operations. As part of the "holding" new combat outposts were being built all over the brigade area of operations (AO). As a result of both the "surge" and our own demands for increased combat outposts construction supplies were in great demand and limited in availability. There were few engineer assets to construct any facilities. Due to these shortages we were unable to build housing structures and instead lived in the battalion tactical operations center (TOC) DRASH tent for nearly six months. PSF 2 had four living containers (a 20' US MILVAN lined with plywood walls, lights, and a heat & A/C unit) from a previous site we relocated. The containers were transformed into a kitchen, an arms room, officer's quarters and office space, and one as a living container for PSF soldiers. To

---

[12] *Ibid.*

create extra living space we acquired a second DRASH tent from our battalion for the PSF. This proved to be advantageous for the building of rapport between units, it showed the PSF they would have all the same accommodations and amenities as US Soldiers or better, since they had the four additional containers we did not.

Once the life support area (LSA) was established we began an aggressive training program with the PSF. We began with fundamental military classes including rank structure and chain of command, military discipline, and drill and ceremony. We integrated the PSF into our platoon PT program three times a week to increase their physical wellbeing and over time trained their sergeants to conduct PT on their own. Athletic events such as soccer or ultimate Frisbee were great cardiovascular workouts that breed newfound respect through competition.

Training PSF on search procedures.

Often when playing PSF vs. US each side seemed to be competing for their entire nation and would put in an extra bit of effort for national pride. We taught the PSF property accountability and proper PMCS of all vehicles, weapons, communication equipment and other items. Together we developed an arms room, property books, hand receipts for all items signed out, and a daily inventory system. In order to make the point crystal clear that no PSF Soldier was to take their issued Sk-80 or AK-47 home with them, but instead turn in their weapon at the end of their shift they would be docked pay for each missing item per day. This proved to be the perfect discipline motivator as we very seldom had anything come up missing from the arms room.

PSF conducting PT.

JSS Arcala was built along the MSR and was a permanent vehicle checkpoint to search all east/ west traffic between Syria/ Jordan and Baghdad. With most intelligence indicating the VBIEDs (vehicle borne improvised explosive device) and suicide vest entering Ramadi were coming from the east, places like Fallujah and Samara, the checkpoint would serve as a gate to stop such forms of attack from entering Ramadi. The check point did its job well. It received three VBIED attacks since its emplacement and stopped all such attacks within the city of Ramadi. Thus, a major focus for our training efforts was to teach proper vehicle and personnel search procedures. We taught weekly classes on these topics, progressing from basic to more in-depth and advanced techniques to the point that the PSF eventually were able to give the class themselves and properly train their new members. We received one Backscatter x-ray van and trained the PSF to use the van. It was a huge force multiplier for their search capabilities especially with vehicles carrying cargo. The ability to x-ray vehicles allowed for non-evasive searches of spaces like door panels, ceiling, inside seats, and wheel wells. This proved to be a great quality assurance tool verifying the vehicles that did go through were not a threat to any other coalition forces or civilians.

Through brigade we were able to obtain a simplified version of Iraqi law and the judicial process. With this information we began weekly training sessions on law and how it applied to the PSF as law enforcement officials. We conducted classes on how to properly detain personnel, humane treatment of detainees, forms for the processing of detainees, and the trial process. We had to continually impress upon them not to abuse their authority. It was essential for them to win the trust and respect of their fellow citizens as fair and impartial protectors of justice, rather than serving as another force of oppression.

My platoon developed a constant rotation of personnel onto the vehicle checkpoint to over watch operations and ensure through searches were conducted in a fair and impartial manner. Additionally, we had a GBOSS forward looking infrared (FLIR) camera system with two monitors in our TOC. The system has two cameras mounted on top of a tower which are connected to the monitors. With these cameras we were able to over watch all aspects of operations day or night, no matter the weather conditions. This major force multiplier not only provided a means of 24 hour observation, but also a great tool for teaching and reinforcing behavior. When we would observe the PSF not performing to standard we would bring the company commander into our TOC and show him the unsatisfactory conduct of his troops. This then would allow the commander the ability to conduct remedial and corrective training on the failing soldiers, and as always if that failed, the threat or actual deduction of pay would always prove its point and help correct below standard behavior.

After we got the wheels rolling with check point operations we began an intensified training effort with our Iraqi partners. We began to include them in all of our weekly training mentioned above from small arms ranges and reflexive fire drills, medical training, battle drills and patrolling techniques, to operation of the Backscatter van and search techniques. Soon we had a rigorous weekly cycle with the PSF which included PT, technical and tactical classes, classes on professional development (Iraqi law, judicial procedures), in addition to their 24/7 manning of the check point and conducting patrols of a 35 KM stretch of the MSR with us daily. We conducted in-depth after action reviews (AAR) with the PSF to stimulate professional growth and development.

The check point at JSS Arcala also proved to be a rich tool for gathering accurate intelligence and dissemination of positive information operations. Within the first month regular traffic patterns became obvious through the check point. Certain vehicles and personnel regularly passed through as part of their daily or weekly routine, especially van loads of students to Al Anbar University and truckers carrying commerce between Jordan/ Syria and Baghdad. When the local citizens noticed the PSF were treating them with respect and dignity in the execution of their searches they began to provide small bits of information that when put together would paint a clear picture of AQI operations in the AO. Often the intelligence we received would be from an adjacent unit's area of operations and when units cross talked it helped narrow the safe zone along unit boarders that AQI would exploit as safe havens.

Further expanding our intelligence gathering capabilities our battalion put up large bill boards with pro Iraqi propaganda and tip hotline numbers and e-mail addresses for anonymous tips. The battalion also had thousands of flyers printed and the PSF passed them to citizens as they traveled through the check

171

point. I firmly believe this was a powerful tool for positive change and allowed frightened citizens a voice in their pursuit for a secure country. In counterinsurgency operations the people are the objective, whichever side can put together the most convincing argument that their ruling of the region/ country will be best for the general populations interest will ultimately win. Mobilizing the population is political power. If the U.S. and PSF could work together in such a positive way it would mobilize the local citizens, ally them with us, and thereby deny safe haven to insurgents who would otherwise seamlessly blend into the local populace.

In Roger Trinquier's classic *Modern Warfare: a French View of Counterinsurgency*, Trinquier concludes "that the guerrilla's greatest advantages are his perfect knowledge of an area (which he himself has chosen) and its potential, and the support given him by the inhabitants."[13] To counter this, the U.S. must recognize what Trinquier did, "his total dependence upon terrain and population is also the guerrilla's weak point." That is why it was so important the PSF became a ready and relevant security force. They speak the language, they know the locals, and if motivated they could do a more effective job in gathering intelligence to shape operations and deny AQI the ability to control terrain or the hearts and minds of the local population.

Through aggressive, intelligent, and disciplined efforts even Soldiers with no official Military Transition Team (MTT) training can turn a group of ordinary men into a ready and relevant security force. If this force is disciplined to conduct itself properly and respects the people whom they are paid to protect, they will become a catalyst for incredible change within their area of operations. Iraqi forces with purpose, direction, and motivation are capable of defeating AQI elements and are an essential element to denying them safe terrain. Aggressive pursuit of intelligence in conjunction with the spread of positive

---

[13] Roger Trinquier, *Modern Warfare: A French View of Counterinsurgency*, trans. Daniel Lee, with an introduction by Bernard B. Fall (New York: Praeger, 1964), p. 6.

information has the potential to persuade citizens to aligning themselves with coalition views and turning away from the oppressive restraints of AQI.

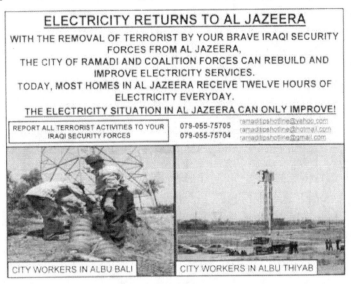

Sample flyer distributed at JSS Arcala (Front).

Sample flyer distributed at JSS Arcala (Back).

Local Interactions, a Critical Element in COIN

The fact that Iraqi Security Forces are working with your unit is an indicator of local cooperation. The power brokers in a tribal society, especially in Al Anbar, are the sheiks. If thousands of men are volunteering to join the ranks of Iraqi police and other city workers it is through the approval of their tribal leadership. This means that frequent visits to the home of various sheiks is mandatory in order to display proper respect for their tribal society. You must be a quick learner and have good interpersonal skills to be successful in this arena.

The common Iraqi greeting tradition of handshakes, hugs, and kisses on the cheek is a bit overbearing for the "personal space" of most sensitive American's, but is required. Soldiers of all ranks must quickly become adept at the "man kiss" and know it is a cultural act demonstrating respect. When meeting with tribal leaders you should clear out about half of a day from your calendar in order to respect their cultural norms of long conversations and lengthy meals. These events usually begin by discussing business matters, then progress to a lengthy meal, and end with multiple cups of chi tea and about a cigarette per cup of tea. Soldiers must understand the Iraqi mannerisms of eating with their hands and not show signs of disgust at what Americans would normally consider unsanitary. The sheik will want to get to know his American partners in-depth and usually at the end of the meal will discuss personal matters over chi in an attempt to forge a strong friendship. These are great opportunities for Americans and Iraqis to find similarities among themselves and to understand one another at a higher level. It is through this process that the tribal leaders will see we are men just like them and that our joint partnership will be more advantageous to success in their area than through an alliance with AQI.

By early July 2007, 1BCT, 3ID had completed a massive clear and hold operation encompassing the entire AO and had set the conditions for major reconstruction operations. The heart of this endeavor was a unified effort from the sheiks of Ramadi; together an amazing transformation would unfold. From the rural outskirts of the city to downtown massive city renewal project began including: trash and rubble removal operations, repaving of streets and sidewalks, installation of solar power street lights, rebuilding damaged buildings, filling in potholes and craters, filling in bullet holes in buildings, and repainting of streets, walls, bridges & overpasses, and homes. Brigade level efforts to renew city services like police, fire, ambulance and hospital services, development of a small business bureau, repair of sewer, water, and power lines all slowly progressed and within six months a new city was reborn. Markets and restaurants were thriving again, museums, banks, and schools operational and US forces were freely patrolling areas on foot that previously were not safe even in an Abrams.

1ˢᵗ Lieutenant Trottier having lunch with a local Iraqi Sheik.

The end result of such unified efforts is a win/ win situation for all participants. In January 2007 the city of Ramadi had four major operating bases and dozens of company outposts. By creating the conditions for peace 1BCT 3ID demonstrated it is possible to reduce the American foot print in Iraq. By March 2008 three of the four major operating bases in Ramadi were closed and operations and logistics consolidated onto one facility, Camp Ramadi. Numerous company outposts were demilitarized and turned over to Iraqi control, further reiterating to the locals the US is in Iraq as a force for positive change not oppression or colonial control as AQI likes to preach.

Ramadi, February 2007.

Ramadi, January 2008.

Conclusion

At the platoon level Soldiers and their leadership need to be aggressive, intelligent, and disciplined. Soldiers in Ramadi applied these fundamental into all their operations to transform a city into an example of success in Iraq. If future platoon leaders continue to provide purpose, direction, and motivation, emphasize continual training, and apply the fundamentals learned in the school house they will be successful. Future leaders in Iraq must be "pentathletes" capable of a wide spectrum of operations. They must be flexible and adaptable to mission changes, but always cognizant of political and cultural implications of their actions. Our behaviors represent the desires of a whole country and must be carefully guided. Ramadi is an example that this war is heading in a positive direction. With intelligently sustained operations from the platoon level on up the chain of command the desired end state of a free and stable Iraq is possible. **HX**

CHAPTER 10

THE ARMY RESERVES AT WAR COMBAT ENGINEERS BUILD, TRAIN AND MATURE UNDER FIRE

By MAJ Rick Rouzer, U.S. Army

Counter-insurgency is challenging and complex. Much of the challenge comes, not from the enemy, but from within. Often, our own procedures (or our reactions from failing to implement procedures) can create the greatest obstacles, inhibiting mission success.

In the beginning of the war, when Reserve and Guard requirements to support the war in Iraq became significant, units would be stripped of personnel and equipment in order to backfill like-units that received deployment orders. This process defies logic because eventually the losing unit- the unit previously stripped of its resources- will receive deployment orders as well. This perpetuates the need to repeat the process, resulting in a significant reduction in the total number of Army Reserve deployable units at the end of the line.

It is possible that planners anticipated the end of hostilities- or at least the end of the requirement for Guard and Reserve support of the war- before the list of available units was nothing more than a group of guidons sitting alone in empty facilities across the states. But that would presume that a plan existed, and there was no proof of that during the early years of the war.

What I observed was a wave of taskings to provide personnel and equipment that started at the eastern shore and moved westward at an increasing rate. The initial requirement to cross-level troops and the growing list of vacancies as each unit was added to the Commanding General Unit of Interest List, was facilitated by several issues unique to the Guard and Reserve communities.

In all cases, the result of breaking and remaking units in this manner affected the training and development of the mobilized units, and were relevant to their degree of success while in theater. In some extreme cases it is indeed possible that the process influenced the mortality rate of soldiers assigned to the most-affected units, though I have no proof that actual data exists.

By the summer of 2004 active component units were already completing their second tour in the sand box, and the fight in Afghanistan had been pushed aside to focus available assets on completing the invasion of Iraq. The unique capabilities of the Reserve and Guard units had been part of the fight from the start, but an increased footprint was needed to help the AC units coordinate a two-war effort with no end in sight. Logistically, having the two efforts resourced concurrently is reminiscent of World War II (minus the exit strategy, the booming economy or the flood of available recruits).

The 2005 rotation plan was designed to include more Reserve units than that of any year of combat since WWII. And the responsibilities of the Army National Guard and Army Reserves commands would increase. The 42nd Infantry Division was slated to defend an area of operation- making them the first National Guard Division to deploy as a command since 1945. In mid 2004 the units for the next rotation were selected, just as the Reserve unit alert list reached the west coast and the Pacific basin.

In August of 2004, while serving in the engineer section of the Reserve command in Hawaii, I was asked to take command of a detachment scheduled to deploy to Tikrit, Iraq, in four months. The fact that this unit was alerted while in need of a commander was insignificant compared to everything else they needed. On the day I accepted command the unit had no NCOs, 30% of its mission essential equipment, no crew served weapons or radios, and just six soldiers who had drilled with the unit.

Due to the unit's location on the island of American Samoa (located halfway between Hawaii and New Zealand), I was commanding the last unit in the Reserve chain, geographically speaking. In other words, there are no Reserve or

Guard engineer units located west of Samoa, so there was no unit remaining from which we could acquire troops and equipment. In less than 18 months, the Reserve engineers had run out of deployable units.

How did this happen? It started two decades earlier when the Vietnam era ended, and with it we ended the use of the draft. For the first time in our modern history, the United States was relying on an all-volunteer Army.

This massive organizational reconstruction, accompanied with the longest stretch of relative peace since the Civil War, caused a change in command priorities. Soon the need to conduct realistic and challenging training was replaced with the need to ensure soldiers stayed in the Reserves and National Guard. In the absence of a real enemy, attrition was the Commander's greatest adversary. Units were graded- and with the advent of the tiered system, funded- based on the need for that unit's particular wartime capabilities and the needs of the Department of Defense.

Unit Commanders had to report to commands; commands had to report to regions; regions had to report to the Chief, Army Reserve, or the Adjutant General (TAG) in the National Guard. No Commander wanted to admit that they didn't have the authorized number of qualified soldiers, as this would indicate that they could not staff their units; so when all else failed they changed their numbers to match the requirement.

The result was that, when preparing quarterly unit status reports, Guard and Reserve units reported personnel numbers that included the troops they saw each drill assembly weekend, as well as men and women they hadn't seen in years- if ever. These faceless names filling the rolls were referred to as "administrative ghosts".

And the problem with these ghosts is that they cannot be relied upon to fill positions in the event of mobilization. They only serve to inflate the personnel numbers, providing the appearance of a more robust unit than actually exists. Every unit had them- some had considerably more than others. Everyone knew it was happening, yet since our funding was based in part on our personnel numbers, and we were not at war, the chain of command looked the other way. In the meantime, planners in the Pentagon were basing their scenarios on numbers that would never add up.

During peacetime this may have seemed inconsequential to many. It was just part of playing the "readiness game". But when peacetime ended, and we started to call these units up, the truth quickly became apparent. Units that previously reported 90% staffing actually required 40% backfill before they could deploy.

For units deploying early in the process, the situation was slightly better. They mobilized with the MOS trained soldiers they recruited over the years, and the slots they needed to backfill were staffed with the most-eager volunteers and the most qualified soldiers with special skills available to the National Guard and Reserves.

Still, the unit training schedule was dictated by the most-recently assigned soldiers, who knew nothing about the unit or the mission. By the time the new soldiers were up to speed, the established soldiers were bored, having no real mission to execute while the new soldiers played catch-up.

And the attrition rate for soldiers in Reserve units was higher than expected, due to misguided peacetime priorities. Too many of the older soldiers were not in good physical shape, and the demands of mobilizing quickly wore them down. Many had to be replaced weeks into the process due to new or pre-existing injuries. This, too, was common in most units. This, too, slowed the unit training cycle. It was clear that the process needed to change if Reserve units were needed to sustain the fight for the duration of the war.

Some soldiers could not acquire a security clearance. Others- single parents and households where both parents were soldiers- had no family care plan and no one to watch their kids. Some were pregnant, or became pregnant during the MOB process. Every issue added names to the list of non-deployables, and every name on the list had to be replaced. The Army Reserve Recruiting Command could not assess new soldiers fast enough to keep up with the needs of the deploying units. And each iteration cut further and further into the well of available experienced soldiers.

By the time I assumed command of my small Samoan detachment, the 25th Infantry on Schofield Barracks had deployed, the Hawaii National Guard was at the MOB station preparing to deploy, and the Army Reserve Engineer Battalion in Hawaii had just arrived in Baghdad to begin their 12-month tour. Five months earlier the battalion had mobilized well under its required personnel strength. My detachment was depleted of 88% of its qualified soldiers in order to "fix" the battalion. A significant number of additional soldiers were needed to round out the battalion, stripping the pool of available engineers just prior to our mobilization.

Still, the requirement had to be met. Like every command before, we had to find bodies to fill the vacant unit positions. Fifty of the fifty-six unit slots were currently vacant, including all but three of the NCO positions.

Nothing that I have expressed to this point is unique to my situation. These issues were common to every commander. They were systematic problems caused by years of creative number crunching, and a failure to retain focus on the objective-which had always been to prepare to fight in war.

There were, however, several concerns that applied specifically to my unit, or were worsened by our position in the deployment chain. And every dilemma caused me consternation with respect to our ability to deploy and attain mission success.

First, my unit was reassigned from Minot, North Dakota in 1999. The detachment had been in Samoa, under the Hawaiian command, for only five years. The unit's allowable level of organization (ALO) was 2-B, meaning we were not the first priority for money or equipment. As a result, we were drastically short of tools, vehicles and individual equipment. The unit was authorized three plumber's tool kits, three electrician's tool kits and three carpenter's tool boxes. At the time of our alert, we had one of each- a direct result of too many priorities and too little funding during peacetime.

The second issue is that we were deploying to theater to serve as a construction engineer detachment under the division.

We were required to report to the engineer brigade across town, but we worked independently for the division and the war-fighters at four patrol bases in Samarra. We were based in Tikrit at one of Sadaam Hussein's palace compounds. This mission required that we conduct our own patrols and that we respond to enemy attacks when they occurred. Never taken into consideration was the fact that we were not designed to do any of this.

When my unit was originated and our mission was determined back in 1999, we were identified as a rear area base support unit- a mission currently filled by contracts with Kellogg, Brown & Root (KBR). We were intended to support the base where we resided, with no patrolling responsibilities and no enemy interaction. Therefore, our MTOE included 56 M-16 rifles for self defense in case of an enemy infiltration to the rear area. We had no machine guns, no pistols, no patrol vehicles and no radios to mount in them. We had tool boxes, contact trucks and walkie-talkies. This discrepancy can be accounted for by the change in enemy tactics from a war with a front to a fluid-asymmetrical- battlefield with the potential for insurgents to attack anywhere, anytime.

And, of course, we had tailored our Mission Essential Task List (METL) to match our anticipated requirements, so we had no training in any of these force protection tasks. Though, that mattered less now that I had no troops. Still, in addition to everything else, I had to rewrite the unit mission and the commander's guidance in six weeks, while restaffing and equipping the unit, and preparing for mobilization.

The local command, which had helped several units prepare for mobilization by this time, had already begun to address the staffing issue before approaching me. They collected several dozen volunteers from other non-engineering units, and paid for them to attend retraining courses. Soldiers who previously worked in personnel offices, communications centers and motor pools, were now going to be carpenters and plumbers in what would be for many, their first field environment. Most had no related experience beyond their basic MOS training.

Some soldiers were now available to my unit from the battalion already in theater. One was pregnant when they mobilized, but was available for our rotation. Several had been recruited as engineers and hadn't completed training in time to go with the battalion. They, too, were available now.

Unfortunately, most of these soldiers were 20 years of age or younger, and most possessed the rank of PFC (E-3) or below. I had a small unit, but it still included 37 NCO slots. Somewhere we had to find experienced soldiers to help train the eager young men and women whose names filled my roster.

Three days after receiving my orders we started a 3-week annual training rotation at Schofield Barracks in order to receive requisite pre-mobilization training. I arrived with nine Sergeants (E-5), two Staff Sergeants (E-6), five Sergeant's First Class (E-7, all instructors from the local training command), a First Sergeant (E-8) and a Chief Warrant Officer (CW3). Nine of the 17 NCOs and the warrant were cross-leveled from other commands.

We also had 51 soldiers, Private Second Class (E-2) thru Specialist (E-4). For the next three weeks we ordered tools, trained on whatever equipment was available, and pared down our personnel list to the best 56 of the 70 present.

It is rare for a commander to be able to choose his troops from a pool of available soldiers. But any benefit from this was negated by the fact that the 55 I kept did not know each other, or me, and they did not know the mission. In addition, only one E-5, cross-leveled from Missouri, had ever deployed previously. We were building a unit from scratch without benefit of a recipe.

Once annual training was concluded and the unit personnel were selected, I sent everyone home for two weeks to return on 1 October to start the mobilization process. We made considerable progress in the previous six weeks, but there was still much to do- and much more to overcome.

Mobilization Stations are very busy installations. They are constantly awaiting the arrival of the next units, training the next to deploy and receiving the returning units who have completed their tour. The list of requirements has grown each subsequent training cycle, and the number of personnel assisting the soldiers training and screening grows correspondingly. There is no way to anticipate everything a unit could experience, and there is no one who wants to guess which task is less worthy of the limited time available. Anything can happen to any unit in an asymmetrical theater of war.

The 25th Infantry Division could not assist us because they were already deployed. And with a unit of just 56 soldiers, we did not warrant the transport and commitment of our own engineer training team, so we got what was available.

Just a month before we mobilized, the 100th Infantry Battalion (the last infantry unit in the United States Army Reserves) also mobilized at Schofield Barracks. The 196th Infantry Training Command is an active component unit whose duties, among many others, is to evaluate and train the soldiers and leaders of the 100th Infantry and to ensure their skills meet the requirements of the AC units they will support in theater. The 196th has many soldiers with several Army branch qualifications. But on Oahu the majority of available trainers was branched infantry and assigned to support the 100th.

Being too small of an organization to justify a dedicated training team (keeping in mind that the most glaring of our deficiencies was our lack of combat training) we, too, were assigned support from the 196th Infantry trainers. They did a great job... of trying to make us infantry soldiers.

This was not the fault of the trainers. They were committed, experienced, supportive and attentive. In many ways they preferred working with us. Our unit was demographically younger on average, and more energetic than most established units; I espoused the importance of demanding physical training, which they also valued; we were learning tactics for the first time, unlike the 100th soldiers who had done the same thing for so many years they were bored and often proved to be uninterested in the training. Also, we were smaller and easier to control. Anywhere they had an opening for training, whether on a range or in the back of the auditorium, we would fit into the remaining slots. This dynamic allowed them to maximize their time and equipment and pushed us through our training more quickly.

The downside of training under an infantry team was that they treated us too much like an infantry unit and, at best, that was our secondary mission. For instance, we spent two days low crawling on the IMT course, and I never saw anyone in theater low crawl. We spent a full day on the grenade range, and no one in our brigade owned a grenade. We spent three days conducting dismounted land navigation operations, and we never had to leave our vehicles while outside the Forward Operating Base (FOB). Not to mention the fact that our vehicles had the Blue Force tracking system.

In many ways, our training was based, not on what we needed, but on what the trainers knew and what training was available at the time. After the first six weeks I felt we were all better infantrymen, but I wasn't sure we were any better at engineering. Ultimately, it was my First Sergeant and Warrant Officer who sought out and found the best engineer training. They located and met with the garrison Department of Public Works (DPW), who agreed to take small groups of soldiers with them on trouble calls. This was real-life experience and the tasks they were executing closely resembled the majority of our deployment missions.

In addition, I was previously assigned to the unit we were replacing in theater. Their commander was a good friend of mine, and we conversed regularly prior to our deployment so that I could get first-hand knowledge of what we would be doing. Early on, when I was still choosing my soldiers, he told me to bring extra electricians, which proved to be valuable considering we arrived with 9 of the 15 electricians assigned throughout our Area of Operation (AO). He also told me to leave my concrete mixer and my asphalt roller in Hawaii. They were our two biggest construction vehicles, and slowed any movement to or from the theater. It turned out that defense contractor KBR was doing that mission, so taking these pieces was an unnecessary addition to our requirements.

Finally, he told me to get as much air conditioner repair training as possible. Engineer utilities detachments like ours do not have AC repair slots. KBR was doing that in theater, too. But KBR, no matter how resourceful or professional, would not go where we would be doing most of our work, and nothing we did would be more appreciated than keeping the water running, keeping the electrical powered, and providing AC where the war-fighters slept. The Schofield DPW helped us with that as well. And once in theater, so did a company called Mantech.

It is important to mention that all my requests to conduct command visits with our war-trace, to participate in VTC briefs, or to send a unit representative to participate in the headquarters site visit to Iraq were disapproved by the training team leadership. They believed the time needed to conduct coordination events would negatively affect our training schedule at the MOB station- which was their primary responsibility. If not for my personal relationship with the unit we were replacing I would not have possessed much of the knowledge that ensured our engineer mission success in theater. This was another glaring flaw in the MOB process early on.

Of course, not every infantry task is exclusively executed by the infantry. Many of their most basic skills are common requirements for all soldiers, and are often categorized outside of the Infantry doctrine as Force Protection measures- a catch-all phrase for any survival task fundamental to basic soldiering in a theater of war. React to enemy attack; basic radio operations; set up a hasty ambush; call in for air support and vehicle recovery are important to all units. But the three I found to be most beneficial were tactical patrolling, crew serve weapons training and medical skills training. And in these areas our trainers proved to be a Godsend.

During WWII a large percentage of allied fatalities were preventable. Injured soldiers often bled out waiting for medical attention. In Korea we set up aid stations, like those seen in the TV show "M*A*S*H", and helicopters were used to get the injured to the doctors faster. Another tried-and-true innovation of that era was triage, the screening and classification of wounded soldiers, which also proved to significantly improve the mortality rate. But still, we were losing too many soldiers due to blood loss.

The Army devised a program to train soldiers in basic medical techniques. All soldiers learn these skills in basic training, and it became part of the list of required skills that all units practice annually. But to expand on the capabilities of assigned soldiers, and to help reduce the load on combat medics during intense activity, the combat lifesaver (CLS) program was developed. This quickly became a valuable program, and reduced the number of battlefield- and training- fatalities by a notable percentage.

I had completed the CLS course as a First Lieutenant in 1998, and I understood the importance of having as many CLS qualified soldiers as possible. The Army standard for deploying units was one CLS per squad. For my small unit, that meant we needed a minimum of six. But thanks to the efforts of our command and the trainers, and my desire to ensure the safety of my soldiers, we ran several iterations of the course and eventually deployed with 22. I can confirm that at least two of my soldiers are alive today because of that training.

Crew-serve training and radio communication training were the most difficult for my unit. One reason was that our modified table of organizational equipment (MTOE), the document used to resource a unit, did not include any type of crew-served weapons, so we had no previous training and we had no idea what weapons we would be using in theater. The same was true of our radios. We owned none, and there are many types in the system. It was difficult for the trainers to determine what training would be most beneficial; again, the type of equipment that we would be issued following deployment was not yet identified. In both cases, the cadre simply expanded the training for each, and covered as much as was conceivable. We stopped only when I determined the soldiers had taken in all they could, and anything more would confuse them.

This situation relates to what was perhaps our greatest hindrance during mobilization. Since we did not own much of what we knew we needed (in particular the crew-served weapons, vehicles and radios) I was prompted to submit an Operational Needs Statement (ONS). This is a written request by the Commander, identifying items needed to ensure mission capabilities and success.

This did not apply to our construction tools. Everything we requested through the garrison support unit that fit in our tool kits was received. The ONS request is specifically designed for sensitive items and equipment in limited supply. I asked for machine guns, night-vision goggles, vehicle-mounted radios, tactical walkie-talkies with frequency-hopping capabilities, pistols for the patrol gunners and extra combat lifesaver bags.

What I got back was a promise my ONS would be filled in Kuwait. There was nothing left to give us, for the same reason there were limited troops available to fill my unit. The units that deployed before us had it all.

Unfortunately, Kuwait never had any of the items I requested. When I handed the support NCO my ONS he told me we would inherit some equipment from the unit we replaced. The rest we would have to live without. So, when we did arrive in Iraq we had no up-armored tactical vehicles, no crew-served weapons, no radios and no idea of what we would eventually end up with.

Based on what my unit was originally provided in personnel, equipment and training, we should have had a decidedly different result to our deployment. It is only through the greatest qualities of the United States military- individual initiative and collective perseverance- that we can claim unequivocal mission success. By the end of our tour we had turned every obstacle into an opportunity.

This air of optimism started with the training we arranged with the DPW at the MOB station. The positive momentum was further increased when we arranged to construct two huts near the weapons ranges. These projects coordinated so I could evaluate the ability of the troops to work as teams. The project work chart designed for the construction of these huts estimated six day duration for completion. Both were completed in four.

When we got to Iraq we made our first patrol in vehicles that could not protect my gunners (see attached photo). This motivated us to go out and search for the equipment we needed. Luckily, my unit possessed a commodity that other units were willing to trade for: Engineer skills. We built a jump-TOC for a

Communications unit and, in exchange, received radios, a crew-served weapon, and internet access for our building. The latter did nothing to directly improve our patrols, but it helped with unit morale a great deal.

We offered to provide maintenance support to a PSD (a team whose primary function is to help others transverse the roads) and got another up-armored vehicle, as well as periodic training on new patrol tactics throughout the year. We built plywood dividers in the living quarters of an Armor unit and received two more weapons. We helped install the plywood desks in a TOC and received several tactical walkie-talkies. Within 6 weeks, we had acquired- through horse trades- everything we needed in order to conduct our patrols with the maximum self defense capability.

A patrol gunner during our first trip through Samarra.

We continued this tactic with our assigned missions as well. The Brigade Class IV yard had limited capabilities to anticipate our mission requirements. The turn-around for parts orders was three months, and we could not anticipate our needs that far in advance.

Instead, we found local vendors and utilized our FOO monies (discretionary money for the commander's use in theater) to supplement what we got from the brigade. I also worked a deal with KBR. We shared some welding rods and sheet metal- most of which we inherited from our predecessors- and they would provide us construction materials needed to support the war-fighters in Samarra. Whatever materials KBR loaned us, we would requisition through the brigade S-4 and return to them when they arrived months later.

The key to everything we did- whether it was construction, patrolling or improving the environment on our forward operating base (FOB) - was accomplished through our own ingenuity. And that capability was developed through necessity at the MOB station.

As a matter of fact, the most important event that occurred during the MOB process- and this was quickly noticed and appreciated by the trainers- was the growth of the young soldiers, and the development of the natural leaders. Many established units had less to overcome than my detachment, but they had their share of issues to resolve. For many, the primary issue was what to do with problematic soldiers in key unit positions.

The First Sergeant and I had to address this issue as well, but not to the extent of some of our sister units. My shortage of senior NCOs provided the opportunity for us to promote from within, and three months at the MOB station gave us tremendous insight on who was best suited for promotion. So instead of inheriting an established- and worn out- NCO corps, we got to build our own.

The result was a group of leaders who had proven themselves with us and with the assigned troops; NCOs who were chosen in a fair and equitable competition for the right to lead; soldiers promoted during mobilization- and later in combat, not during peacetime.

By the end of our tour we had progressed from a hodge-podge of individuals to a cohesive and high-functioning unit that successfully completed more than 800 missions and 300 patrols. We supported 40 units on 12 FOBs and patrol bases. We closed three bases, including our own (which had the distinction of being the largest successfully closed at the time) on our way out the door. And we built a strong and mutually beneficial relationship with everyone in which we had contact.

The most significant aspect of our deployment was our involvement in five separate enemy incidents. Ten of my soldiers were injured; four of which earned the Purple Heart. Two soldiers received injuries significant enough to be sent home. But at the end of the year I had returned every one of them home alive. They hid from nothing; they volunteered for missions others would not accept; they faced fear daily and they endured almost nightly enemy harassment on our FOB. And through it all they never failed to complete a single mission.

These are not the traits of a unit thrown together at the MOB station. These are the traits of a strong and established unit, with soldiers who possess the Army values, solid training skills, and who are vested in each other and the war-fighters they supported. And by the time we returned to a heroes-welcome back in Hawaii that is exactly what I had.

But I cannot take credit for our successes. In truth, I was lucky. I knew other Commanders, good men, with the capability to lead but without the troops I was blessed to command. Ours was a team effort, facilitated by a difficult start and a strong desire by all to serve our mission well.

Yes, I was very lucky. Many units could not have overcome the situation we inherited at the start. It was obvious to all that we were not mobilizing from a position in which we could predict success. Of course, this only enhanced the image of our unit and the opinion of others when we eventually exceeded, not only our expectations but, the expectations of older and more-established units. Our success was very personal, because it was facilitated by the individual abilities and the collective determination of our soldiers and unit leaders.

Recent changes to the deployment cycle address many of the issues Reserve units have faced during the first five years in Iraq. We now deploy on a 5-year cycle. Units possess a basic understanding of their anticipated mission as much as four years prior to mobilization. They conduct progressive levels of training, where the final touches are added at the MOB station instead of the massive training that has previously been required.

The soldiers in these units are frozen in position two years before deployment, so the majority will remain with the unit throughout. Some soldiers will still be lost during the process, but Commanders should be able to anticipate more reliable numbers, and deploy with familiar faces.

Still, more changes need to occur. MTOE units should not be used to backfill units with similar requirements. Soldiers in good commands with effective training and retention practices should not be fodder for the preceding units in the deployment cycle. Vacant slots should be filled, first, with TDA and IMA soldiers, and then with available AC troops. All deployable units should remain intact, as much as circumstances allow.

Annual funding needs to be increased for Guard and Reserve units. Currently these units receive fewer dollars per soldier for training, equipment, sustainment, travel and support functions. These soldiers and their units are now major players in the big plan. The Active Component cannot deploy for more than 30 days without Reserve or National Guard Support and Service Support units. Funding levels should reflect the requirements and demands of these units.

All military units have limited equipment, funding, recruiting pools and time for training. But the supply for each is dire in Guard and Reserve commands. If the force structure plan continues to depend so highly on these units for war-fighter support, then they need to be provided the greatest opportunity for success. After all, these units are staffed by citizen soldiers-men and women who spend the majority of their time teaching, coaching, building, nursing, designing and repairing, just like their civilian counterparts. The main difference is that they have accepted the call- the toughest part-time job in the world. The least they deserve from us is a plan that ensures the opportunity for success. **HX**

CHAPTER 11

OPERATION BATON ROUGE: PERSPECTIVES FROM AN IRAQI SECURITY FORCES ADVISOR

By John DeRosa

"A combat advisor influences his ally by force of personal example. You coach, you teach, and you accompany in action. Finally, an advisor provides the connection and expertise to bring to bear fires, service support, and other combat multipliers. All accolades go to the leader your support."

Brigadier General Daniel P. Bolger.

In the dawning of October 2004, the Second Brigade Combat Team (2BCT) of the First Infantry Division, The Big Red One (BRO), led a group of approximately 5,000 soldiers comprised of 3,000 Americans and 2,000 Iraqis on a major offensive against insurgents in Samarra, Iraq. The mission of OPERATION BATON ROUGE was "to kill or capture anti-Iraqi forces (AIF) and return the city to competent civilian control."[1] Intelligence suggested that the AIF numbered 200 to 500 made up of local Baathists and former military officers fighting for a return of a Sunni-dominated government. The rest were foreign "jihadis" and hard-core Iraqi Islamists heeding the call of terrorist leaders like Abu Mousab al-Zarqawi.

---

[1] "The Fight for Samarra: Full-Spectrum Operations in Modern Warfare," MG John R.S. Batiste and LTC Paul R. Daniels, *Military Review*, May-June 2005, pg. 13-21.

The coalition forces' offensive operations lasted three days and on October 4, were able to claim victory. OPERATION BATON ROUGE was touted as a resounding coalition success. Over the three days, "over 125 AIF were killed, 60 wounded, and 128 detained."[2]

The focus of this chapter is the challenges of a very specific group of BRO soldiers, Iraqi Security Forces (ISF) Advisors during Phase III (Search and Attack) of OPERATION BATON ROUGE. The introduction of ISF into the operation was to increase the size of the attacking/stabilizing force to prevent a power vacuum and demonstrate a credible ISF.[3] Specific to this article, the integration of the 1st Ministry of Interior (MOI) Special Police Commando Battalion (hereafter "the Commandos") proved to be a successful Iraqi solution to the Samarra problem.

Mission planning for OPERATION BATON ROUGE. The objective was "to kill or capture anti-Iraqi forces (AIF) and return the city to competent civilian control

---

[2] *Ibid.*

[3] *Ibid.* pg. 18.

Initial Planning

A key component of OPERATION BATON ROUGE was the introduction of ISF into city to enable civilian control of a deteriorated security environment. Initial plans for BATON ROUGE called for the implementation of "Police-In-A-Box" concept. "Police-in-a-Box" was a concept based on police sub-stations built in transportable shipping containers (with ancillary equipment of weapons, radios, etc.) complemented with newly trained Iraqi Police Officers. Each TF element was to go in and clear their sector of AIF to establish control. During Phase IV (Stabilizing) TF ISF Advisors would escort Police-In-A-Box elements from nearby staging areas to conduct a link-up and establish Iraqi led policing operations.

Task Organization (Ground)

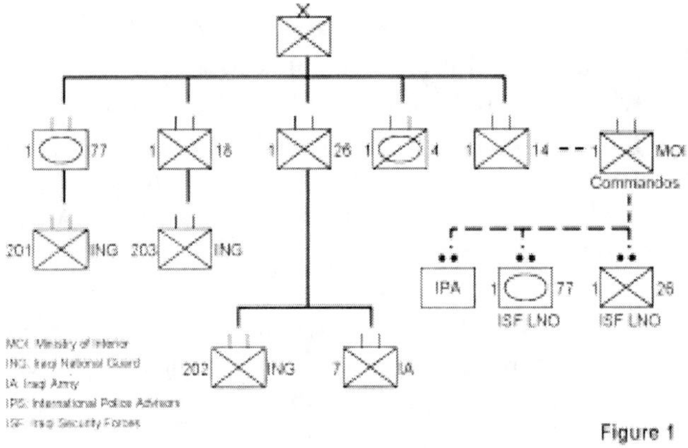

Figure 1

Our TF mission analysis of Phase IV assigned our civilian International Police Advisors (IPA) to each of the TF's company teams to be liaisons to the IPS. [4] Our TF Operations SGM (TIGER 37) and I would coordinate the ISF efforts for the TF CDR.

The IPAs were U.S. State Department contractors who were American police officers peppered across Iraq to oversee

---

[4] Task Force STEEL TIGERS, 1st Battalion, 77th Armor (Schweinfurt, GE).

the training and mentoring of the Iraqi Police Service. Overall they were well intentioned Americans looking to shoulder some of the burden in reconstructing Iraq. Despite some small scale successes, my impression was that they were recruited more for a U.S. interagency solution than out of any competence for the job—with no area expertise and little or no real knowledge of the mission that the Iraqi security and police forces actually had to perform. Most IPAs migrated from recent service under the United Nation's Mission in Kosovo. Generally, the IPAs struggled with conflicting priorities, a lack of integrated communications, and non-standard equipment.

Our contingent of ISF Advisors and IPAs arrived prior to our TF LD at Forward Operating Base Brassfield-Mora to stage and link up with IPS counterparts.[5] We were advised by the lead ISF Advisor from TF BLUE SPADERS that Phase IV was still being ironed out at BCT HQ. Any insight into the developing plan would not be established as we had no contact with BCT S-5/ISF cell. Adding another layer of friction was that contact with our TF (which was located south of Samara) went through FBCB2 to our attacking elements or bounced via Mobile Subscriber Equipment back to our home at FOB Paliwoda then via FM to TF because of urban communications limitations.

Unfortunately, "Murphy" decided to show up and assist the planning cell for Phase IV development. That evening we found out the hold up in Phase IV planning, coalition forces had yet secured compliance with the Iraqi Ministry of Interior. There would be no IPS available to implement the "Police-in-a-Box" concept. The newly independent Iraqi bureaucracy would allot ISF to the division only days prior to execution.[6] Due to the delayed introduction to the fight, before mentioned "Commandos" became more of an exploitation force versus policing.

---

[5] FOB Brassfield-Mora overlooked nearby Samarra and was the home of our sister TF, the BLUE SPADERS of 1st Battalion, 26th Infantry.

[6] *Ibid.*

Phase III (Search and Attack)

sketch not to scale

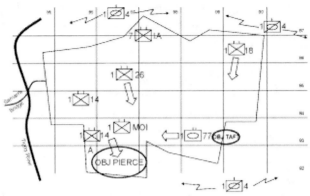

Figure 2

Negotiations with 2nd BCT CDR, TF 1-14 IN CDR, the Salah Ad Din Deputy Governor, and the Commanding General and Battalion Commander of Commandos ended with an agreement that the Commandos would work with autonomy in cooperation with TF 1/14 IN (see figure 1: Task Organization).[7] They would enter operations during Phase III (Search and Attack) conducting raids, snatch and grabs, and deliberate clearance of zones in the city. The Commandos would follow TF 1/14 IN after they crossed the Tigris River Bridge west of Samarra and completed a FPOL with TF 1/26 IN, then conduct cordon and search operations to the south in vicinity of OBJECTIVE PIERCE (see figure 2: Phase III (Search and Attack).

The Commandos

Only together only a few weeks, the commandos moved to support OPERATION BATON ROUGE given only 48 hours notice. The Commandos were focused on urban raid operations and counterterrorist missions against hijackers and kidnappers. A

---

[7] TF GOLDEN DRAGONS, 1st Battalion, 14th Infantry, 25th Infantry Division (Schofield Barracks, HI).

rough, para-military looking unit, their uniforms consisted of a woodland camouflage pattern with black leather gloves, jackets, and balaclavas. They used American-supplied pickups with camouflage paint and machine guns mounted in a "field expedient" fashion.

> From this regiment we have police who have previous experience fighting terrorism and also people who received special training under the former regime—people who used to be in the army." Police Commando Commanding General MG Adon Thabit[8]

The Commandos would be effective in Samarra because of their predominantly Sunni background. Sunnis historically were in high security roles under Saddam Hussein and therefore most experienced. They have deep family ties in the Sunni Triangle and relied on those ties as an ad hoc intelligence network. They were very skilled in identifying civilians who represented a threat.

Mission and Link-Up

The contingent of TF STEEL TIGERS and BLUE SPADERS ISF Advisors and IPAs would coordinate between the Commandos and higher/adjacent units overseeing movement and resolving CF/ISF issues. We would drive out immediately to link up with the Commandos that were being staged at a nearby annex of FOB Brassfield-Mora, FOB 7. Upon arrival at FOB 7 we quickly broke into teams to work with the Commandos.

We went about our prep for combat and integrated with our assigned company leadership. Our first priority was to find English speaking commandos. Of our team of six now split between three companies, we only had one translator. With my assigned commando company I found a senior lieutenant that

---

[8] "Iraq Interior Ministry Forms Police Commando Battalions," SGT Jared Zabaldo, Armed Forces Information Services: News Articles, 20 October 2004, http://www.defenseling.mil/news/Oct2004.

spoke broken English and all had common understanding of military phrases from their training with US Special Forces.

As with all Iraqis paramilitary types I have encountered, there was always at a lack of equipment. The most prominent Arabic word I learned from my deployment was *"areed"*; which loosely translates to "I need". In my work with the ISF I learned to let them present their dissertation on how a*reed* would solve all their problems. My mission was to give them what I had and get them to execute/adapt/overcome.

The next morning the Commandos made a huge convoy—the likely target of an ambush—and departed the moonscape of FOB 7 to Patrol Base RAZOR to begin the FPOL into Samarra. We staged at PB RAZOR for what seemed like an eternity. Each commando company seemed to know exactly where we were going and sped off into the city. As I suspected, the convoy attracted contact as we entered the city. Again, another eternity was sweated out on the bridge entering Samarra as we waiting for the lead elements to sort out actions on contact.

Soon after, we arrived at our chosen assault position. Unfortunately for the children of Samarra, a local school was chosen. It had a large courtyard for staging vehicles, its completely walled compound proved to be relative protection from small arms fire, and a roof top view of the sector. Our defensive positions overlooked a cemetery leading to a jumbled mess of a casino, hotels and apartment buildings. Traffic from the adjacent units was relatively regular.

Establishing security is where I found conflict with T.E. Lawrence aforementioned advice to "let them do it." An IPA on loan from their regional headquarters did not like our stern interaction with the commandos. It seems the established priorities of work (1. establish security 2. nothing else happens until security is established) is in contrast to his "diplomatic agenda." We were in the middle of a firefight and he was still trying to establish bonds with his company. Diplomatic cigarette breaks were getting in the way of completing the mission. Since our position was not as commanders, we struggled to lead by "force of example." After much coaching and refinement, security is established.

With security finally established, the companies break to establish patrols and traffic control points in their assigned sectors. Our company closed ranks to fill in the gaps left by the patrolling company. TIGER 37, his driver, and I share our NODS with the commandos' snipers. In a play on "diplomacy," we ask to see one of the more outgoing sniper's dragonov. As we pass off this as show and tell, we use the scope to clear his fields of fire.

Patrols

The traffic around our assault position attracts attention of the insurgents. And IED erupts about 200 meters from our position on a passing American patrol. The patrol spots our rooftop security positions and reacts to what it believe is the point of origin. The American patrol peppers our position with machine gun fire. What follows may not be recommended example of how to conduct MOUT. We cannot raise the patrol because we don't know which unit, let alone patrol element it is. As our TF 1-26 counterparts call higher, the patrol halts its firing. TIGER 37 moves to the school house rooftop to gain a better vantage point. I on the other hand leave the sanctuary of the school house walls to help establish recognition as a coalition forces position. With the TIGER 37 on the roof and I at the entrance, we wait. Their turrets swivel north and away. After what seems like another eternity passes they resume their patrol. Either higher got the call or they recognized us as US soldiers and recognized us as another unit in the mess of Samarra.

Over the course of the night AIF probe our school house assault position. The company commander sends a patrol to follow the egress route of the AIF. The commandos follow the AIF through a cemetery up to a hotel. The hotel turns out to be an AIF hideout. The commandos capture the AIF by surprise. Twenty-five AIF are rounded up. From their obvious physical characteristics they are foreign fighters. The commandos point out the non-Iraqi Arabs; but the African-born fighters are easy to recognize. It's such a big haul that PB RAZOR sends a patrol of 5-tons to conduct a detainee transfer. The commandos receive instant credibility after this snatch.

Objective Pierce

After consultations with the TF 1/14 IN CDR, the Commandos are tasked to conduct combined operations with TEAM REAPER (A/1/14IN) to conduct a cordon and search to clear the south-west portion of Samarra, named OBJ PIERCE. OBJ PIERCE is a heavy industrial area of Samarra. The automotive garages, ice factories, warehouses, and even a pharmacy was being exploited by the AIF because of the industrial nature made it a prime hiding spot for IED making caches and workshops.

The cordon was established by a tank platoon to the west, Bradley platoon in the north, and Apaches/Kiowa helicopters in the south. The search was conducted west to east in the north with TEAM REAPER. In the south my assigned company would be the lead element of the commandos. Well versed in urban combat, the commandoes executed with fervor. Their snipers quickly secured observation posts on the highest structures to provide over watch. Often, since they lacked integrated communications, the snipers would reveal themselves to direct their counterparts to movement and hazard identification. We follow our company through our sector dismounted. With the initial sweep not drawing contact with AIF, we maneuvered to the north on-line with TM REAPER. Now, with an attachment of three sappers from the 65th EN, we conduct a deliberate clearing of OBJ PIERCE going door-to-door/hole-to-hole.

This is where the discipline of the commandos broke down. The uneventful initial clearing lulled them out of their game. Security devolved as they were more interested in the breaching done by the sappers. With the help of my translator (Omar) we snaked through our assigned sector. Used to working with American soldiers, even Omar lost his temper often cursing the commandos into action like a crusty NCO of old. Once the excitement of the sapper's work wore off, the commandos focus increased and a rhythm of searching developed. Occasionally a commando would find a resident still at home/work willing to open doors/gates to allow our searches rather than test our sappers' entry techniques.

The combined U.S. and ISF clearance of OBJ PIERCE was a distinct element of BATON ROUGE. Immediately, the "good news drum" began its beating. At the completion of this operation, the photo op begins. The commando leadership was quickly paraded in front of the CNN cameras with TF DANGER and DAGGER leadership to tout a successful Iraqi solution to the Samarra problem.

ISF Advisor & IPA giving instruction to translator.

Transition to Phase IV

After we pass the reins of control of OBJ PIERCE to TF 1-14 IN, we re-group and refit at the Samarra mayor's office, the makeshift HQ of the commando senior leadership. With their recent successes, the CF leaders offer the commandos the opportunity to continue operations off their own internal intelligence. These guys are from Samarra; they have a score to settle.

The following 24 hours is filled with raids/snatch and grabs—each more successful than the previous. One captive rumored is to be one of the captors in one of the al-Zarqawi beheadings; he confesses under interrogation.

Since Phase IV is not what is originally planned, we return to FOB Brassfield-Mora to link up with a TF 1-77 platoon resting and refitting for an extended stay in support of TF 1-26. A "doctrinal" FPOL occurs the next day as we ride shotgun with the platoon as it returns back to the TF sector. After a brief stay with one of our companies' interim patrol bases, we catch a patrol to the TF Trains outside Samarra just in time to start the road march back to FOB Paliwoda.

After Action Review

Clearly any lens of history is speckled with the mud of reality. However, in light of the ongoing combined operations between coalition and indigenous security forces (whether in Iraq or Afghanistan) it is important to reflect on OPERATION BATON ROUGE from the perspective of ISF Advisors. The commandos were not the only combined U.S. and ISF operations conducted during this operation. Each task force brought components of their sister Iraqi Army/National Guard infantry battalions from their assigned AORs. This review does not address those significant endeavors.

The delay in task organization complicated "multinational integration." The Dagger BCT and specifically TF Dragon did not receive the Commandos until just hours before execution. Our (TF Steel Tigers) experience with our partner ISF identified rehearsals helped better integrate their capabilities into the operation. Moreover, the ad hoc task organization of advisors to ISF complicated operations initially. While the Commandos executed with surprising success, we did not fully maximize their capabilities during the initial fight.

The Commandos are trained almost exclusively to conduct offensive operations and expect to conduct only these types of operations. Their training regimen prior to BATON ROUGE was primarily focused on raids and sensitive site exploitation. Establishing a patrol base and conducting traffic control points taxed their relatively small organization (nearly half the size of the Iraqi Army Battalions in this operation).

Indigenous Security Forces already possessed valuable intelligence networks. Many of the Commandos (notably their Commanding General) were displaced from Samarra under the former regime. Their knowledge of local families, criminals, and neighborhoods, allowed them an instinctive identification of any outsider (specifically foreign fighters and Abu Musab al-Zarqawi's operatives). Much of their exploitation success is directly tied to their home-grown intelligence networks.

ISF lack cultural initiative, specifically as it relates to priorities of work. Reflecting on T.E. Lawrence's previously stated advice; decisions are created by committee after lengthy discussions. The Commandos would not execute priorities of work unless their American counterpart had significant "influence of personality" or were directed by higher headquarters. A lot of this is accounted for by the slow and deliberate Arab culture (desert life forces a methodical pace to Arab Armies). We relied on our own initiative as army leaders to direct willing ISF NCOs to establish priorities of work then having to follow up with impromptu OPDs with the Company Commanders and their lieutenants.

A focus point of ISF weak leadership was junior officer leadership (lieutenants). During Saddam's reign, all hints of initiative or charisma were smothered.[9] In my assigned company we were "blessed" with a "Mulazim Awal" (1st Lieutenant) that was respected and well liked (and to my advantage spoke broken English). I tended to use him much like a company executive officer. He helped bridge the gap between the commanders and the soldiers. However, the majority of the other "Mulazims" (Lieutenants) lacked any initiative to execute or to learn.

The Commandos displayed a distinctly high level of morale and courage. I would be remiss to disregard the combat

---

[9] "So you want to be an Advisor," BG Daniel P. Bolger, *Military Review*, March-April 2006, pg 7.

performance of these brave men. When the time to LD came, the Commandos were all business and they knew their business.

American Advisors developed tactics, techniques and procedures to overcome communication difficulties with the Commandos such as language barriers and incompatible communications. I personally recruited an Iraqi translator from our home FOB knowing that our mission was to liaise with ISF.[10] "Omar," despite his role, displayed immense courage during BATON ROUGE. I often had to force myself to remember he was a civilian on the battlefield. At task organization, my first task was to find the best English speaking commandos and linked them up with my IPA counterparts.

Unfortunately, FM crosstalk did not exist. The Commandos, the IPA, and U.S. soldiers each had separate radio systems. You can imagine the command and control nightmare during the cordon and search of OBJ PIERCE between the three groups. We relied on the tried and true "command voice" and hand-and-arm signals to direct operations.

ISF did not own the night. Communications were not the only equipment shortfall in BATON ROUGE. In our short task organization with the Commandos, we recognized that facets of operations are outside the scope of their equipment. The Commandos were not equipped with appropriate night vision devices to conduct operations during hours of darkness. The commandos relied on instinct and bare knuckles vs. laminated maps (w/G.P.S.), encrypted radios, and night vision optics.

Poor U.S. inter-agency coordination. Perhaps an insignificant reflection on OPERATION BATON ROUGE was the lack of formal interagency coordination between U.S. military and supporting civilian agencies, specifically the Department of State contracted "International" Police Advisors. Despite the recognized directive that military commanders were the senior U.S. representatives in each sector of Iraq, there was no one place, agency or force that directed interagency

---

[10] First, I had to strong-arm a friendly neighborhood field ordering officer, so I could offer a bonus above his normal salary. I will not name names or a position in case he is ever audited.

cooperation. Cooperation was based on ad hoc personal relationships. Seams in interagency cooperation were most strained as each commando company was split to conduct individual missions. The IPAs seemed more focused on their long term strategic goals of rebuilding Iraqi police units leaning more toward "community police patrols." This was in contrast to the 2BCT commander's intent of using the Commandos as a short-term exploitation force in raids and sensitive site exploitation. To the credit of a minority, they ceded operational control to US military officers when the commandos were given direct tasks from higher headquarters. **HX**

"Do not try to do too much with your own hands. Better the Arabs do it tolerably than that you do it perfectly. It is their war, and you are to help them, not to win it for them. Actually, also, under the very odd conditions of Arabia, your practical work will not be as good as, perhaps, you think it is." *T.E. Lawrence*

CHAPTER 12

Improvised Explosive Devices (IEDs)

by Eric Chevreuil

A simulated IED emits a firestorm as Soldiers in the Iowa National Guard's 1-133 Infantry Battalion experience the concussion and noise of an explosion during Theater Immersion Training at Camp Shelby, Miss., in 2006. The Iowa unit rounded out the 1st Brigade, 34th "Red Bull" Division, of nearly 4,000 Soldiers who deployed to Iraq US (Army photo, June 14, 2006).

ROADSIDE BOMBS, TERRORISM, AND LESSONS LEARNED

Improvised Explosive Device (IED) attacks have proven to be the highly lethal and efficient way for insurgent groups to kill U.S. soldiers, destroy vehicles, create a feeling of insecurity on the battlefield, and bring a very disturbing message home, to America. IEDs are a strategic weapon of choice for insurgent groups.

The Internet and the peer to peer networks that allow the fast exchange of news not available mainstream, have numerous Jihadist propaganda "home videos" available for download, and allow interested parties to access them faster in a "centralized location" that does not require the knowledge of, nor the visiting of monitored official websites of known terrorist organizations. The distributed training potential to terrorists of such videos is obvious.

The Effect of the IEDs

The videos show a wide range of effects that depends on the size of the explosive device and the type of target.

Small charges: Small explosion are shown to be highly lethal on foot patrols or unprotected crews of armored vehicle; depending on the distance from the explosion, some survivors are always seen, moving or crawling for shelters. The same explosive devices against small vehicles or trucks all the way up to tractor-trailers show intensive internal damages in the cabins caused by the blast. Maybe that is the reason why since Afghanistan, Russian soldiers would rather sit on top of their APCs than inside! Most of the time the vehicle is seen idling to a stop further away from the blast, smoldering, doors and hoods wide opened. The videos also show the admirable resistance to blasts of the so-called Armor Survivability Kit (ASK), most of the HUMVEEs are fitted with; the kit has obviously been designed to resist any blast, from small or big explosive devices...and the doors are "unharmed", even when the whole vehicle is completely destroyed and its crews killed! Up-armoring HUMVEEs with the ASK is basically like putting a bulletproof vest on an eggshell.

Big charges: Explosion of devices made with bomb or artillery shell warheads are huge and their blast tremendous. On the one hand, foot patrols, soft skinned vehicles, light armored vehicles or check points are literally vaporized. On the other hand, heavier armor such as tanks and APCs are propelled into the air or brought to a sharp and final flaming stop. In all reviewed cases, after a big explosion, none of the heavy vehicles restarted and moved on -- a sign of extensive mechanical and human damages.

An Iraqi family stands outside their home, damaged by fire from a recent vehicle-borne IED. Iraqi Police and U.S. Soldiers assisted several families by supplying water, beds, school supplies and shoes on July 6, 2006 (US Army photo).

Lessons Learned From the Analysis of Hours of Videos

- Always assume that there is a video camera within a mile range of the explosion: All the videos seen account for dozens of destroyed vehicles and many more killed exposed infantry personnel. Video footages are not professional and obviously made with portable camcorders, thus seriously limiting the distance and the quality of the propaganda shots.

- Half of the videos were edited with text, music, and basic special effects for propaganda purposes. The other half was just depicting raw footages, posted "as is."

- Most of the videos were shot at a really close range of the explosion and are affected by the shock wave or flying debris. Furthermore, when the sound track is available, it is easy to "guesstimate" the distance and in many case the sound and the explosion are practically simultaneous.
- Many videos show the bomb making process. Most of them show the use of unexploded ordnance such as bombs, artillery shells, and mortar shells. A few show "homemade" explosive devices contained in bags. Some of the detonators are made with medical syringes. In one instance, in Chechnya, a Lada 4 door sedan is loaded with 3 155mm artillery warhead and abandoned on the side of a street, hood open like if it broke down. Another video shows the setting of a 250 lb bomb on a roadside and its detonation against a M1 in Iraq.
- The IEDs were always well camouflaged and never laid in the open. The videos showing the actual setting of the devices showed them being buried and covered with rocks or gravel for adding lethality. Camouflage was cleverly done because many videos show foot soldiers walking by or actually combing the area in front of tanks and not finding anything.
- The explosive devices are used as regular landmine or roadside bombs detonated by crude mechanical or electrical pressure plates (medical syringe, basic wiring…) or remotely. Almost everything that generates a radio signal can been used as the method for remote detonation, from short-range, hand held transmitters (walkie talkies), to wireless remote control for toys, garage door opener, movement sensors or cell phones. On some videos, the dialing of a cell phone is clearly audible before the explosion of the device. With a cell phone, timing is critical to hit the target. Operator has to take into account the distance and velocity of the vehicle from the IED, the time to pre-dial the phone number, and finally, the burst of time between the pressing of the dial button to the "ringing" of the phone: the explosion. All

videos involving cell phones showed a total mastering of these delays.

- The bomb size does not matter for the choice of the target. Videos show that huge bombs are blown on foot patrol and sometimes lesser one on soft skinned vehicle. The opportunity primes over the target. Most of the videos show soft skinned vehicles like a HUMVEE or a truck. Tanks or APCs seem to be targeted only when the roadside bomb is a huge one, when crew is exposed, infantry riding atop or walking by.

- On some cases, daisy chained bombs are used to cover a whole stretch of road, a whole length of the convoy. This occurrence seems rare because it needs a lot of vulnerable clandestine time in the settings, many IEDs, and the technical skills to link them together and set them up for a simultaneous explosion.

- Analysis of the targeted vehicles show that most of the time, the target is just a target of opportunity, a single vehicle, a vehicle carrying many exposed infantrymen or a vehicle close to the front or rear of the convoy. The destruction and video team are static and potentially exposed while waiting for a target. Most of the videos show an isolated vehicle being targeted. When a convoy is spotted, the bomb is detonated on a vehicle with exposed personnel.

- Watching these video is a gut wrenching experience because the viewer knows that somewhere, in the field of vision of the camera, lays the explosive device that is going to seal the fate of unaware US or Russian soldiers. Eventually, after a couple of reviews of the films, one can get a sense of where the explosion is going to occur. Most of the time, there is some kind of "landmark" on the side of the road, or in the line of sight between the road and the destruction team. A couple of videos show an easy culprit: a telephone or power line pole.

- The videos also show that it is easier to get a successful hit on a slow vehicle or on a vehicle that has a constant speed. The critical challenge for the bomber is to accurately figure out the distance-velocity factors for a successful detonation of the device.

- Roadside bombs are as successfully used in open country than in urban area. In order to score, the terrorists need to know that there is enemy traffic on the specific road they are targeting, or they need to create the opportunity and attract enemy traffic. Another way is to "bring" the roadside bomb to the enemy. Some videos actually show suicide bombers driving through check points and detonating their cars, or terrorist firing a RPG to one of 2 HUMVEE from the unprotected rear of a mobile check- point.

Other films show Chechen fighters filming themselves from within a car. They actually slow down to let the unsuspecting target get closer and open up through their rear tinted window with AK47 and SMG. The same applies to drive by shooting, when they pass a truck and open up on the unprotected crew.

What To Do

Here are things that could be done to make the life of the bombers a little more difficult:

- Deny them financing, propaganda, recruiting, training: Internationally: track and shut down financial sources, take down all websites, jam or shut down radio and TV stations, shut down print shops, arrest vocal proponents of the Jihad and destruction of our countries, shut down recruiting stations in Muslim countries, infiltrate organizations and dismantle them, sanction countries sheltering all of the above tools or organizations.
- Educate people about the threat and deny the terrorists the Western media as a propaganda tool: There is a difference between reporting events and helping the enemy.
- Deny them shelter by the population: Employ Psy Ops, intelligence, infiltration, and preemptive elimination and arrest of terrorists and collaborators. Bounties and

monetary incentive to deliver terrorists and information about terrorists to the authorities are important to turn the population against the IED bombers.

A Buffalo vehicle belonging to the Army Reserve's 467th Engineer Battalion uses its hydraulic arm to probe a trash pile thought to contain an IED on August 1, 2006 (US Army photo).

- Deny them access to the unexploded hardware: Friendly forces must conduct a systematic destruction of all unexploded hardware. Monetary incentives to report unexploded ordinance will assist this effort. A "buying plan" for unexploded ordinance should be part of the operation. Make it illegal to be in the possession of unexploded hardware or weapons.
- Deny them the night: Use unmanned sensors and night vision devices to monitor of the roadsides. Employ drones, satellites, aerial surveillance, curfew on the main roadsides, static random sniper ambushes, mobile ambushes, intrusion detection devices along roadsides to keep watch of high traffic routes.

- <u>Deny them opportunities</u>: Plan random and irregular schedules for convoys, alternate routes, clear roadsides from wrecks and abandoned vehicles, destroy on site any abandoned vehicle, and maintain 360-degree security for all the mobile or static checkpoints.

- <u>Deny them the casualties</u>: Armor up and move swiftly. Drive fast in the middle of the road, keep distances between vehicles, keep distances between soldiers on foot patrol, setup irresistible "honey pots" close to the front of the convoy (troop transporters with dummy soldiers in the back and heavily protected drivers for example), change speed on regular basis, randomly take alternate routes off the main one, never setup mobile check points at the same location, never setup relief or "rendezvous" at the same location, avoid routine, jam all ranges of wireless and cell phone frequencies, wear full de-mining like body suit and facial shield. Employ fully armored vehicles in convoys.
- <u>Deny them the post explosion "dance of victory" and videotaped desacralization of the corpses</u>: Never assign a

single vehicle to a mission. Plan sufficient back up vehicles and manpower to control a potential explosion area.

- <u>Propaganda</u>: Take active measures to deny them the ability to place and keep IED ambush videos on the Internet.
- <u>Bring the war to them:</u> Deny the enemy their sanctuaries. Adopt the Israelis tactics of pinpointed retaliation. ▪X

CHAPTER 13

TACTICS FOR SMALL WARS

By COL Kevin C.M. Benson,
U.S. Army(Retired)

War no longer exists.
General Sir Rupert Smith, 2005[1]

[M]ake the existing state of war and martial law so inconvenient and so unprofitable to the people that they will earnestly desire and work for the reestablishment of peace and civil government.
Brigadier General J. Franklin Bell, 1902[2]

Army Chief of Staff General George W. Casey, Jr., in an essay in *ARMY* magazine, wrote, "Today, we are at war and live in a world where global terrorism and extremist ideologies are realities. . . . I believe the next decades are likely to be ones of persistent conflict."[3] The small wars conducted during a period of persistent conflict will require the use of force to attain policy objectives. The use of force alone may not produce decisive results, but it must absolutely establish conditions for policymakers to declare victory or at least a form of status quo that can be called victory. The art and science of tactics must recognize the changing conditions requiring the use of force.

---

[1] General Sir Rupert Smith, *The Utility of Force The Art of War in the Modern World*, New York: Alfred A. Knopf, 2007, p. 3.

[2] Brigadier General J. Franklin Bell, cited in Max Boot, *The Savage Wars of Peace Small Wars and the Rise of American Power*, New York: Basic Books, 2002, p. 123.

[3] General George W. Casey, Jr., "The Strength of the Nation," in *ARMY*, October 2007, p. 20.

Officers in our Army, engaged as they are, must participate in the debate that will precede the refinement of existing doctrine. The Department of Defense recently sent a report to the Congress on the state of the implementation of Department of Defense Directive 3000.05, *Military Support to Stability, Security, Transition and Reconstruction (SSTR) Operations*. A footnote in the report states that the Army will have "a coherent body of current stability operations doctrine spanning tactical and operational levels" by 2008.[4] This coherent body of stability operations doctrine will be incomplete if it does not include an update of Army Field Manual (FM) 3-90, *Tactics,* and an exploration of the science of employing units in battle and in relationship to the enemy, terrain and the civil population amid which the Army will fight.

Army and joint doctrine still articulate the levels of war: strategic, operational and tactical. The art and science of tactics includes levels of command from squad to corps, albeit with a different focus at each level. Nonetheless, the changing conditions of war or the use of force necessitate that the Army consider what tactics are in the persistent conflict or small wars of the 21st century. There must be open debate within the profession as we come to grips with the changing conduct of war and how to educate ourselves to plan and execute the tactics required for success in the small wars of the 21st century.

The current definition of tactics in FM 3-90 is "the employment of units in combat. It includes the ordered arrangement and maneuver of units in relation to each other, the terrain, and the enemy to translate potential combat power into victorious battles and engagements."[5]

---

4   Report to Congress on the Implementation of Department of Defense Directive 3000.05, *Military Support for Stability, Security, Transition and Reconstruction (SSTR) Operations*, report dated 1 April 2007,http://www.defenselink.mil/policy/downloads/ Congressional_Report_on_DoDD_300005_Implementation_final_2.pdf.

5   Headquarters, Department of the Army. Field Manual 3-90, *Tactics*, July 2001, p. 1-1. Hereafter cited as FM 3-90.

FM 3-0 defines tactics as "the employment and ordered arrangement of forces in relation to each other (CJCSI 5120.02A)."[6]

To fight in the small wars of the 21st century, the Army must redefine tactics as "the employment of units before, during and after combat. It includes the ordered arrangement and maneuver of units in relation to each other, the physical, human, and information terrain, and the enemy to ensure successful battles and engagements."

Tactics is the business of corporals to lieutenant generals, although the 2008 FM 3-0, *Operations*, states that divisions are the principal tactical headquarters in the Army and corps will primarily orient on joint task force missions.[7] The current definition in FM 3-90 focuses on three elements: terrain, friendly forces and enemy forces. In 21st century tactics, actions before, during and after combat must be taken into account as commanders arrange and maneuver forces. A series of tactical victories will not produce victory, although victory cannot be achieved without tactical success. Tactical victory is a necessary but not sufficient condition for strategic success. Wars are won at the operational and strategic level, so tactical success must be linked to attaining higher-level objectives. Tactics must be redefined and restructured for warfare in the 21st century.

---

[6] Headquarters, Department of the Army, Field Manual 3-0, *Operations*, p. 6-3. Hereafter cited as FM 3-0.

[7] The February 2008 version of FM 3-0 is ambiguous on this topic. On page C-4 it states that "when required, a corps may become an intermediate tactical headquarters" and goes on to state that the corps is also "a primary candidate headquarters for joint operations" as either a joint task force or land component command headquarters. Our doctrine is ambiguous, appearing to place the primary focus of the U.S. Army Corps at the joint task force level. This has profound implications for the conduct of operations, not to mention the curriculum at the Command & General Staff College. There could be war plans in the future that have a land component command/field army directing multiple corps thus squarely placing corps again at the high end of the tactical level of war. We ignore tactical operations at the corps level at some risk. On page C-5 the manual clearly names the division as the Army's primary tactical warfighting headquarters.

Tactics executed before combat begins must include the arranged arrival of forces into a theater of operations or their posture to enter a theater of operations. This arrangement of forces must support the operational and strategic goals set in the opening phase of an operation and could lead to the prevention of combat. This tactical execution before combat must end with forces postured for a successful transition to combat operations. Errors in the initial placement of forces are difficult if not impossible to overcome during the duration of a campaign.[8]

Tactics executed during combat, from squad to division and corps, must sustain a series of successful battles and engagements that are linked to attaining operational and strategic objectives. While no plan can look with certainty beyond initial contact with the main body of enemy forces, the successful execution of tactics during combat and stability operations will establish conditions for victory.[9] Victory in the 21st century also requires the successful execution of tactics after combat.

The arrangement of forces on the ground relative to the remnants of enemy forces and the population of the country in which operations are conducted, as well as the swift return of security for the people, ensure the successful execution of tactical operations are linked with attaining operational and strategic objectives. Attaining these objectives ensures that U.S. policy objectives are met, which is the real victory. Making all of this come to pass will require many actions from within our Army. Setting conditions for successful tactical execution will require many activities ranging from force structure decisions to changing doctrine and the necessary education effort to teach the level of understanding required for changed tactics.

To successfully address the tactics required to win in small wars the Army will need a truly network-enabled force with an ability to have broadly shared database access from

---

[8] The final line in this paragraph is drawn from a quotation attributed to Moltke the Elder, a lesson I learned from Dr. Jim Schneider of the School of Advanced Military Studies (SAMS).

[9] This sentence is also drawn from Moltke the Elder and Dr. Schneider's classes in SAMS.

corps/division to the company/battery/troop and platoon levels. This is not merely a statement of material need, technique and procedure; it is a method of war that recognizes the power of sharing information rapidly with machines serving the Soldier. Leaders and commanders at these levels must be mentally agile enough to use and contribute to these databases and to act on changing information.

This network-enabled force must be empowered to act and rely on commander's intent. To capitalize on commander's intent, tactics—offensive, defensive and stability—must be designed for exploitation operations when information that can be acted on regarding the enemy is discovered. Tactics and tactical thinking must evolve from linear to non-contiguous in every way. To evolve from a linear mindset to a non-contiguous mindset, the Army must change its schools and training.

Army schools must re-imagine how to teach tactics, from the basic noncommissioned officer and officer courses through the staff and war colleges. Basic and advanced courses must teach small-unit offensive, defensive and stability operations tactics based on sharing information via the network and focused on exploitation when the opportunity presents itself. The staff and war colleges much teach higher-level division and corps tactics. These institutions must develop true commander's intent tactics. There must be a common understanding of what tactics are at these levels and how to structure and sustain battles. The linkage to operational-level effects happens at division level now that corps will focus almost exclusively at the operational/joint task force (JTF) level. Redefined tactics require education in how to produce the theater-level effects operational commanders require.

The paradigm of tactics must shift. FM 3-0 makes it clear that tactics must include a view toward a blend of offense, defense and stability actions. We must expand our understanding of tactics to address the tactics of stability operations. Offensive and defensive operations could well be the shaping operation in a division tactical concept with stability operations as the decisive operation or main effort. Current tactical doctrine states, "Tactical commanders focus primarily on employing combined arms in an area of operations." FM 3-0 goes on to state that "tactical commanders [may] receive missions that divert combat power from tasks that seem more urgent at lower levels."[10] This reality of combat presents certain tensions for commanders, who are admonished to recognize and resolve such tension. Normally commanders should expect to have clearly defined tasks—defeat the enemy and occupy objectives—but "normal" is an ill-defined word in the 21st century, so tactical thinking must adapt to 21st century conditions to continue to meet this requirement for tactical commanders. Getting to "normal" will be the challenge. FM 3-90, *Tactics*, competently addresses offensive and defensive operations—based on 20th century experience. Updating tactics to reflect the integration of stability operations is the key.

FM 3-0 cites the Joint Publication 3-0 definition of stability operations:

> . . . various military missions, tasks, and activities conducted outside the United States in coordination with other instruments of national power to maintain or reestablish a safe and secure environment, provide essential governmental services, emergency infrastructure reconstruction, and humanitarian relief.[11]

FM 3-0 states, "Stability operations promote reconciliation, strengthen and rebuild civil infrastructures and institutions, build confidence, and support economic reconstruction to prevent a return to conflict."[12] The operational-level field manual makes very clear the expectations of successful stability operations; how to meet these expectations is left to the realm of tactics.

---

[10] FM 3-0, p. 6-2.

[11] FM 3-0, Glossary p. 13.

[12] FM 3-0, p. 2-9.

The current edition of FM 3-90, published in July 2001, contains very thorough explanations of the tactics of offensive and defensive operations. Stability operations were not a part of the lexicon of tactics at the time. A step toward incorporation of stability operations tactics into the 21st century American way of war will be an expansion of the definitions of common doctrinal terms and the development of new terms to fit the tasks. FM 3-90 must be rewritten to be in accord with the new direction stated in FM 3-0. Full-spectrum operations require full-spectrum tactics. As a means of exploration, changes to the concept of mission command, commander's intent, gaining and maintaining enemy contact, exploitation and pursuit, and area defense, among others, must be made to better fit into a framework where the main effort in a division area of operations is stability operations.

The elements of mission command are straightforward and require no adaptation for the conduct of stability tactics. The execution of mission command requires a clearly articulated commander's intent; subordinates empowered to exercise initiative through the commander's intent; mission orders, which include a brief concept of the operation that ties all task execution together; and minimum control measures. Mission command also requires a statement of resource allocation and the naming of main and supporting efforts.[13] While the elements of mission command remain straightforward, applying them in the execution of the tactics for small wars will require education and practice. Attaining the goal of a clearly articulated commander's intent will require some thought for the tactics of the 21st century.

Commander's intent was defined the 2001 edition of FM 3-0 as "a clear, concise statement of what the force must do and the conditions the force must meet to succeed with respect to the enemy, terrain, and the desired end state." FM 3-0 now defines commander's intent as "a clear, concise statement of what the force must do and the conditions the force must establish with

---

[13] FM 3-0, p. 3-6.

respect to the enemy, terrain, **and civil considerations that represent** the desired end state." [Emphasis added][14] The subtle changes in definition will require deep thought on just how to articulate the meaning of the civil considerations that represent the desired end state.

The blending of offense, defense and stability operations within the tactical realm will be enhanced by a clear expression of intent. Principal stability tasks for Army forces as expressed in FM 3-0 are civil security, civil control, restoration of essential services, support to governance, and support to economic and infrastructure development.[15] Tactical units will naturally gravitate toward civil security and civil control as they most readily rely on techniques and procedures with which Soldiers and leaders are familiar, to wit: security. The experiences the Army gained in Bosnia, Haiti, Somalia and Iraq will carry over into an understanding of what these tasks mean to a tactical unit. Civil security operations are designed to protect the populace from internal and external threats. Civil control operations are designed to regulate "selected behavior and activities of individuals and groups."[16] Effective and actionable intelligence will play the dominant role in designing these operations, resulting in tasks ranging from information efforts to dissuade people from certain activities to establishing traffic control points to slow the pace of traffic or movement of people. The doctrinal term "secure" can be used in expressing the commander's intent as well as tasks to subordinate units in the concept-of-operations paragraph of an order.

"Secure" is defined in our current lexicon as "A tactical mission task that involves preventing a unit, facility, or

---

[14] FM 3-0 2001, p. 5-14, para. 5-61 and FM 3-0 2008, p. 5-10, para. 5-55, emphasis added. This is yet another undebated change in doctrine, along with the notion that objective equals center of gravity at the tactical level.

[15] FM 3-0, pp. 3-13 and 3-14.

[16] FM 3-0, p. 3-13.

geographical location from being damaged or destroyed as a result of enemy action."[17]

Tactics for the 21st century require an expanded definition of "secure." A small-wars definition could be a tactical mission task that involves preventing a unit or facility from being damaged or destroyed, or a geographical location and its population from being disrupted as a result of enemy action. The word "disrupted" will assist in analysis as it requires understanding of a pre-hostilities base line of what was "normal" for that particular geographical location. Understanding of a pre-hostilities base line of normality will also ensure that the accumulated tactical successes are linked to post-hostilities transitions that will ensure that tactical success is linked with attaining operational and strategic objectives. Success in conventional operations requires gaining and maintaining contact with the enemy to prevent surprise. This concept must be adapted to 21st century tactics.

The concept of gaining and maintaining contact is presented in FM 3-90 as a vital component to success in offensive operations and as an enhancement of the security of the attacking force. Gaining and maintaining contact contributes to the commander's situational understanding of his battle space. Updating this concept for 21st century tactics requires thought about how to apply it to stability operations and tasks. Clearly the struggles for the hearts and minds of the people are paramount for ultimate success in 21st century operations. Gaining and maintaining contact with the people is a requirement for the success of stability operations and the situational understanding required for these forms of operations.

Stability operations are designed to establish or reestablish a safe and secure environment for the people of a country in which U.S. forces are operating. Stability operations might also be executed to assist in the reconciliation of local or regional adversaries, establish or reestablish systems of political, legal, social and economic import and assist in the transition of

---

[17] FM 3-90, Glossary p. 24.

responsibility to a functioning host-nation government.[18] The requirement to gain and maintain contact with the people clearly is important in accomplishing any of these tasks. FM 3-24, *Counterinsurgency*, explicitly states, "Cultural knowledge is essential to waging a successful counterinsurgency. American ideas of what is 'normal' or 'rational' are not universal."[19] Cultural knowledge enhances and is enhanced by gaining and maintaining contact with the people. This notion is then an imperative for 21st century tactics and the development of division-level plans and orders that combine offense, defense and stability operations in reaching the objectives set by the operational-level headquarters. Reaching these objectives demands that the understanding of exploitation and pursuit operations also must be expanded for execution of 21st century tactics.

Exploitation and pursuit are types of offensive operations. Exploitation "rapidly follows a successful attack and is designed to disorganize the enemy in depth." Pursuit is "designed to catch or cut off a hostile force attempting to escape, with the aim of destroying it."[20] A pursuit usually follows a successful exploitation such as was executed by Napoleon's cavalry after the battle of Jena-Auerstadt and by Patton's Third Army after the breakout from the Normandy beachhead. The definitions need to be updated for 21st century tactics, especially regarding stability operations.

Exploitation in stability operations can be viewed as the follow-through after assessing the success of a stability task or tasks (for example; civil security and restoration of essential services). Exploitation of success in a stability operation will be primarily in the form of information operations. Just as conventional exploitation requires a mobility advantage over the enemy, exploitation in stability operations requires an

---

[18] FM 3-0, pp. 3-12/13.

[19] Headquarters, Department of the Army. Field Manual 3-24, *Counterinsurgency*, Washington, D.C., December 2006, p. 1-15, para. 1-80.

[20] FM 3-90, p. 3-4, paras. 3-9 and 3-10.

information advantage over the adversaries; also required is an intellectual advantage in understanding the culture of a region in order to broadcast successes in a manner that will be received by the people of the local area and the wider region. Building on the situational understanding of an area, achieved through maintaining contact with the populace, exploitation of success is broadcast through means most suitable for positive receipt by the populace. From increased interaction with the populace and building on the exploitation of positive events that materially affect the lives of the populace, pursuit can be executed in the form of offensive operations to further drive the adversaries from a wider area and away from population centers. A network-enabled force with a depth of situational understanding will be able to pursue an enemy force through the exploitation of documents and a shared database of enemy patterns of activity. Exploitation operations will build on successful execution of stability operations and result in the physical pursuit of enemy forces as the effect of positive contact with the people builds situational understanding. Here again these tactical tasks must be in concert with the operational-level objectives and tied to setting conditions for strategic effects.

Stability operations cannot take place in the presence of organized enemy forces, either conventional or irregular. These threats to the populace and the friendly forces conducting stability operations must be reduced or eliminated. The conduct of defensive operations to ensure the continued security of both the friendly force and the populace will be in the form of area defenses.

Defensive operations and tasks to sustain security are not the same as civil security tasks conducted in stability operations. Defensive operations defeat enemy attacks, buy time, allow a higher commander to economize forces, and develop conditions for offensive operations. Defensive operations also retain decisive terrain or deny vital areas to the enemy. Conducting defensive operations to retain key terrain and deny the enemy access to the people and sources of supply is the aim of shaping operations in a division area where the main effort is conducted by forces executing stability operations.[21] A successful defense is necessary for the conduct of civil security tasks as the forces conducting the defense will focus on external threats to the population, while forces conducting civil security operations will focus in internal threats. This difference in task and purpose will require thought on the part of a staff and commander.

FM 3-0 articulates the conduct of full-spectrum operations as shown in figure 3-1.[22] The mission of the division will determine the relative weight of effort among the tasks assigned to subordinate brigade combat teams. The division mission may further influence subordinate brigade combat teams own weighting of efforts on offense, defense and stability operations tasks relative to the situation in the brigade zones of action. In the specific case of a division conducting stability operations with a requirement to defend population centers, the task of defense will of necessity include civil security and civil control tasks.

Defense within a division area may not involve establishment of final protective fires, dug-in fighting positions for combat vehicles, mines and obstacle belts, but will

---

[21] FM 3-90, pp. 8-1–8-4, paras. Introduction, 8-1–8-6.

[22] FM 3-0, p. 3-1, fig. 3-1.

incorporate actions such as civil control. Established and roving checkpoints will limit the mobility of the enemy. Unmanned aerial vehicles and reconnaissance patrols will monitor named and targeted areas of interest. The conduct of a defense in support of a stability operation will conceptually resemble a defense at the operational level and the offense at the lower tactical levels. The mobility advantage of Soldiers and information over the enemy force will enhance contact with the people and result in a continual update of the understanding of the situation. Agility in information-sharing among networked units will enable pursuit of enemy forces after the conduct of raids. The function of the division, brigade and even battalion headquarters in this type of defense will be to sustain the fighting done by company teams and ensure information is as agile as the engaged forces.

The small wars the Army will face in the 21st century require a new appreciation of the conduct of tactics. Doctrine is introducing the blending of offense, defense and stability operations in a box as a device to portray the combination of activities. Thinking about the tactics required to accomplish the necessary tasks will require the officer and noncommissioned officer corps to think "outside the box."

The Army must have a coherent body of doctrine for 21st century operations. The Army officer corps must participate in the debate and discourse that will precede the refinement of existing doctrine. This coherent body of doctrine will be incomplete if it does not include an update of FM 3-90, *Tactics,* and an exploration of the science of employing units in battle and in relationship to the enemy, terrain, and the civil population amid which the Army will fight. The concept of stability operations should be addressed in a dedicated field manual however the tactical considerations of employing Army units in the conduct of full spectrum operations must be considered as a whole, not in piecemeal. The longer we engage in the fiction that tactics are only considered in combat the longer we will continue to confuse the field Army. Tactical tasks must not be addressed in different field manuals. **HX**

(This chapter was previously published as an *Association of the United States Army Institute of Land Warfare* paper.
Reprinted with permission.)

US Navy Hospital Corpsman 3rd Class Edwin L. Daniel, assigned to 3rd Platoon, Foxtrot Company, 2nd Battalion, 7th Marine Regiment, examines an Afghan citizen before dispensing aspirin during a patrol in the Helmand province of Afghanistan, Oct. 22, 2008.

CHAPTER 14

AFTER INSURGENCY: HOW THE LONG WAR WILL CHANGE AMERICA'S MILITARY AND AMERICA

By James Jay Carafano

The most interesting questions about counter-insurgency warfare have little to do with the winning hearts and minds in Afghanistan and Iraq; chasing down al Qaeda-affiliates in North Africa; coaching Southeast Asia militaries in crushing Jemaah Islamiyah; or cajoling Pakistani forces to take on the Taliban. The real issue to ponder is how the American experience in the Long War will shape the future of the American military. What a nation remembers when it walks away from the last battle is the first skirmish in the next conflict.

Like many of the far flung places where US troops are conducting occupations, taking on insurgents, or assisting friends and allies in counterinsurgency campaigns, the future is a foreign country—a hard place to know till you get there. What America's military will look like when the future comes will in part be shaped by how the impressions of the present are applied to preparing for the challenges ahead.

Myth History

Interpreting the current conflicts will, of course, scope much of the effort over thinking about future war. It is not clear, for example, that today's armed forces will be able to dispel enduring myths about the American way of war—including absurd beliefs like: Americans cannot accept high causalities, fight long wars, defeat insurgencies, or efficiently conduct an occupation. All these claims are rubbish.

Most modern military myths are rooted in historical interpretations of the Vietnam conflict that say more about the politics of the time than the reality of the war. Once the cause in

Vietnam garnered the distain of the right and the left—victory was not an option. Congress voted to withdraw aid from the South and the country was swamped by invading troops from the North. History blamed everybody, but Congress.

History started to go wrong as the politics of the war turned sour. By 1968, presidential electioneering and opposition to the draft fueled the anti-war movement to a fever pitch. On Jan. 31 of that year, during the annual cease-fire to mark Tet, the traditional Vietnamese celebration of the Lunar New Year, the North Vietnamese Army launched a cross-border invasion timed with an uprising by Viet Cong insurgents in cities throughout the South. The Tet Offensive proved a crushing military defeat for the enemy. The North Vietnamese Army endured a severe beating and the Viet Cong insurgency was so decimated that it never truly emerged again as a serious military or political force. But that's not how it played in the United States. Here, thanks to deeply flawed media reporting and inaccurate first impressions, many thought American forces had suffered a catastrophic defeat.

As historian Lewis Sorley explained in, *A Better War*, this incorrect impression may have cost the South Vietnamese their country. Around that time, the U.S. military had begun to turn over responsibility for ground defenses to the South Vietnamese, and they proved capable of defending their own country as long as they received material and firepower support equal to the aid the North was getting from the Soviet Union and China. Likewise, American assistance for the counterinsurgency effort began to payoff, by 1968 the assistance effort, CORDS, had been reorganized and began to show results. By the time U.S. forces withdrew in 1973, Saigon had regained control over vast swaths of the countryside—and while the country was hardly an ideal democracy, at least it had a stable and functioning government.

Likewise, the notion that Americans cannot fight sustained and bloody wars is equally ridiculous. While the homefront apparently turned its back on the war after 1968, ground operations "surged"—combat activities increased, expanded into neighboring countries and causalities went up, all the while the pace of Vietnamization accelerated. In short, U.S. commitments continued for seven years after Tet, spanning two presidential terms, proof enough that Americans can prevail in long and even unpopular wars.

After Tet, however, outside the White House little political will existed for continued support for the South on the political left or right. Neither a Nixon administration crippled by Watergate, nor a Ford presidency looking to find its footing in Washington could muster the votes to continue aid. It was then—and only then—that South Vietnam collapsed. Myth-history, however, argues that defeat was inevitable, offering a laundry list of shortcomings that don't square with the reality of the course of the war on the ground.

The Rhythm of Habits

Vietnam does, in fact, fit rather squarely into the American military experience, but not in the way conventional myth-history suggests. Americans, of course, have fought a number of long wars going back to the American Revolution, and many of them have been very unconventional conflicts. Likewise, the U.S. military has been saddled with dealing "post-conflict" missions and uneasy occupations that included an unsettling admixture of war and peace. The American response in unconventional warfare in this respect is fairly consistent— every one of them was an ad hoc affair, and when the military was done it largely purged any lessons that might have been learned. And then after the next war, when transitioning from war-fighters to peacekeepers or engaging in counterinsurgency warfare, the armed forces would reflexively start over all over again as though they had never done it before. That is the rhythm of habits.[1]

Perhaps the best example of America's long tradition of not preparing well for complex contingency operations is the

---

[1] For further discussion of the "rhythm of habits," see James Jay Carafano, *Waltzing Into the Cold War: The Struggle for Occupied Austria* (College Station: Texas A&M University Press, 2002).

role played by the U.S. Army in postwar occupations. The Army's experience and knowledge about peace operations have never been incorporated into mainstream military thinking in any major, systematic way. For example, the official report on the U.S. participation in the occupation of the Rhineland after World War I noted that "despite the precedents of military governments in Mexico, California, the Southern States, Cuba, Puerto Rico, Panama, China, the Philippines, and elsewhere, the lesson seemingly has not been learned."[2] This assessment could have well been written after any of America's unconventional campaigns.

After World War I, the tradition of forgetting continued. The Army's Field Service Regulations of 1923 (doctrinal guidance crafted to capture the lessons of World War I) made no mention of the occupation of the Rhineland or that there might be a need to conduct similar operations in the future. The manual simply affirmed that "the ultimate objective of all military operations is the destruction of the enemy's armed forces in battle."[3] FM 100-5, the Army's capstone field manual for the conduct of operations during World War II, did not mention the conduct of occupation duties.

Following World War II, the Pentagon largely forgot about the problem and continued to reinvent solutions each time it faced a new peace operation. Fighting the battles of the Cold War remained the military's overwhelming preoccupation.

Arguably, America's military after the Cold War had a better appreciation for its post-conflict responsibilities. It could not forget these missions entirely because they had become a fact of life in the post-Cold World disorder. On average, the U.S. military has conducted an operation related to peacekeeping, peacemaking, or post-conflict occupation every two years since

---

[2] U.S. Army, American Military Government of Occupied Germany, 1918-1920: Report of the Officer in Charge of Civil Affairs, Third Army and American Forces in Germany (Washington, D.C.: U.S. Government Printing Office, 1943) p. 64.

[3] U.S. Army, Field Service Regulations, 1923 (Washington, D.C.: U.S. Government Printing Office, 1924), p. 77.

the end of the Cold War. Yet, this modicum of experience proved wholly inadequate to prepare for Afghanistan and Iraq.

With the Soviet menace gone, there was greater pressure to employ U.S. forces for a range of operations, which the Pentagon termed "military operations other than war." Yet the military did little to prepare for this proliferation of challenges. In 1995, the Pentagon produced its first joint doctrine for military operations other than war. Even the term "operations other than war" was problematic, implying a range of military tasks less strategically important than conventional war-fighting and grouping post-conflict operations and counterinsurgency warfare (essentially an extension of the war-fighting mission) in with a plethora of tasks that included everything from peacekeeping to helping out after hurricanes.

Soldiers from 1st Battalion, 66th Armored Regiment conduct a cordon and search operation in Sheik Hamid, Iraq on October 11, 2006 (US Army Photo).

Counterinsurgency warfare was lumped into the pile of other military activities that according to the Pentagon mattered less. There was scant discussion, training, or doctrine on unconventional warfare outside of the Special Forces community. The Army's rich experience from Vietnam learned the hard way, "on the job," had largely been purged from modern military memory.

Back to the Future

It remains to be seen whether today's military is more successful at institutionalizing the hard learned lessons of the Long War. Myth-history bodes against it. In many ways, today's popular culture mirrors the post-Vietnam era. After long years of war many Americans are disillusioned with the use of military force. A general malaise about the state of the U.S. economy has left many apathetic over the need to invest in defense. Finally, Americans are more complacent about threats in the world and skeptical of the capacity of military power to solve problems.

These public attitudes coupled with the sad state of the federal government's fiscal policies do not bode well for sustained defense budgets that would allow the military the opportunity to institutionalize the lessons of the Long War. Government in the developed world has expanded substantially during the past century. The United States stands at the apex of this trend. One of the best measures of the burden that the federal government, as a whole, imposes on the national economy through its spending policies is the percentage of gross domestic product (GDP). During America's first 140 years, the federal government rarely consumed more than 1 or 2 percent of GDP. In accordance with the U.S. Constitution, Washington focused on defense and certain public goods while leaving most other functions to the states or the people. That changed in the 20th century. Between 1962 and 2000, defense spending plummeted from 9.3 percent of GDP to 3.0 percent. Nearly all of funding shifted from defense spending went into mandatory spending (mostly entitlement programs), which jumped from 6.1 percent of GDP to 12.1 percent during that same period.

This importance of Washington's fiscal evolution cannot be understated. For most of the nation's history, the federal government's chief budgetary function was funding defense. The two-thirds decline in defense spending since 1962 has substantially altered the make-up and structure of the U.S. national defense. Today, spending on defense and homeland security in the United States stands at about 4.0 percent of GDP, the highest level of investment since the end of the Cold War. However, this represents, on average, less than half what the nation spent before the fall of the Berlin Wall. And, unlike the Cold War period, post-Cold War defense spending is faced with unprecedented competition for federal dollars with mandatory government spending on entitlement programs.

Mandatory outlays for programs such as Social Security, Medicare, and Medicaid are consuming, and will continue to consume, ever-larger percentages of federal spending and total GDP. As a result, they will apply increasing pressure to crowd out the resources available to the government's traditional primary mission--providing security to the nation.

As a result, future defense budgets may look more like the anemic spending of the Carter years with inadequate funding to pay for current operations, maintain a trained and ready force, and modernize the force. The post-Iraq military could turn out a lot more like the "hollow force" of the 1970s. In that environment the military might well find itself under pressure to shed missions and capabilities—and like after Vietnam once again sacrifice its capacity to conduct the full range of military tasks. Keeping the rhythm of habits from repeating itself will be a significant challenge for the military after Iraq and Afghanistan.

Brave New World

If the military did have the resources and support it needed to chart its own future, it is worth pondering how the armed forces might institutionalize lessons of the Long War. Militaries only retain the capability to do well that which they retain the missions, strategy, education, and organization that sustain the knowledge, skills, and attributes necessary to get the job done. Institutionalizing the capacity to conduct counterinsurgency and post-conflict missions could well require a set of initiatives that cut across the services' education, career professional development patterns, and organization. These innovations might include the following.

A Soldier from the 61st Cavalry Regiment, 101st Airborne Division and an Iraqi soldier work together to secure the streets of Baghdad on September 5, 2006 (US Army Photo).

Leader Education

In the present military education system much of the edification relevant to building these attributes is provided at the war colleges to a relatively elite group being groomed for senior leader and joint duty positions. This model is wrong on two counts. First, these skills are needed by most leaders and staffs in both the active and reserve components, not just an elite group within the profession. Second, this education comes too late in an officer's career. Virtually every other career field provides "graduate level" education to members in their mid-20s to 30s. Only the military delays advanced education until its leaders are in their mid-40s. Strategic leader education that prepares officers and NCOs for the full scope of military missions should occur by the mid-point in the average service career.

Special Schools

The armed services also need special schools specifically designed to teach the operational concepts and practices relevant to missions such as counterinsurgencies, homeland security, and post-conflict operations. The services already have advanced schools (such as the Marine Corps' School for Advanced Warfighting) for instructing in the operational arts at their staff colleges. These courses train the military's finest planners. Similar instruction is needed for the full-range of military operations.

Combatant Commands.

The combatant commands should be reorganized to include interagency staffs with specific responsibility for developing complex contingency plans in the same manner as current operational staffs plan for warfighting contingencies.[4] In the event of war, the post-conflict interagency group can be attached to the operation's joint force commander to provide the nucleus of an occupation staff.[5]

In addition, the joint force command should include a general-officer deputy commander who would oversee the work of the planning group and assume command of the occupation force after the conflict or during other complex contingencies. These staffs and command positions could provide a series of

---

[4] For more detail recommendations see James Jay Carafano, "Missions, Responsibilities, and Geography: Rethinking How the Pentagon Commands the World" *Backgrounder* *#1792* (August 26, 2004) at http://www.heritage.org/Research/NationalSecurity/bg1792.cfm.

[5] For one proposal, see John R. Boullé III, "Operational Planning and Conflict Termination," *Joint Force Quarterly* (Autumn/Winter 2001-2002), pp. 99-102.

operational assignments for the career development of a cadre of officers especially skilled in complex contingency duties.

The military should also retain force training and force structure packages appropriate to complex contingency tasks. There are three ways to obtain commands suitable to post-conflict missions: (1) training and equipping allies to perform these duties, (2) retraining and reorganizing U.S. combat troops for the task, and (3) maintaining special U.S. forces. As a great power, the United States needs all three of these options to provide the flexibility that will enable the nation to adapt to different strategic situations which might require different levels of commitments from U.S. forces.

Simply relying on U.S. Special Forces is inadequate. Special Forces are not "scalable" to deal with large contingencies such as cases on the scale of Iraq and Afghanistan. Special units could be assembled from existing National Guard and Reserve units including security, medical, engineer, and public affairs commands. Since many of the responsibilities involved in post-war and counterinsurgency duties are similar in many ways to missions that might be required of homeland security units, these forces could perform double duty, having utility both overseas and at home.

The Shape of Things

One of the most vociferous debates will be over the balance of the future force, and whether more Active or more Reserve forces will provide the military the best balance of capabilities for conventional warfare and complex contingencies.

The lessons of Iraq and Afghanistan suggest contrasting Active and Reserve forces is really a false debate. Both have proven their worth in the Long War. In particular, the Reserves have given the "full measure of devotion" serving in numbers unprecedented since World War II. The U.S. Army simply could not conduct its missions worldwide without the contributions of its Reserve Components.

The accomplishments of the Reserves certainly validate the underlying premise of the Total Force Concept. For example, in the period from September 11, 2001, to the end of 2003, over

319,000 citizen soldiers—27 percent of the Reserve Components—performed active duty. The Total Force has proven itself an effective means to rapidly expand military capacity to meet changing national security requirements.

On the other hand, stresses on the Reserves also reflect the lack of adequate investment in the Total Force. The National Guard alone has had to transfer over 74,000 individuals from one command to another just to fill the ranks of units with sufficient trained and qualified personnel before they deployed. Equipment shortfalls are also significant. Since 9/11, the Army has transferred over 35,000 pieces of equipment from non-deploying units to forces in Iraq, leaving the stay-behind commands lacking more than a third of their critical equipment. Most troubling, the Army lacked the means to mobilize and demobilize forces effectively. Reserve commands, in practice, cannibalized the force to meet short-term deployment needs. These shortfalls reflected years of chronic underfunding and the lack of effective personnel policies for managing, training, sustaining, mobilizing, deploying, and reconstituting Reserve forces.

Sustaining a large and capable Reserve Component in the years ahead will require significant investments. For example, recruiting efforts will have to be increased, pre-mobilization training and medical and dental readiness improved, and pay and benefits enhanced. The current mobilization process also has to be scrapped and restructured.

Reserve Component equipment will also require substantial attention. "Absent a concerted effort to fully resource modernization and recapitalization," the 2003 report of the Reserve Forces Policy Board concluded, "unit equipment will continue to age and become obsolete.... Over the next ten years, without a change of equipment policies aging RC equipment inventories will increase substantially."[6] The additional wear and tear on equipment as a result of deployments supporting the

---

[6] Reserve Forces Policy Board, *The Annual Report of the Reserve Forces Policy Board* (Washington, D.C.: Office of the Secretary of Defense, 2003), p. 10. See also, Bette R. Sayre, ed., *National Guard and Reserve Equipment Report for Fiscal Year 2004* (Washington, D.C.: Department of Defense, February 2003), p. 1-1.

global war on terrorism has only made the need for substantial investments more of an imperative.

These are investments worth making, but achieving them will require the Pentagon to think differently about how it maintains its Reserve Components, as well as robust defense budgets adequate to meet the needs of both the Active and Reserve forces. The Reserves will have to be moved to the heart of the Department of Defense's transformation efforts rather than relegated to the periphery.

New Patterns of Military Service

Simply recapitalizing the reserves, however, may not be enough. Over the long term, the traditional notions of Active and Reserve forces may have to be completely rethought. Increasingly the military may move toward a concept called continuum of service that blurs the distinction between the two.

One reason that the continuum of service may come to dominate future military service is that career options for personnel are not keeping pace with skyrocketing defense man-power costs, expanding use of Reserve forces, and the rapid changes in the American workplace. The Pentagon may need a new paradigm for compensating its military personnel that allows them to move seamlessly through active duty, the Reserves, the National Guard, and civilian employment without concern for how their career decisions will affect their health care and retirement benefits. This may require a "rucksack" of benefits that they select themselves and can carry with them would be a critical tool in recruiting and retaining a trained and ready volunteer military.

The key to recruiting and retaining a quality, all-volunteer force may be to adopt career models that are consistent with both the changes in the American workforce and the nation's national security needs. The chief characteristic of this system must be flexibility that allows individuals to decide when and how to volunteer their time and talents, providing more opportunities to move back and forth between active and reserve service and civilian employment, to shift career fields within the military, and to choose options for voluntary deployments.

Among other things, establishing an effective continuum of service will require a package of incentives that best serve the nation and the individual. The right mix will require a combination of immediate targeted compensation (e.g., cash bonuses, career options, and educational opportunities) and the confidence to accept voluntary deployments knowing that the decision will not adversely affect health care and retirement. The Pentagon needs to be able to offer each soldier a "rucksack" that could accompany that individual whether or not the soldier chooses to serve on active duty or in the ready or inactive reserve.

These new patterns of military service may be particularly vital for sustaining the capacity to conduct counterinsurgency operations and other complex contingencies. These activities frequently require diverse work skills and knowledge requirements which may not be resident in the Active force at the outset of a crisis.

Soldiers from the 1st Armored Division search for insurgents who shot at them the previous day in Tameem, Iraq on August 18, 2006 (US Army photo).

Lifeline of a Guiding Idea

Another mark of how the military prepares for the future is how well it will participate in the process of creating "national security" doctrine. Counterinsurgencies and other unconventional operations often require "interagency" coordination, cooperation among federal agencies, non-governmental agencies, and international institutions, a process often referred to as something akin to "herding cats."

Calls for interagency reform often myopically focus on Washington, proposing solutions that centralize power in the office of the White House. These answers are remarkably wrongheaded. Indeed, the lessons of the Long War counsel exactly the opposite. Field operations have to be conceived, organized, and executed in the theater, not air-conditioned offices too remote to deal with real issues in real-time. Likewise, the more complex and wide-spread operations are the more decentralized execution is required. In this environment, effective doctrine is essential. Doctrine does not tell people how to think, but it helps understand how to analyze problems and address them with common trust and confidence.

There is certainly a need for sound doctrine that addresses how to achieve success in complex contingency settings; efforts to regain security, prosperity, and freedom in ungoverned areas; or assisting territories in recovering after catastrophic disasters—whether they result from natural disasters or malicious human activity like insurgencies. There are plenty of lessons from the Long War to help forge this doctrine. These principles can be organized into three categories: Principles of Process—preparing government to undertake complex operations; Principles of Purpose—organizing for complex activities; and Principles of Peace—guidelines for the transition to establishing safe, free, and prosperous societies.

Principles of Process

Regardless of the mission, when the federal government as a whole has to work toward a common purpose, when it needs to team with friends and allies or state and local governments and non-governmental organizations, it needs a consistent approach to start with. In looking at the lessons of Long War consistent themes emerged again and again. Washington habitually fails to invest in its human capital. When a crisis or contingency occurs, Washington plays Russian roulette. By happenstance, the people in charge may or may not have the skills to do the job. Process cannot replace people. At the highest levels of government, no organizational design, institutional procedures, or legislative remedy proved adequate to overcome poor leadership and combative personalities. Presidential leadership is particularly crucial to the conduct of interagency operations. Guidelines that address these key shortfalls, the problems that can and should be fixed before the crisis or contingency, should be part of any doctrine. These should include the following:

- **Principle 1: Develop Human Capital.** Organizing these efforts requires a core of professionals skilled in interagency operations. The professionals that lead the effort must have three essential skills: familiarity with a number of diverse related disciplines (such as health care, law enforcement, immigration, and trade) and practice in interagency operations, working with different government agencies, the private sector, and international partners; competence in crisis action and long-term strategic planning; and, a sound understanding of the free-market economy, constitutional rights, and international relations.
  - Establishing this corps requires a professional development program with the following attributes. Education—a program of education, assignment, and accreditation that cuts across all levels of government and the private sector with national responsibilities has to start with professional schools specifically designed to teach interagency skills. Assignment—qualification will also require interagency assignments in which individuals can practice and hone their skills. These assignments should be at the "operational" level, at which leaders

learn how to make things happen, not just set policies. Identifying the right organizations and assignments and ensuring that they are filled by promising leaders should be a priority. Accreditation—national standards and congressional involvement are crucial to ensuring that programs are successful and sustainable. Before leaders are selected for critical (non-politically appointed) positions in national and homeland security, they should be accredited by a board of professionals in accordance with broad guidelines established by Congress.

- **Principle 2: Create Common Space.** It is senseless to talk about "unity of command" among governmental and non-governmental organizations. It is even unreasonable to talk about "unity of effort." It is, however, a reasonable expectation to create a "common space" in which legitimate organizations can have an opportunity to engage in those activities they believe will be helpful in creating a safe, free, and prosperous society. There is no one-size-fits-all prescription for how to achieve these conditions. Indeed, there are many situations in which security is minimal, infrastructure inadequate, and civil society crippled--where creating the common space will be extremely difficult. However, given the existing situation, U.S. efforts should strive to set the conditions for the common space. Teaching leaders and planners how to create the common space must be a priority.

- **Principle 3: Fight the Fog of Peace.** It is often forgotten that there is a "fog of peace" that is equally as infamous as Clausewitz's "fog of war"—which rejects the notion that outcomes can be precisely predicted or that there is a prescribed rulebook for success that any military can follow. Large-scale operations will inevitably include ambiguous and confusing situations with unclear, contradictory, or incomplete information.

Operations should be designed to anticipate and account for the most common elements of the fog of peace. Any doctrine which does not incorporate this principle will produce plans that consistently fail to meet the conditions on the ground.

o Principles of Purpose: Any doctrine must drive leaders toward establishing and sticking to a unifying purpose for activities. Nation-building, for example, is a terrible goal. Nations build or rebuild themselves. Indeed, nation-building is such a complex phenomenon that even practitioners are unsure how they achieved success. U.S. goals should always be more modest and circumspect. What Iraq and Afghanistan have taught is that there are three tasks before reconstruction or nation-building can begin their priorities that have to be accomplished.

(1) Avert a humanitarian crisis. Military forces must ensure that the population does not die en masse from disease, starvation, or exposure.

(2) Establish, reestablish, or support legitimate government. It is essential to have political leadership that people widely perceive as credible to lead the long-term reconstruction effort.

(3) Provide domestic security forces to support the government. It is not essential that the nation is free of violence, but the new leadership must have adequate forces at its disposal to begin to establish a functioning civil society. Once these tasks have been completed, post-conflict operations are essentially finished. The struggle for safety, growth, security, and liberty is not over, but the nation's fate is largely in the hands of its new leadership.

- **Principle 4: Determine Clear, Concise National Objectives.** Before deciding to engage in operations, the President must articulate specific, clear, credible national interests and objectives. During the operation, the authority in charge of U.S. operations should continue to measure its actions against those objectives. This is essential both for the efficient allocation of resources and to sustain public support. Throughout operations objectives may change. Measuring success will change as well.

- **Principle 5: Establish Interagency Coordination.** Operations require more than Department of Defense participation. They require that multiple U.S. agencies coordinate their activities, especially in the post-conflict phase of the regime change. Issues include restoring basic public services such as water, power, waste management, and public safety. Transportation and power generation infrastructure damaged by military operations will need to be rebuilt. Refugees will need to be returned to their homes, prisoners of war repatriated, and members of the old regime tried for their crimes when necessary. For the new regime to become self-sufficient, the economy must be restarted and the country put back to work. All of these tasks will require some degree of coalition participation and interagency coordination.

- **Principle 6: Ensure Unity of Effort.** By their nature, operations are multi-agency tasks and usually involve a coalition of other countries as well. Despite the multiplicity of actors, a single agency or headquarters must command the operations. Splitting authority for operations in Iraq, for example, between military commanders and a civilian administrator was a mistake. In future U.S. operations, the military should remain in charge until the disease-and-unrest formula has been accomplished. The decision to make the transfer to civilian authority should be made by the President.
  - o Principles of Peace: Moving beyond the simple, but difficult tasks of dealing with an immediate

crisis or violence an insurgency long-term recovery is essentially the responsibility of the indigenous population. Here U.S. operations must shift from a lead to a supporting role. While the United States might provide a range of support activities from aid to security assistance, the fundamental purpose of these efforts must be ideological.

o The ultimate route to a safe, free, and prosperous nation is building a strong civil society--and that is essentially an ideological struggle: Institutions come from ideas. There are three principles that can be applied to winning the war of ideas.

- **Principle 7: Understand the Country.** An ideological struggle requires knowing the political, social, cultural, economic, demographic, environmental, and geo-spatial factors that affect the operation. An ideological struggle requires knowing how ideas are sent, received, and understood.

- **Principle 8. Delegitimize Bad Ideas.** An ideology offers solutions to political, cultural, security, or economic ills. When that ideology is destructive to the civil society, it has to be effectively combated.

- **Principle 9. Create Credible Alternative and the Will to Prevail.** Winning requires offering ideas that provide the tools for building the institutions that will result in a strong civil society and demonstrating the perseverance to establish these institutions.

These principles should serve as the foundation for all U.S. complex contingency operations. Together they argue for a simple goal—advance the cause of freedom. Here concerted action means a lot more than just holding elections, though free and fair elections, of course, are an important step in building civil society. These principles must be infused in all U.S.

operations, advancing legal and economic institutions, liberties regarding free speech and the practice of religion, justice and reconciliation. All these activities are part of cutting the path to a free, safe, and prosperous society.

Public Wars—Private Sector

The future of the relationship between the military and other components of the interagency community and doctrines that evolve to define that relationship are not the only bonds that will determine the armed forces interpret and adopt the lessons of the Long War. Equally important will be how the military of the future draws on its current experiences to determine how it will engage with the private sector in responding to complex contingency missions. The future of this relationship is up for grabs as well.

Sgt. Nicholas Fate, from 1st Brigade Combat Team, 4th Infantry Division, provides perimeter security while fellow Soldiers search for weapons caches in a field near Mushahda, Iraq July 21, 2006 (US Army photo).

The global free market has become a reality, and commensurate with this economic condition is the emergence of an unprecedented capacity for the private sector to expand, innovate, and adapt to market needs—including an ability to provide what once were considered military services offered solely by national powers.

The trend for militaries to increasingly outsource logistical and support functions is well established. Added to that, however, is the emerging use of private sector companies to provide traditional combat services, ranging from training soldiers to patrolling streets.[7]

The increasing importance of privatized military services was particularly apparent during post-conflict operations in Iraq. Among the many tasks that the private sector can perform, security assistance is the most essential. Establishing security is a precondition for conducting post-conflict operations. In particular, establishing effective domestic security forces must be the highest priority. Private sector firms have a demonstrated capacity to provide essential services including administrative support, training, equipping, and mentoring, as well as to augment indigenous police and military units. In Iraq, these services were essential for both standing-up the Iraqi security forces and augmenting the security provided by U.S. military troops. Private sector assets can assist in providing an important bridging capability during the period when American military forces withdraw and domestic forces take over.[8]

Despite the heated political rhetoric and controversy over the employment of contractors in Iraq, the reliance on private sector assets in war is likely irreversible. Unlike the public sector, the private sector is bred for efficiency. Left to its own devices it will always find the means to provide services faster, cheaper, and more efficiently than governments. In

---

[7] Described in P.W. Singer, *Corporate Warriors: The Rise of the Privatized Military Industry* (Ithaca: Cornell University Press, 2003).

[8] James Jay Carafano, "The Pentagon and Postwar Contractor Support: Rethinking the Future," *Heritage Foundation Executive Memorandum* No. 958, February 1, 2005, at www.heritage.org/Research/NationalSecurity/em958.cfm.

addition, as governments lose their monopolies over the technologies and means to generate combat power, their capacity to retain military prowess as a public activity will also be lost.

As long as free markets proliferate, the reemergence of the private sphere of war is inevitable. Nations that seek to hold back against this trend and limit the participation of the private sector will be left behind because they will lack the capacity to keep up with states that can harness the power of the marketplace.

On the other hand, there is good reason for liberal, developed states not to fear the reemergence of a prominent role for the private sector in war. There is little likelihood that the private sector's place in war will attend the rise of a new "Middle Ages" with sovereigns losing their capacity to manage violence. "Capitalism," as Fareed Zakaria cogently argues, is not "something that exists in opposition to the state . . . [A] legitimate, well-functioning state can create the rules and laws that make capitalism work."[9] Unlike medieval kings, modern nations can use the instruments of good governance to bind the role of the private sector in military competition. These instruments include institutions like a well-established judicial system; an activist legislative branch with its own investigatory instruments (such as the Government Accountability Office); and an independent press and public interest groups (like the ACLU). These assets offer unprecedented means to balance the public and private spheres—not just to constrain government conduct, but also to limit the excesses of the commercial sector. In fact, these capabilities might argue that in the long term, liberal, free market democracies will prove far more effective at mastering the capacity of the private sector in the 21st century than authoritarian states with managed economies.

That said, however, the role of the private sector in war raises innumerable legal, ethical, and practical issues that must

---

[9] Fareed Zakaria, *The Future of Freedom: Illiberal Democracy at Home and Abroad* (New York: Norton, 2003), p. 76.

be dealt with. Marrying the private sector's capacity to innovate and respond rapidly to changing demands with the government's need to be responsible and accountable for the conduct of operations is not an easy task.

Pfc. Josh Kendrick, from Company C, 1st Battalion, 66th Armor Regiment, 1st Brigade Combat Team, 4th Infantry Division, launches the Raven, an unmanned aerial vehicle, to provide area reconnaissance during Operation Bold Action near Tarmiya, just north of Baghdad on April 14, 2006 (US Army photo).

The proliferation of the private sector in military operations will require militaries to think differently about how best to integrate the private sector into public wars. Someone must have clear responsibility for the doctrine, detailed coordination, force requirements, and technologies needed to conduct these operations. Today, in the halls of the Pentagon and the staff rooms of the combatant commands, roles and missions are dispersed too diffusely and only intermittently gain the attention of senior leaders. One of the services needs to be tasked with developing a core competency contracting in complex contingency environments.

The American military has an innate prejudice against contracting security operations, which it comes by honestly. The modern state was built on transforming military activities from a private enterprise to a public responsibility. Civil supremacy and control of the military is the hallmark of 20th century Western democracy. Yet the 21st century is a different place. The private sector of the 21st century has the means to compete with the military. The Pentagon needs to become more comfortable with the idea that companies can provide security services without threatening democratic institutions. The doctrine of the armed forces needs to acknowledge the importance of getting post-conflict activities right, including integrating the role of the private sector. This is a prerequisite for getting the military to make companies part of the plan rather than an afterthought.

The Pentagon will also be unable to exploit the capacity of the private sector if doubts persist about the efficacy and legitimacy of contractor support. In any private sector activity, people understand the marketplace and make smart decisions when there is transparency. Security services are no different. Companies providing contractor support must help build trust and confidence in their services. They must establish best practices and professional standards--measures by which their actions should be judged.

Finally, contracting in Iraq was on a scale and complexity never imagined by Pentagon planners. Simply having the capacity to manage the contracts being let could have solved many of the most perplexing challenges. The military needs to build into its force structure the means to rapidly expand its ability to oversee private sector support. This might be done through building additional force structure in the National Guard or a reserve civilian contracting corps.

The Next Brave New World

Other lessons learned from the Long War may have a lot more to do with Wall Street than the Pentagon. If history is any judge the impact of the wars in Iraq and Afghanistan on the American entrepreneurial spirit are likely to be profound. The cyclical impact of major wars and the private sector has been an enduring feature of American history. Their influence on one another has been particularly dramatic since the onset of the Industrial Revolution. When major wars occur, the American military draws on the American citizenry to energize the American military machine, adopting the best civilian practices to military purposes. In turn, the military trains its citizen soldiers in the application of these skills. After the war, the nation's citizen-soldiers return to the workplace and apply their new knowledge, skill, and talents to the marketplace. The result is an explosion of innovation, economic growth, and cultural change.

At the outbreak of World War I, the United States stood as the world's preeminent industrial power. When America entered the war, it harnessed industrial age practices to the purpose of war better than did any other nation on earth. In turn, the military unleashed over three million veterans schooled in industrial-age warfare on the American marketplace. At the same time, it helped kick-start new industries, such as commercial aviation. American industrial dominance in the world not only grew, but, by the advent of the Second World War, had trained a new generation of soldiers for the battlefield.

GIs differed from doughboys in that the generation that fought the second war to end all wars was the first generation of soldiers who went to war comfortable with modern technology. Unlike their fathers, the technology of the twentieth century was a ubiquitous part of their lives—telephones, cars, radios, and electricity were common place. GI soldiers likely tinkered with jalopies in their garages, fiddled with ham radios, or read comic books about the fantasy worlds that modern technology might bring. They were a generation well suited to harnessing the unprecedented armada of machines that World War II saw brought to the battlefield. Their tinkering, innovating spirit made the American military the master at adapting and improvising with technology on the battlefield.

In turn, the technologies of the Second World War empowered intermediate levels of command in a manner unprecedented in military history. At Normandy, not far beyond the beachhead, a commander of few hundred men could control ground once held by an entire medieval army and call in more air and artillery support than could a corps commander during World War I. The increasing independence of military commands at the company, battalion, and brigade level called on the military increasingly to employ the principles of "middle management" developed in the private sector.

In the postwar period, the military once again unleashed its veterans on the marketplace, 12 million strong, armed with a confidence in technology, and possessed of leadership and work skills ideal for postwar industries. This work force, bolstered further by the education opportunities created by the GI Bill (government grants of payments to veterans for attending college or trade schools) and new industries evolving from technologies developed during the war, started the nation on the greatest economic expansion of its history.

The Korean conflict was close enough in time and space to be considered an extension of the World War II experience. Vietnam, on the other hand, was something different. In some respects, the war in Vietnam was America's first post-industrial military experience. By the advent of the conflict, industrial-age warfare and the ubiquitous place of technology on the battlefield were old hat. What Vietnam did bequeath to the veterans of that generation, however, was a life-long lesson in individual responsibility. In Vietnam, more than in any other modern American war, very junior officers and soldiers had a tremendous amount of individual responsibility. In addition, the changing nature of the war over the years and the varying character of combat from province to province precluded military leaders from becoming dogmatic in the practice of leadership. The school of war in Vietnam made an ideal breeding ground for individual entrepreneurs for the post-industrial age.

Unlike the economic expansions after the great world wars, however, the contributions of Vietnam veterans went largely unnoticed. Two factors account for that. The first was great global economic downturn of the 1970s—hardly a market conducive to showing off the capabilities of new age entrepreneurs. The second was a lack of opportunity to exploit new markets and new opportunities. Both those conditions changed in the 1980s. The U.S. economy rebounded and the advent of commercial computers created the opportunities of the information age.

The traditional image of Vietnam veterans as drug-crazed losers or apathetic dropouts suffering from post-dramatic shock syndrome is largely a myth. They were foot soldiers in the information revolution. For every Steve Jobs and Bill Gates that graced the cover of trendy magazines, there were innumerable Vietnam-era veterans that served as corporate leaders fueling America's leap into the post-industrial age in the computer industry as well as in many other business sectors.

What the generation of veterans from the long wars in Iraq and Afghanistan will bring back to American society remains one of the most intriguing questions of the day. The contributions of this generation will no doubt be—different. This will be America's first veteran generation in which all the veterans will not have worn uniforms. Many of them will be veteran contractors. Unlike returning military veterans, contract veterans already have both feet in the private sector. Thus, the "cycle-time" of good ideas from the battlefield to the home field might be far faster than in previous wars.

The impact of technology on veterans, both in and out of uniform, may prove to be different as well. Technology in combat today is not only ubiquitous—it is networked. In other words, technologies exist as part of integrated systems that share information and capabilities. Technology is in many cases virtually invisible as users manipulate, improvise, change, and adapt complex systems with virtually no conception whatsoever of the fundamental science behind the equipment they are employing.

Network warriors, whether civilian and soldier, are approaching technology in fundamentally different ways than their fathers, or, for that matter, their older brothers or sisters. They are comfortable in chaos, learning networks, and self-organizing communities that build groups based on interests rather than rules.

Combined with their fresh vision of technology is a new level of entrepreneurship unseen since Vietnam. Iraq and Afghanistan are corporal's wars in which significant responsibility is routinely devolved not just to junior officers, but to small groups and even to individual soldiers. Individual warriors walk away from modern battlefields with more confidence in their individual talents and potential than have those of any other generation in history.

How soldiers and civilians will harness the skills of the information age honed in war remains to be seen. The outcome is likely to be dramatic.

Captain Derrick Draper, from the 172nd Stryker Brigade Combat Team, maintains radio contact with an Apache attack helicopter during a mission near Tal Afar, Iraq on July 11, 2006 (US Army photo).

Next-War-itis

Many in the military are already thinking about the lessons of the Long War and where they fit in planning for the future. They need to do a better job than those who thought about the future before 9/11.

The military must fight the future—and it does all the time. Today, there are more men and women on operational missions around the world than at any moment since the end of the Cold War. Still, yet the majority of the military spends its days preparing for the next battle, not fighting the one at hand. Cadets study. Troops train. Some stateside commands develop new requirements for new equipment; others refurbish equipment the military already has. Military scientists push the envelope, applying new knowledge to combat capabilities. Few organizations spend more time and other resources worrying about what challenges and pondering what possibilities tomorrow will bring.

Far too often, and far too glibly, pundits accuse the military of preparing to fight the last war. Nothing could be further from the truth. Few organizations are more adept at learning and adapting to new requirements than are the American armed services. That said, the military is hardly immune from the affects of the historical, intellectual, and cultural forces that filter how institutions sees the challenges ahead.

The Army's Training and Doctrine Command (TRADOC) musings on the future national security environment in 2007 offer a case in point. PowerPoint slides now assume that the Army will have to participate in "persistent" operations requiring years of effort and at least tens of thousands of boots on the ground. They demonstrate an all-too-obvious lesson from the current conflict, but they are no more insightful than are the slides of a few years ago that trumpeted the need for an "expeditionary Army" such as the forces that were needed to win the first conventional battles in Iraq and Afghanistan. In contrast, new Navy and Air Force briefings highlight the potential for conflict with China—a mere coincidence that this theater places a higher premium on air and sea forces. All these "death by

PowerPoint" presentations suffer from the tendency to envision the future merely by extending the trends of the present. The military must do better. These tepid efforts will wither in the face of the great forces that are likely to drive how the lessons of the Long War are adopted by the military.

The effort offered here lays out some of the challenges ahead maps a route fraught with intellectual, fiscal, cultural, and institutional obstacles. Hard thinking and clear-headed advocacy is the best preparation for navigating this treacherous terrain and preparing for the next fight. **HX**

Far too often, and far too glibly, pundits accuse the military of preparing to fight the last war. Nothing could be further from the truth. Sgt. Tommy Hughes, a UH-60 Black Hawk Helicopter Crew Chief from the 36th Combat Aviation Brigade, participates in a pre-Iraq deployment exercise at Fort Hood, Texas (US Army photo).

APPENDICES

APPENDIX A − The Foreword for Army and Marine Corps Field Manual 3-24: Counterinsurgency.

This manual is designed to fill a doctrinal gap. It has been 20 years since the [US] Army published a field manual devoted exclusively to counterinsurgency operations. For the Marine Corps it has been 25 years. With our Soldiers and Marines fighting insurgents in Afghanistan and Iraq, it is essential that we give them a manual that provides principles and guidelines for counterinsurgency operations. Such guidance must be grounded in historical studies. However, it must also be informed by contemporary experiences.

This manual takes a general approach to counterinsurgency operations. The Army and Marine Corps recognize that every insurgency is contextual and presents its own set of challenges. You cannot fight former Saddamists [Baathists] and Islamic extremists [e.g., the Taliban and Al Qaeda] the same way you would have fought the Viet Cong, Moros, or Tupamaros. The application of principles and fundamentals to deal with each varies considerably.

Nonetheless, all insurgencies, even today's highly adaptable strains, remain wars [fought] amongst the people. They use variations of standard themes and adhere to elements of a recognizable revolutionary campaign plan. This manual therefore addresses the common characteristics of insurgencies. It strives to provide those [who are] conducting counter-insurgency campaigns with a solid foundation for understanding and addressing specific insurgencies.

A counterinsurgency campaign is, as described in this manual, a mix of offensive, defensive, and stability operations conducted along multiple lines of operations.

It requires Soldiers and Marines to employ a mix of familiar combat tasks and skills more often associated with non-military agencies [e.g., constabulary roles]. The balance between them depends on the local situation.

Achieving this balance is not easy. It requires leaders at all levels to adjust their approach constantly. They must ensure that their Soldiers and Marines are ready to be greeted with either a handshake or a hand grenade while taking on missions only infrequently practiced until recently at our combat training centers. Soldiers and Marines are expected to be nation builders as well as warriors.

They must be prepared to help re-establish institutions and local security forces and assist approaches in rebuilding infrastructure and basic services. They must be able to facilitate establishing local governance and the rule of law. The list of such tasks is long.

Performing [these tasks] involves extensive coordination and cooperation with many intergovernmental, host-nation, and international agencies. Indeed, the responsibilities of leaders in a counterinsurgency campaign are daunting. However, the discussions in this manual alert leaders to the challenges of such campaigns and suggest general for grappling with those challenges.

Conducting a successful counterinsurgency campaign requires a flexible, adaptive force led by agile, well-informed, culturally astute leaders. It is our hope that this manual provides the guidelines needed to succeed in operations that are exceedingly difficult and complex. Our Soldiers and Marines deserve nothing less.

Signed by:

David H. Petraeus, Lieutenant General,
US Army Commander, US Army Combined Arms Center,
and
James F. Amos, Lieutenant General,
US Marine Corps Deputy Commandant,
Combat Development and Integration.

APPENDIX B – General David Petraeus Multi-National Force-Iraq Commander's Counterinsurgency Guidance, July 15, 2008.

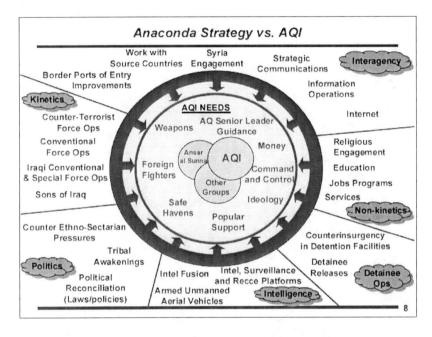

Anaconda Strategy: General Petraeus' visualization of the COIN battlefield in Iraq.

HEADQUARTERS
MULTI-NATIONAL FORCE – IRAQ
BAGHDAD, IRAQ
APO AE 09342-1400

15 July 2008

Multi-National Force-Iraq Commander's Counterinsurgency Guidance:

- **Secure and serve the population.** The Iraqi people are the decisive "terrain." Together with our Iraqi partners, work to provide the people security, to give them respect, to gain their support, and to facilitate establishment of local governance, restoration of basic services, and revival of local economies.

- **Live among the people.** You can't commute to this fight. Position Joint Security Stations, Combat Outposts, and Patrol Bases in the neighborhoods we intend to secure. Living among the people is essential to securing them and defeating the insurgents.

- **Hold areas that have been secured.** Once we clear an area, we must retain it. Develop the plan for holding an area before starting to clear it. The people need to know that we and our Iraqi partners will not abandon them. When reducing forces, gradually thin our presence rather than handing off or withdrawing completely. Ensure situational awareness even after transfer of responsibility to Iraqi forces.

- **Pursue the enemy relentlessly.** Identify and pursue Al Qaeda-Iraq and other extremist elements tenaciously. Do not let them retain support areas or sanctuaries. Force the enemy to respond to us. Deny the enemy the ability to plan and conduct deliberate operations.

- **Employ all assets to isolate and defeat the terrorists and insurgents.** Counter-terrorist forces alone cannot defeat Al-Qaeda and the other extremists. Success requires a comprehensive approach that employs all forces and all means at our disposal—non-kinetic as well as kinetic. Employ Coalition and Iraqi conventional and special operations forces, Sons of Iraq, and all other available non-military multipliers in accordance with the attached "Anaconda Strategy."

- **Generate unity of effort.** Coordinate operations and initiatives with our embassy and interagency partners, our Iraqi counterparts, local governmental leaders, and non-governmental organizations to ensure all are working to achieve a common purpose.

- **Promote reconciliation.** We cannot kill our way out of this endeavor. We and our Iraqi partners must identify and separate the "irreconcilables" from the "reconcilables" through thorough intelligence work, population control measures, information operations, kinetic operations, and political initiatives. We must strive to make the reconcilables part of the solution, even as we identify, pursue, and kill, capture, or drive out the irreconcilables.

- **Defeat the network, not just the attack.** Focus to the "left" of the explosion. Employ intelligence assets to identify the network behind an attack, and go after its leaders, explosives experts, financiers, suppliers, and operators.

- **Foster Iraqi legitimacy.** Encourage Iraqi leadership and initiative; recognize that their success is our success. Partner in all that we do and support local involvement in security, governance, economic revival, and provision of basic services. Find the right balance between Coalition Forces leading and the Iraqis exercising their leadership and initiative, and encourage the latter. Legitimacy of Iraqi actions in the eyes of the Iraqi people is essential to overall success.

- **Punch above your weight class.** Strive to be "bigger than you actually are." Partner in operations with Iraqi units and police, and employ "Sons of Iraq," contractors, and local Iraqis to perform routine tasks in and around Forward Operating Bases, Patrol Bases, and Joint Security Stations, thereby freeing up our troopers to focus on tasks "outside the wire."

- **Employ money as a weapon system.** Money can be "ammunition" as the security situation improves. Use a targeting board process to ensure the greatest effect for each "round" expended and to ensure that each engagement using money contributes to the achievement of the unit's overall objectives. Ensure contracting activities support the security effort, employing locals wherever possible. Employ a "matching fund" concept when feasible in order to ensure Iraqi involvement and commitment.

- **Fight for intelligence.** A nuanced understanding of the situation is everything. Analyze the intelligence that is gathered, share it, and fight for more. Every patrol should have tasks designed to augment understanding of the area of operations and the enemy. Operate on a "need to share" rather than a "need to know" basis. Disseminate intelligence as soon as possible to all who can benefit from it.

- **Walk. Move mounted, work dismounted.** Stop by, don't drive by. Patrol on foot and engage the population.

Situational awareness can only be gained by interacting with the people face-to-face, not separated by ballistic glass.

- **Understand the neighborhood.** Map the human terrain and study it in detail. Understand the local culture and history. Learn about the tribes, formal and informal leaders, governmental structures, religious elements, and local security forces. Understand how local systems and structures—including governance, provision of basic services, maintenance of infrastructure, and economic elements— are supposed to function and how they really function.

- **Build relationships.** Relationships are a critical component of counterinsurgency operations. Together with our Iraqi counterparts, strive to establish productive links with local leaders, tribal sheikhs, governmental officials, religious leaders, and interagency partners.

- **Look for Sustainable Solutions.** Build mechanisms by which the Iraqi Security Forces, Iraqi community leaders, and local Iraqis under the control of governmental institutions can continue to secure local areas and sustain governance and economic gains in their communities as the Coalition Force presence is reduced. Figure out the Iraqi systems and help Iraqis make them work.

- **Maintain continuity and tempo through transitions.** Start to build the information you'll provide to your successors on the day you take over. Allow those who will follow you to "virtually look over your shoulder" while they're still at home station by giving them access to your daily updates and other items on SIPRNET. Deploy planners and intel analysts ahead of time. Encourage extra time on the ground during transition periods, and strive to maintain operational tempo and local relationships to avoid giving the enemy respite.

- **Manage expectations.** Be cautious and measured in announcing progress. Note what has been accomplished, but also acknowledge what still needs to be done. Avoid premature declarations of success. Ensure our troopers and our partners are aware of our assessments and recognize that any counterinsurgency operation has innumerable challenges that enemies get a vote, and that progress is likely to be slow.

DAVID H. PETRAEUS
General, United States Army
Commanding

General David H. Petraeus, commanding general, Multi-National Force- Iraq, receives a mission update from Sgt. 1st Class Trey Corales, scout platoon sergeant, 2nd Battalion, 35th Infantry Regiment, 3rd Brigade Combat Team, 25th Infantry on February 16, 2007.

APPENDIX C – General Ray Odierno's Multi-National Force-Iraq Commander's Counterinsurgency Guidance, September 16, 2008.

HEADQUARTERS
MULTI-NATIONAL FORCE – IRAQ
BAGHDAD, IRAQ
APO AE 09342-1400

16 September 2008

Multi-National Force-Iraq Commander's Counterinsurgency Guidance

We serve during a pivotal period in the campaign for a secure, stable, and prosperous Iraq. Our Coalition Forces and Iraqi partners have sacrificed much, and together we have achieved remarkable gains. Today, the Iraqi people enjoy greater freedoms than at any point in several generations, and there is tremendous hope for the future in this ancient land. As we look ahead, we continue to see an evolution of progress in Iraq. As Iraqi Security Forces stand on their own, Coalition Forces will increasingly *"Enable from Overwatch."*

Together, Coalition and Iraqi forces will continue to protect the populace while fostering reconciliation, promoting good governance, and encouraging Iraqi men and women to build upon their newly-won hope by investing in their communities. Given Iraq's changing environment, accomplishing this will require a subtle shift in "how we think" about our mission, "how we operate" to accomplish that mission, and the principles that define "who we are."

"How We Think"

- **Protect and serve the population.** The Iraqi people are the decisive "terrain." Enable our Iraqi partners to provide security and help the people of Iraq to invest and take pride in their communities. Foster local governance, provision of basic services, maintenance of infrastructure, and economic revitalization.

- **Understand the complexity of the conflict.** The environment in which we operate is complex and demands that we employ every weapon in our arsenal, both kinetic and non-kinetic. To fully utilize all approaches, we must understand the local culture and history. Learn about the tribes, formal and informal leaders, governmental and religious structures, and local security forces. We must understand how the society functions so we can enable Iraqis to build a stable, self-reliant nation.

- **Give the people justice and honor.** We want the hands that bring security to be the hands that help bring justice and honor as well. In this complex struggle, strive to be the "honest broker." Ensure that complaints and abuses are dealt with quickly and publicly. Provide an environment that creates honorable work, rewards honorable behavior, and emphasizes honorable treatment for all.

- **Foster GoI legitimacy – Make it easy for the people to choose.** Exemplify professionalism in all your actions and promote the same in our Iraqi partners. Continually develop the capability and legitimacy of the ISF, and give the Iraqi people hope by showing them that loyalty to the national government is the best way to improve the lives of their families.

- **Promote reconciliation.** Separate those who promote and practice violence from those now willing to reconcile and become productive members of Iraqi society. Encourage and enable the Iraqi government to reintegrate those committed to peaceful coexistence with their neighbors.

"How We Operate"

- **Conduct operations by, with, or through our Iraqi partners – *"Enable from Overwatch."*** Understand Iraqi systems and capabilities, and help Iraqis make them work – always look for sustainable solutions. Coalition and Iraqi units must live, work, and fight together, with the Iraqis more and more in the lead. Ultimately, the legitimacy of the ISF in the eyes of the Iraqi people is essential to long-term success.

- **Walk.** Move mounted, work dismounted. Patrol on foot and engage the population – with the ISF in front whenever possible. Situational awareness can only be gained by interacting with the people face-to-face. Every patrol should have tasks designed to augment understanding of the area and the enemy.

- **Defeat the network, not just the attack.** Defeat enemy attacks before they happen by identifying the network behind attack preparations -- pursue and take apart the network's leaders, bomb makers, financiers, suppliers, and operators. Use both lethal and non-lethal means to destroy the network and prevent it from regenerating.

- **Share intelligence.** Establish collection systems, and promptly and regularly share information up and down the chain of command and with our Iraqi partners. Know that small pieces of information paint the big picture.

- **Integrate civilian and military efforts.** As we move closer to sustainable security, civilian and governmental agencies will naturally take on more responsibility as we reduce our military presence. Coordinate operations and initiatives with our embassy and interagency partners, our Iraqi counterparts, local civilian leaders, and non-governmental organizations to ensure all are working to achieve a common purpose. At all levels, continue to build Iraqi capacity to independently execute governance functions.

- **Transfer security responsibility.** Enable Iraqi units to accept security responsibility as local conditions permit. Don't rush to failure -- closely supervise deliberate, well-coordinated transitions that preserve security gains and maintain momentum. "Thin" our presence in sector, but stay engaged, and maintain situational awareness and vigilance in protecting our force.

"Who We Are"

- **Be first with the truth.** Communicate accurate information – good or bad – to the chain of command, to Iraqi leaders, and to the public as soon as possible. Pre-empt rumors and beat the insurgents, extremists, and criminals to the headlines. Hold the press (and ourselves) accountable for accuracy and context. Challenge enemy disinformation. Turn our enemies' extremist ideologies, oppressive practices, and indiscriminate violence against them.

- **Have realistic expectations.** We have made great gains, but much remains to be done. The enemy still has a vote, and progress may sometimes be slow. Make no premature declarations of victory, but identify and share successes and champion their cause.

- **Live our values.** Stay true to the values we hold dear and that distinguish us from our enemies. This endeavor is often brutal, physically demanding, and frustrating. We all experience moments of anger, but we can neither submit to dark impulses nor tolerate unethical actions by others.

- **Leaders make the difference.** Warfare has never been more complex and never has it required more imaginative leadership. Empower subordinates and push decisions, resources, and authorities to the lowest level possible. Provide appropriate right and left limits for our leaders and give them the flexibility necessary to be imaginative and adaptive. Communicate with your subordinates daily to ensure awareness. Leaders are the barometer for their unit. Do what's right and trust your fellow troopers to do the same.

Many challenges still lie ahead. I salute your professionalism, your skill, and your extraordinary dedication in this complex environment. The world watches our progress with great anticipation. You are the authors of one of our era's proudest chapters of military history, and I am honored to lead MNF-I as we put to practice these tenets of counterinsurgency.

RAYMOND T. ODIERNO
General, United States Army
Commanding

Appendix D – The Insurgency and Terrorist Tactics, Official update from the Operation Iraqi Freedom Multi-National Force Iraq, July 15, 2008.

The Insurgency

The insurgency in Iraq consists of myriad anti-Iraqi Forces and their supporters who are engaged in guerilla warfare against Coalition and Iraqi security forces and use terrorism to strike fear in the Iraqi populace. Their tactics include, but are not limited to, suicide bombings, improvised explosive device attacks, kidnapping, rudimentary sniper techniques, mortar attack, rocket attacks, and murder.

Insurgent activity is centered in the Sunni-dominated parts of Iraq, primarily the areas to the northwest of Baghdad and between the cities of Tikrit, Ramadi, Samarra and Fallujah. Sunni Arabs, including Ba'athist and former elements of Saddam Hussein's regime, Saddamists, sometimes collaborate with international Sunni Arab terrorist networks, providing funds and guidance across family, tribal, religious and peer group lines. The foreigners include jihadists led by Abu Musab al-Zarqawi's terrorist network, al-Qaida in Iraq, AQI. Together, these groups work to perpetuate a reign of terror designed to breed havoc in Iraq.

Some of these anti-government elements are clearly groups drawn from the former regime, the Ba'th Party, the paramilitary Fedayeen, and the Republican Guard. Some are anti-Saddam nationalist groups with no desire to see Saddam restored but resentful of U.S. and Western presence; others are Islamist groups, some members of which have been trained overseas or are foreign nationals, the latter including Syrians, Saudis, Yemenis, and Sudanese. Some activities have been the work of criminals or criminal organizations, large numbers of criminals being released at the end of the war and some certainly hiring themselves out for attacks on Coalition forces.

Other Iraqi jihadists groups are active, notably Ansar al-Sunnah, which operates primarily in Kurdish-dominated northern Iraq. The foreign jihadists enter Iraq from Saudi Arabia,

Syria, Jordan, and Iran. Most of the victims of jihadists suicide bombings have been civilians, innocent bystanders. This has been especially true since Coalition and Iraqi security forces developed tactics and deployed better equipment to protect themselves from the attacks. Among the Sunnis, a variety of groups have been identified. They are united only in the sense of having what have been called "negative" goals in opposition to U.S. presence; in seeking some return to the former status quo in which the Sunni minority have exercised power since the Ottoman period.

There are also armed militias attached to the two main Shiite political parties, the Supreme Council for the Islamic Revolution in Iraq and al-Dawa, and there is clearly potential for Shiite participation in violence. The pattern of Iraqi activity thus far looks remarkably similar to that in Palestine with roadside bombs, which have also been used by Hezbollah in Lebanon, and other so-called improvised explosive devices; ambushes of soft-skinned vehicles; opportunistic rocket-propelled grenade and shooting attacks on military personnel; attacks on civilian members of the Coalition authorities and foreign personnel working in some way for the Coalition; attacks on Iraqi "collaborators," most recently police and army recruits' and attacks on economic targets such as power stations, oil installations, and pipelines. There has also been an increase in the number of attacks upon "soft" targets, principally civilian gatherings.

Terrorist Organizations
- al-Qaida Organization in the Land of the Two Rivers
- Mujahideen Shura Council
- Ansar al-Sunnah
- Islamic Army in Iraq

Although some named terrorist groups operate in Iraq, these categories are constantly shifting. The following is a brief introduction to some of the most well-known terrorist groups in Iraq.

Al-Qaida Organization in the Land of the Two Rivers
(al-Qaida in Iraq—AQI)

Al-Qaida Organization in the Land of the Two Rivers (AQI) is the name of the terrorist group led by Abu Musab al-Zarqawi before being killed in a Coalition forces airstrike on June 7, 2006.

Abu Ayyub al-Masri replaced al-Zarqawi as leader of the group whose name implies that they consider themselves as the center of Jihadist activities in Iraq.

The goals of this group are to overthrow the Iraqi government and establish an Islamic state in Iraq by forcing out the U.S.-led coalition. Elements of the Kurdish Islamist group Ansar al-Islam, and indigenous Sunni Iraqis form the ranks of this group.

AQI has issued claims of responsibility in Iraq for attacks on American and Iraqi security forces, often claiming several attacks in one day. The group uses a variety of tactics that include RPG attacks against armored vehicles, guerilla style attacks by armed militants, suicide bombings, and the kidnapping and beheadings of foreigners.

Al-Qaida in the land of the Two Rivers, which is believed to derive most of its domestic support from Sunni Arabs, has focused on attacking Shiite Arabs and the fledgling Iraqi police force. This group is blamed for the bombing of a Shia shrine in Samarra in February of 2006 and June of 2007, which set off a series of deadly reprisal killings between Sunnis and Shias.

In addition to these frequent smaller scale attacks in Iraq, the group claimed responsibility for the bombing of three hotels in Amman, Jordan that left 67 people dead and injured more than 150.

In January 2006, the group was one of six insurgent organizations to unify under the Mujahideen Shura Council. As of now, all attacks perpetrated by al-Qaida in Iraq are claimed in the name of the Council.

Mujahideen Shura Council

The Mujahideen Shura Council, "Freedom Fighter Consultation Council," is an umbrella organization made up of several terrorist groups in Iraq, including AQI.

The Mujahideen Shura Council first appeared in spring 2005 when it claimed the kidnapping of Australian citizen Douglas Wood. Wood was a contractor with the American firm Bechtel. The group demanded the departure of all foreign forces in Iraq. Wood was freed by Iraqi forces in an operation in June 2005 after being held several weeks.

Despite the high-profile nature of this incident, the Council did not claim responsibility for any more attacks for several months.

In January 2006, several Sunni insurgent groups announced that they were joining to form the Mujahideen Shura Council. They claimed to unite in order to continue the struggle and force out the "invading infidels." The groups that formed the council included: al-Qaida Organization in the Land of the Two Rivers, Jaish al-Taifa al-Mansoura, al-Ahwal Brigades, Islamic Jihad Brigades, al-Ghuraba Brigades, and Saraya Ansar al-Tawhid.

The idea of the Council is to unify insurgent efforts in Iraq against government and Coalition forces. It may also be an attempt to mend a rift between various Sunni insurgent groups. But it is clearly an attempt to unify disparate groups with a radical Sunni ideology driven to destroy the Iraqi government and its international support.

The formation of the Council is also possibly to shore up support for the insurgency by distancing itself from the extremely violent tactics and targeting of innocent Iraqis by al-Qaida. The Council allows AQI to continue its methods without claiming direct responsibility. It is now the organization claiming attacks by its member factions. Thus, the goals of the Council and its members are the same: the removal of U.S. troops from Iraq and the formation of an Islamic government in place of the current government.

Ansar al-Sunnah

Ansar al-Sunnah ("Followers of the Tradition") is a group of Iraqi Jihadists attempting to establish an Islamic state with Shariah law in Iraq. They aim to achieve this by defeating Coalition Forces in the country. To them, Jihad in Iraq is obligatory for all Muslims, and anyone opposed to Jihad is their enemy. The group's membership is varied, but includes radical Kurds in the Ansar al-Islam, foreign al-Qaidaand other Sunni terrorists.

The Ansar al-Sunnah has targeted coalition military, Iraqi soldiers and governmental institutions, and other political establishments in Iraq which the group treats as puppet regimes of American occupation. The group claims many attacks, many of which are unsubstantiated.

Ansar al-Sunnah has reportedly teamed up with the banned Arab Socialist Ba'th Part and AQI where they pledge to continue and increase attacks on the coalition and Iraqi government forces.

Islamic Army in Iraq

The Islamic Army in Iraq, IAI, conducts a brutally violent campaign against foreigners within Iraq, specifically anyone believed to be cooperating with the U.S.-led coalition. IAI has been implicated in several gruesome beheading deaths. The terrorist group aims to drive all U.S. and related Coalition forces, both military and civilian, from Iraq. But IAI does not limit its attacks to just these groups; it has also murdered French journalists, Pakistani contractors, an Italian journalist, and Macedonian citizens working for a U.S. company.

In the past, IAI has kidnapped individuals or group of people and then made demands impossible to meet. Frequently, these demands are indirectly related to the kidnapping victims. For example, IAI captured Enzo Baldoni, an Italian journalist who also volunteered for the Red Cross in Iraq. IAI demanded that Italy withdraw all troops from Iraq or Enzo Baldoni, both an independent journalist and humanitarian volunteer, would be killed. Italy did not recall its troops and Baldoni was murdered. This is a common tactic of IAI. The Islamic Army in Iraq has also attacked French civilians in retaliation for France's law regarding headscarves in schools. IAI does not limit its terrorist attacks to non-Iraqis; the group has also executed Iraqi people who join Iraq's police and military services.

According to old statements by the leader of the Islamic Army in Iraq, the group has thousands of terrorists in its ranks. The group's leader also claims that the group is predominantly Iraqi, not foreign-born. Statements released in November 2004 announced that the Islamic Army in Iraq has collaborated with Ansar al-Sunnah and AQI.

(*Sources: Memorial Institute for the Prevention of Terrorism; SITE Institute; International Crisis Group.*)

Terrorist Tactics

Iraqi guerilla attacks against Mulit-National Force - Iraq, Iraqi government and commercial targets typically take the following forms:

- Attacks on convoys and patrols using improvised explosive devices
- Ambushes on Coalition forces with small arms and/or rocket propelled grenade fire and hit-and-run mortar strikes on Iraqi government, Iraqi security forces, and MNF-I bases are also common.
- Sabotage of oil pipelines and other infrastructure is another tactic often used
- Assassination of Iraqis cooperating with the Coalition forces and Iraqi government
- Suicide bombings targeting international organizations, Coalition forces, Iraqi police, hotels, etc.
- Kidnapping and murder of private contractors working in Iraq for Iraqi government, MNF-I, or for commercial entities.

- Kidnapping private Iraqi citizens as a fundraising tactic.

Improvised Explosive Devices

The majority of insurgent attacks come in the form of IEDs targeting Iraqi and Coalition convoys and patrols. Most IEDs are made from leftover munitions and foreign explosive materials which are often hastily put together. Vehicle borne IEDs, VBIEDs, are devices that use a vehicle as the package or container of the device. These IEDs come in all shapes and sizes, from small sedans to large cargo trucks. There have even been instances of what appeared to be generators, donkey-drawn cards, and ambulances used to attempt attacks on Coalition forces and the new Iraqi government.

The Internet and Psychological Warfare

Terrorism has often been conceptualized as a form of psychological warfare, and terrorists have certainly sought to wage such a campaign through the Internet. There are several ways for terrorists to do so. They can use the Internet to spread disinformation, to deliver threats intended to instill fear and helplessness, and to disseminate horrific images of recent actions, such as beheadings of foreign hostages in Iraq. The insurgents and terrorists in Iraq wage battles with traditional guerilla means as well as by employing psychological warfare on the Internet. Many terrorist groups use message boards, online chat, and religious justifications for their activities. Sites also often provide histories of their host organizations and activities.

HX

Appendix E – Provincial Reconstruction Teams (PRTs) Fact Sheet, U.S. Embassy, Iraq, December, 17, 2007.

A Soldier stands guard in Golbahar, Afghanistan, during a visit by members of the Parwan Provincial Reconstruction Team (PRT) to a local school. The PRT is rebuilding the school in an effort to help bring stability to Afghanistan. The Soldier is assigned to the 1st Battalion, 501st Infantry Regiment on March 26, 2004 (US Army photo).

Provincial Reconstruction Teams (PRTs)

"We're very focused on the need to return control to Baghdad. But we're also very focused on the need to build capacity in the local and provincial governments and to be able to deliver economic and reconstruction assistance there."
Secretary of State, Condoleezza Rice January 11, 2007.

- First established in Iraq in 2005 and inaugurated by Secretary Rice in November that year, the Provincial Reconstruction Team (PRT) initiative is a civilian-military inter-agency effort that is the primary U.S. Government interface between U.S., Coalition partners and provincial and local governments throughout all of Iraq's 18 provinces.
- As of mid-December 2007 there were 28 PRTs located in all 18 of Iraq's provinces -- 15 embedded with military units -- staffed by approximately 700 people. Since 2003, the U.S. Government has spent $32 billion on reconstruction and stabilization efforts in Iraq supported by PRTs.
- The PRTs are an important tool in helping Iraq achieve economic and political stabilization by bolstering moderates, promoting reconciliation, fostering economic development and building provincial capacity.
- They do this by assisting provincial and local governments to deliver essential needs like schools, roads and sewage and water services. A major focus is to build local and regional capacity in governance.
- All provinces in Iraq are now served by a total of twenty-eight PRTs, with the majority of Iraq's population served by ten full-sized teams stretching from Mosul in the north to Basrah in the far south. Coalition participation includes the British-led PRT in Basrah, the Italian-led team in Dhi Qar and the Korean-led team in Erbil. The PRTs work closely with a U.S. or coalition military unit in their area to build capacity in their Provincial governments.
- Ten of the twenty- teams are the new "embedded" PRTs formulated as part of President Bush's New Way Forward strategy. These civilian-led teams work hand-and-glove in BCTs (Brigade Combat Teams) or Regiments (U.S. Marines) to support the military surge in Anbar Province and the greater Baghdad area.
- Manning of the PRTs is diverse: Department of State, USAID, Coalition military personnel, U.S. Department

of Justice, U.S. Department of Agriculture, Gulf Region Division of the U.S. Army Corps of Engineers and contract personnel. The Office of Provincial Affairs within the U.S. Embassy Baghdad provides policy guidance and support to the PRT program.

- PRT support comes from a variety of sources, including Coalition partners and donor nations with the majority coming from the U.S. Principal programs associated with PRTs include U.S. funded CSP (Community Stabilization Program); the PRDC (Provincial Reconstruction & Development Committee) program; the LGP (Local Governance Program); the Civil Society Program; and the INMA Agri-business Program. ▪X

APPENDIX F – Clear-hold-build Short Case Studies: Tal Afar from FM 3-24/MCWP 3-33.5 5-23.

Crouched low, Sgt. Roger E. Tiapula, a communications specialist with Company D, 2nd Battalion, 325th Airborne Infantry Regiment, 82nd Airborne Division, pulls security as his patrol moves down a street in Tall Afar, Iraq, Nov. 12, 2005 (US Army, Photographer: Pfc. James Wilt).

Clear-Hold-Build in Tal Afar, Iraq 2005

In early 2005, the city of Tal Afar in northern Iraq had become a focal point for Iraqi insurgent efforts. The insurgents tried to assert control over the population. They used violence and intimidation to inflame ethnic and sectarian tensions. They took control of all schools and mosques, while destroying police stations. There were frequent abductions and executions. The insurgents achieved some success as the populace divided into communities defined by sectarian boundaries. Additionally, Tal Afar became an insurgent support base and sanctuary for launching attacks in the major regional city of Mosul and throughout Nineveh province.

During the summer of 2005, the 3d Armored Cavalry Regiment (ACR) assumed the lead for military efforts in and around Tal Afar. In the months that followed, the 3d ACR applied a clear-hold-build approach to reclaim Tal Afar from the insurgents.

Destruction or Expulsion of Insurgent Forces (Clear)

In August 2005, the 3d ACR and Iraqi forces began the process of destroying the insurgency in Tal Afar. Their first step was to conduct reconnaissance to understand the enemy situation; understand the ethnic, tribal, and sectarian dynamics; and set the conditions for effective operations. Iraqi security forces and U.S. Soldiers isolated Executing Counterinsurgency Operations the insurgents from external support by controlling nearby border areas and creating an eight-foot-high berm around the city. The berm's purpose was to deny the enemy freedom of movement and safe haven in outlying communities. The berm prevented free movement of fighters and weapons and forced all traffic to go through security checkpoints manned by U.S. and Iraqi forces. Multinational checkpoints frequently included informants who could identify insurgents. Multinational forces supervised the movement of civilians out of contentious areas. Forces conducted house-to-house searches. When they met violent resistance, they used precision fires from artillery and aviation. Targets were chosen through area reconnaissance operations, interaction with the local populace, and information from U.S. and Iraqi sources. Hundreds of insurgents were killed or captured during the encirclement and clearing of the city. Carefully controlled application of violence limited the cost to residents.

Deployment of Security Forces (Hold)

Following the defeat of enemy fighters, U.S. and Iraqi forces established security inside Tal Afar. The security forces immediately enhanced personnel screening at checkpoints based on information from the local population. To enhance police legitimacy in the people's eyes, multinational forces began recruiting Iraqi police from a more diverse, representative mix comprising city residents and residents of surrounding communities. Police recruits received extensive training in a police academy.

A Soldier from the 14th Cavalry Regiment, 1st Brigade, 25th Infantry Division, patrols Tall Afar, Iraq on January 3, 2005 (US Army photo).

U.S. forces and the Iraqi Army also trained Iraqi police in military skills. Concurrently, the local and provincial government dismissed or prosecuted Iraqi police involved in offenses against the populace. The government assigned new police leaders to the city from Mosul and other locations. U.S. forces assisted to ensure Iraqi Army, police, and their own forces shared common boundaries and were positioned to provide mutual support to one another. At the same time, U.S. forces continued to equip and train a border defense brigade, which increased the capability to interdict the insurgents' external support. Among its successes, the multinational force destroyed an insurgent network that included a chain of safe houses between Syria and Tal Afar.

Improving Living Conditions and Restoring Normalcy (Build)

With insurgents driven out of their city, the local population accepted guidance and projects to reestablish control by the Iraqi government. The 3d ACR commander noted, "The people of Tal Afar understood that this was an operation for them—an operation to bring back security to the city."

With the assistance of the Department of State and the U.S. Agency for International Development's Office of Transition Initiatives, efforts to reestablish municipal and economic systems began in earnest. These initiatives included providing essential services (water, electricity, sewage, and trash collection), education projects, police stations, parks, and reconstruction efforts. A legal claims process and compensation program to address local grievances for damages was also established.

As security and living conditions in Tal Afar improved, citizens began providing information that helped eliminate the insurgency's infrastructure. In addition to information received on the streets, multinational forces established joint coordination centers in Tal Afar and nearby communities that became multinational command posts and intelligence-sharing facilities with the Iraqi Army and the Iraqi police. Unity of effort by local Iraqi leaders, Iraqi security forces, and U.S. forces was critical to success. Success became evident when many families who had fled the area returned to the secured city. HX

Appendix G – IED Attack Terminology

AAIED - An Anti-Armor IED that incorporates armor defeating principles such as Explosively Formed Projectiles, Shaped and Plate Charges. They are designed to damage or destroy armored vehicles and/or kill or wound individuals inside armored vehicles.

Cache - A facility or location where supplies are hidden or otherwise concealed and are not readily available. A Cache may consist of weapons or other equipment.

Complex Attack - An attack that involves one or more IEDs, or an IED attack used in conjunction with direct or indirect small arms fire (SAF).

Effective Attack - An attack which meets the intent and produces casualties, or damage to vehicles or infrastructure.

EFP Explosively Formed Projectiles - A specially designed IED which incorporates explosive encased behind a metal plate liner which, through explosive force, reshapes into a projectile capable of piercing armor. The charges are generally cylindrical and fabricated from common metal pipe. The forward end is closed by a concave copper or steel disk-shaped liner shaped like a shallow dish. The shape of this dish creates the shaped charge which focuses the explosive force creating a jet of hot, molten plasma. Detonation is controlled by cable, radio control, TV or IR remote controls, or remote arming with a passive infrared sensor. EFPs can be deployed singly, in pairs, or in arrays, depending on the tactical situation.

ERW - Explosive Remnants of War are any military ordnance left on the battlefield, or in
abandoned munitions storage sites – not necessarily old or deteriorated.

Home Made Explosives - A combination of IED Attack commercially available ingredients combined to create an explosive substance.

IED - An Improvised Explosive Device is a device placed or fabricated in an improvised manner incorporating destructive, lethal, noxious, pyrotechnic, or incendiary chemicals and designed to destroy, incapacitate, harass, or distract. It may incorporate military stores, but is normally devised using non-military components.

Hoax - An object or report designed to simulate an IED, deliberately employed to cause disruption of normal activity and/or to identify Coalition Forces Tactics Techniques and Procedures (TTPs).

LVBIED - A Large Vehicle-borne IED delivered by any large ground-based vehicle (e.g. dump truck, panel truck, bongo truck commercial bus, tanker etc.) and/or serves as the concealment means for explosives with an initiating device.

Magnetic Attachment - A type of IED employment in which the device is attached to the target using magnets.

Underbelly IED - A type of IED employment in which the device targets the undercarriage of a vehicle.

PBIED Person-borne IED - An IED worn by a person, such as a vest, belt, back-pack, etc., in which the person houses the whole IED or principle IED components and/ or serves as the delivery or concealment means for explosives with an initiating g device. A PBIED is often initiated by the person wearing the IED (Suicide) – however, not all PBIEDs are triggered by the person wearing the IED.

Platter Charge or Plate Charge – A hollow charge, or plate charge, used to propel the metal plate towards a target in a manner where the plate remains intact. With detonation the brass plate melts into a projectile which penetrates vehicular armor.

RVBIED Remote VBIED - A VBIED which is driven to the target by Radio or Remote (Wire) Control. The initiation system may or may not be the same as the driving control system.

Shaped Charge - A charge shaped in such a manner so as to concentrate the explosive force in a particular direction (i.e. plasma jet). This plasma jet easily perforates an unprotected steel armor hitting the surface at a speed of 8,000 meters per second and extremely high pressure.

Secondary Device - This is an additional device emplaced in the target area to attack individuals or vehicles after the initial event. A secondary device is often employed to target first responders following an initial IED event.

SVBIED - a Suicide VBIED which requires the driver or passenger inside IED driver, the vehicle, to detonate the explosives. May incorporate a command initiation as a back-up.

Suicide Attack - An IED initiated by an operator at a time of his/ her choosing in which the operator intentionally kills himself/ herself as part of the attack.

Tertiary Device - This is an additional device emplaced in the target area to attack individuals or vehicles after the initial and secondary events.

UBE Unknown Bulk Explosive - A categorization used to define a quantity of explosive if there is insufficient evidence to determine if the explosives are of military, commercial, or homemade origin.

UXO - Unexploded Ordnance is explosive ordnance which has been primed, fused, armed or otherwise prepared for action, and which has been fired, dropped, launched, projected, or placed in such a manner as to constitute a hazard to operations, installations, personnel, or material and remains unexploded either by malfunction or design or any other cause. Some UXO may be placed with the intent to add an initiation system at a later time; at this point it may become an IED. Determination is subject to the Team Leader's judgment and knowledge. If in doubt treat as a worst case scenario and report as an IED.

VBIED Vehicle-borne IED
An IED delivered by any small ground-based vehicle (e.g. passenger vehicle, motorcycle, moped, bicycle etc.) and/or serves as the concealment means for explosives with an initiating device.

The ESA Warfighter Editor, Colonel John Antal, US Army (Ret.) standing next to a Mine Resistant Ambush Protected truck near Kabul, Afghanistan in September 2008. The MRAP is designed to protect troops from all but the largest IED and EFP attacks.

List of Contributors:

Editor-in-Chief

Colonel John Antal, US Army (Retired). Colonel John F. Antal, U.S. Army (Retired) is a noted historian of the art of war and novelist and the Editor of the Warfighter Series. He is the author of nine books on military subjects and over one hundred and fifty articles in professional military journals. He has appeared frequently on the History Channel and Discovery Military Channels TV shows. He is the founding editor of the Armchair General, a military history magazine.

Antal served in the US Army for thirty years before retiring in 2003. Antal has served predominantly in combat tank and infantry units during his Army career and served at every level of command from platoon to regiment. In his last military assignment he served as the G3 Operations officer for the 62,350 soldier III Armored Corps at Fort Hood, Texas. Prior to this assignment he was the commander of the 16th Cavalry Regiment at Fort Knox, Kentucky where he was responsible for armor combat leader training for Army and Marine Corps students from the rank of sergeants through colonel. A former Special Assistant to the Chairman of the Joint Chiefs of Staff, Colonel Antal holds a Master of Military Arts and Sciences degree and is a distinguished graduate of the United States Military Academy, the Army Command and General Staff College and the Army War College.

Managing Editor

PJ Putnam (Fmr. USAF Spec Ops Pilot). PJ Putnam received his commission from the United States Air Force Academy. During his twelve years in the US Air Force, PJ, first, served as a judo/unarmed combat instructor at the US Air Force Academy and, later, as a Special Operations' Helicopter Instructor/Evaluator Pilot having flown over 3,000 hours while stationed at both overseas and CONUS bases.

After PJ broke his neck in an unfortunate car accident, he completed his MBA from the University of New Mexico, graduated *cum laude* with a law degree from Southern Methodist University, and studied international law in Oxford, England. Between schools, PJ worked as a transactional lawyer in an international law firm; the Editor-in Chief of the American Bar Association's *The International Lawyer* law journal; as an executive in an Internet security company; as a volunteer surgery technician in Ecuador; as a business consultant; as a motivational speaker; and, as an entrepreneur. Mr. Putnam is the author of numerous magazine articles and he is awaiting the publication of his first book, *Fiery Vigil*, which details his flying in and around the erupting Mt. Pinatubo, Republic of the Philippines.

If you are interested in writing a chapter for future **Warfighter Series** books, contact COL John Antal, US Army (Ret.) at:

editor@hx-warfighter.com

Authors (In Alphabetical order)

Major General John R. Allen, USMC, currently serves as Deputy Commanding General, II Marine Expeditionary Force and Commanding General, 2d Marine Expeditionary Brigade.

Following commissioning, he attended The Basic School and was assigned to Second Battalion, 8th Marines where he served as a platoon and rifle company commander. His next tour took him to Marine Barracks 8th and I, Washington D.C. where he served at the Marine Corps Institute and as a ceremonial officer. Major General Allen then attended, and was the Distinguished Graduate of the Postgraduate Intelligence Program of the Defense Intelligence College. He would serve subsequently as the Marine Corps Fellow to the Center for Strategic and International Studies (CSIS). He was the first Marine Corps officer inducted as a Term Member of the Council on Foreign Relations.

Returning to the Fleet Marine Force in 1985, he commanded rifle and weapons companies and served as the operations officer of Third Battalion, 4th Marines. During this period he received the Leftwich Leadership Trophy. In 1988, Major General Allen returned to the Naval Academy where he taught international organizations, regional politics, and intelligence in the Political Science Department. In 1990, he received the William P. Clements Award as military instructor of the year.

Major General Allen reported to The Basic School as the Director of the Infantry Officer Course from 1990-1992 and was subsequently selected as a Commandant of the Marine Corps Fellow, serving as a special assistant on the staffs of the 30th Commandant and the Commanding General, Marine Corps Combat Development Command. In 1994, he served as Division G-3 Operations Officer for the Second Marine Division and subsequently assumed command of Second Battalion, 4th Marines; re-designated as Second Battalion, 6th Marines. This unit served with JTF 160 in Operation Sea Signal during Caribbean contingency operations in 1994, and as part of the Landing Force of the 6th Fleet in Operation Joint Endeavor during Balkans contingency operations in 1995-1996. Following battalion command, Major General Allen reported as the Senior Aide de Camp to the 31st Commandant of the Marine Corps, ultimately serving as his Military Secretary. He commanded The Basic School from 1999 to 2001, when he was selected in April 2001 to return to the Naval Academy as the Deputy Commandant. Brigadier General Allen became the 79th Commandant of Midshipmen in January 2002, the first Marine Corps officer to serve in this position in the history of the Naval Academy.

Major General Allen's first tour as a General Officer was as the Principal Director, Asian and Pacific Affairs in the Office of the Secretary of Defense, a position he occupied for nearly three years. Major General Allen graduated with military honors from the Naval Academy with the Class of 1976, receiving a Bachelor of Science degree in Operations Analysis. He is a 1998 Distinguished Graduate of the National War College. He holds a Master of Arts degree in Government from Georgetown University, a Master of Science degree in Strategic Intelligence from the Defense Intelligence College, and a Master of Science degree in National Security Strategy from the National War College. Personal decorations include the Defense Distinguished Service Medal and the Legion of Merit with three Gold Stars in lieu of four awards.

Bevin Alexander is the author of ten books on military history, including *How Wars Are Won, How Hitler Could Have Won World War II, How America Got It Right,* and his latest book *How the South Could Have Won the Civil War.* He was an adviser to the Rand Corporation for a recent study on future warfare and a participant in a recent war game simulation run by the Training and Doctrine Command of the U.S. Army. His battle studies on the Korean War, written during his decorated service as a combat historian, are stored in the National Archives in Washington, D.C. He was formerly on the president's staff as director of information at the University of Virginia, Charlottesville, Va., and is currently an adjunct professor at Longwood University, in Farmville, Virginia.

- He is a specialist on military strategy.
- His book, *Lost Victories*, was chosen by the Civil War Book Review as one of the seventeen books that have most transformed Civil War scholarship.
- He was commander of the 5th Historical Detachment in the Korean War, and received three battle stars for service in the combat zone, 1951-1952. He also received the Commendation Medal for his work as a combat historian.
- He was formerly a teacher at Virginia Commonwealth University, Richmond.

Colonel Kevin Benson, US Army (Retired), retired from the US Army in July 2007 in the rank of colonel, after 30 years of service. His final position prior to retirement from active service was Director, School of Advanced Military Studies. He also served as the Director of Plans, C/J-5, Combined Forces Land Component Command and Third US Army at the opening of hostilities in Iraq, from 2002 to 2003. He works for McNeil Technologies and is currently a seminar leader at the University of Foreign Military and Cultural Studies. He gratefully acknowledges the assistance of COL Robert Burns, Director of the Center for Army Tactics, USACGSC and Prof. Michael Mosser, School of Advanced Military Studies, in the development of this essay.

Major General Daniel P. Bolger of Aurora, Illinois, received his commission from The Citadel in Charleston, South Carolina. He served as a platoon leader, company executive officer, battalion S-4 (supply), and rifle company commander in the 24th Infantry Division at Fort Stewart, Georgia. He went on to teach history at the U.S. Military Academy at West Point, New York. He served as a battalion S-3 (operations) with the 2d Infantry Division in Korea, then joined the staff of the 101st Airborne Division at Fort Campbell, Kentucky. After a year on the U.S. Army staff in Washington, D.C., he took command of an Infantry battalion at Fort Campbell, and afterward served with the Division staff. He commanded a brigade in the 2d Infantry Division in Korea, served with U.S. Joint Forces Command in Norfolk, Virginia, and then returned to the staff of the 2d Infantry Division in Korea. He came back to the 101st Airborne Division as an assistant division commander, followed by service overseas in the current war. He most recently commanded the Joint Readiness Training Center at Fort Polk, Louisiana. Professional education includes the Infantry Basic and Advanced courses, the U.S. Army Command and General Staff College, and the U.S. Army War College.

James Carafano, Ph.D., is a leading expert in defense affairs, military operations and strategy, and homeland security at The Heritage Foundation.

Recognizing that the war against terrorism will be a protracted conflict, Carafano's research focuses on developing the national security that the nation needs to secure the long-term interests of the United States – protecting its citizens, providing for economic growth, and preserving civil liberties.

An accomplished historian and teacher, Carafano was an Assistant Professor at the U.S. Military Academy in West Point, N.Y., and served as director of military studies at the Army's Center of Military History. He also taught at Mount Saint Mary College in New York and served as a fleet professor at the U.S. Naval War College. He is a visiting professor at the National Defense University and Georgetown University.

Carafano is the author of several military history books and studies. His latest is *GI Ingenuity: Improvisation, Technology and Winning World War II* (2006). The book's premise: World War II saw the first generation of young men that had grown up comfortable with modern industrial technology go into combat. These tinkerers, problem-solvers, risk-takers, and day-dreamers were curious and outspoken – a generation well prepared to improvise, innovate, adapt on the battlefield – and win the war.

Carafano also is the coauthor of *Winning the Long War: Lessons from the Cold War for Defeating Terrorism and Preserving Freedom.* The first to coin the term, the "long war," the authors argue that a successful strategy requires a balance of prudent military and security measures, continued economic growth, the zealous protection of civil liberties and winning the "war of ideas" against terrorist ideologies.

In addition, Carafano is the coauthor of the text book, *Homeland Security* published by McGraw-Hill. *Homeland Security* is a practical introduction to everyday life in the new era of terrorism. Numerous key details are addressed, from roles of first responders and volunteers to family preparedness techniques to in-depth descriptions of weapons of mass destruction.

Carafano was also the principal author of the budget analysis in the 2003 Independent Task Force Report, *Emergency Responders: Drastically Underfunded, Dangerously Unprepared*, published by the Council on Foreign Relations. He was also a contributing author to the National Academies Army Science and Technology for Homeland Security 2004 report and co-director of the task force report, DHS 2.0: Rethinking the Department of Homeland Security.

His other works include: Waltzing Into the Cold War, published in 2002 by Texas A & M University; *After D-Day*, a Military Book Club main selection published in 2000 by Lynne Rienner. Carafano is currently writing a book about the role of contractors in support of combat operations. He is also editing the forthcoming book series, "The Changing Face of War," which examines how emerging political, social, economic, and cultural trends will affect the nature of conflict.

As an expert on defense, intelligence, and homeland security issues, he has testified before the U.S. Congress and has provided commentary for ABC, BBC, CBS, CNBC, CNN, C-SPAN, Fox News, MSNBC, NBC, SkyNews, PBS, National Public Radio, the History Channel, Voice of America, Al Jazeera, Telemundo, Al Arabiya and Australian, Austrian, Canadian, French, Greek, Hong Kong, Irish, Japanese, Portuguese, and Spanish television. His editorials have appeared in newspapers nationwide including *The Baltimore Sun, The Boston Globe, The New York Post, Philadelphia Inquirer, USA Today* and *The Washington Times*.

Before becoming a policy expert, he served 25 years in the Army, rising to the rank of Lieutenant Colonel. His areas of expertise included military strategy, joint operations, future combat systems, post-conflict operations, and nuclear weapons. During his service, Carafano served in Europe, Korea, and the United States and was head speechwriter for the Army Chief of Staff, the service's highest-ranking officer. Before retiring, he was Executive Editor of *Joint Force Quarterly*, the Defense Department's premiere professional military journal.

A graduate of West Point, Carafano also has a master's degree and a doctorate from Georgetown University and a master's degree in strategy from the U.S. Army War College. In 2005, Carafano earned Heritage's prestigious Drs. W. Glenn and Rita Ricardo Campbell Award. It is given to the employee who has delivered "an outstanding contribution to the analysis and promotion of the Free Society."

Captain Eric Chevreuil, French Army (Ret.) is currently is a Department of Defense contractor working as a Network System Engineer for ENDWAVE Corporation in Diamond Springs, CA, 95619 and has worked extensively in defeating IEDs. He was a tank company commander, in the 1st Regiment de Cuirassiers, French Army.

John P.J. DeRosa – During Operation Baton Rouge in October 2004, John P.J. DeRosa was assigned as a liaison and advisor to the Iraqi Ministry of Interior, 1st Commando Battalion, on loan from Task Force Steel Tigers (1st Battalion, 77th Armor). Currently, he is the Director of Security, Plans, and Operations, Area Support Team-Balkans, Camp Bondsteel, Kosovo. He received a M.A in National Security Studies and a B.A. in Economics from California State University-San Bernardino. Mr. DeRosa is a regular contributor to professional journals and local newspapers on issues of military operational history, international security, and veterans' affairs. A former armor captain, he served with the 1st Infantry Division in Iraq, Kosovo, and Germany. Additionally, he served as an enlisted soldier in the Hawaii, Tennessee, and New Mexico Army National Guards and as an armor officer in the California Army National Guard.

General James Mattis, USMC, Commander, U.S. Joint Forces Command (USJFCOM) and Supreme Allied Commander Transformation for NATO. General James N. Mattis, USMC is the current Commander, U.S. Joint Forces Command (USJFCOM) and Supreme Allied Commander Transformation for NATO. He previously served as Commanding General, I Marine Expeditionary Force and Commander, U.S. Marine Forces Central Command. He assumed his current assignment on November 9, 2007.

Mattis attended Central Washington University and was commissioned a Second Lieutenant January 1, 1972. As a Lieutenant, he served as a rifle and weapons platoon commander in the 3rd Marine Division. As a Captain, he commanded a rifle company and a weapons company in the 1st Marine Brigade. As a Major, he commanded RS Portland. As a Lieutenant Colonel, he commanded 1st Battalion, 7th Marines, one of Task Force Ripper's assault battalions in Operation Desert Shield and Desert Storm. As a Colonel, he commanded 7th Marines (Reinforced). As a Brigadier General, he commanded 1st Marine Expeditionary Brigade and then Task Force 58 (TF 58), during Operation Enduring Freedom in southern Afghanistan. As the commander of TF 58, he became the first Marine to command a Naval Task Force in combat. As a Major General, he commanded the 1st Marine Division during the 2003 invasion of Iraq and subsequent stability operations in during the Iraq War.

General Mattis played a key role in the April 2004 battle of Fallujah, Operation Vigilant Resolve, by negotiating with the insurgent command inside of the city, as well as playing an important part in the November 2004 battle of Fallujah, Operation Phantom Fury. The General has displayed a deep understanding of the nature of war, an understanding often lost on those of similar rank. As reported in the Los Angeles Times in May 2007, following a Pentagon survey that showed only 55% of soldiers and 40% of Marines would report a colleague for abusing civilians, Mattis told his Marines, "Whenever you show anger or disgust toward civilians, it's a victory for Al Qaeda and other insurgents." Reflecting an understanding of the need for restraint in war, restraint that is a key to defeating an insurgency, he added that, "Every time you wave at an Iraqi civilian, Al Qaeda rolls over in its grave."

The Pentagon announced on May 31, 2006 that Lt. Gen Mattis had been chosen to take command of the I Marine Expeditionary Force based out of Camp Pendleton, California.

General Mattis popularized the slogan **"no better friend, no worse enemy,"** (originally coined by the Dictator Sulla as his own epitaph in 78 BC) for his command. This phrase became widely publicized during the investigation into the conduct of Lieutenant Ilario Pantano, a platoon commander serving under General Mattis.

Ralph Peters, is a retired Army officer and former enlisted man, a strategist and journalist, a novelist and a world traveler— with experience, in and out of uniform, in 70 countries. Peters has appeared on PBS, FOX News, CNN and other networks with commentary on military issues and current affairs. He is the author of 23 books, including the recent book *LOOKING FOR TROUBLE, Adventures in a Broken World*, a memoir of his experiences as a rogue Foreign Area Officer from the dying Soviet Union to the cocaine badlands of the Andean Ridge, and from Pakistan and Southeast Asia to the streets of Los Angeles.

Major James Spies, U.S. Army Special Forces is an Assistant Professor and course directors for the Counterinsurgency (COIN) and Special Operations/ Low-Intensity Conflict (SO/LIC) courses at the United States Military Academy at West Point, New York. He also serves as the Special Forces representative to the Academy. He is also a visiting Assistant Professor at Bard College where he teaches on Irregular Warfare. A Graduate of the Naval Postgraduate School in Monterey California, Major Spies has a Master of Science in Defense Analysis with a focus on Irregular Warfare. He is the author of several articles examining the use of Pseudo Operations in COIN, The tactical Application of the Oil-Spot in COIN, and the similarities between street gangs and insurgent organizations.

Major Klaudius K. Robinson, US Army, of Szcecinek, Poland earned his commission through the ROTC program at Florida Southern College. Commissioned as a 2LT in the Armor branch, he completed and graduated Armor Officer Basic Course and Scout Platoon Leaders Course. Subsequently was assigned as a platoon leader in D Trp, 1-509th Airborne Infantry (OPFOR), Fort Polk, LA where he also served as the Troop executive officer and battalion S-1. Upon successful completion of the Armor Captains Career Course, Combined Arms Services Staff School, and Tank Commanders Certification Course, then CPT Robinson was assigned to 3-67 AR with the 4th Infantry Division at Fort Hood, TX where he deployed in support of Operation Iraqi Freedom I. While deployed he served as the battalion A/S-3 and for several months as the battalion S-3 planning and executing numerous operations including several air assaults.

After returning to Fort Hood, then CPT Robinson assumed command of a newly established brigade HHC for seven months. He was offered command of B Trp 8-10 CAV, and after accepting, he commanded for two years including a second deployment in support of Operation Iraqi Freedom during the "Battle for Baghdad" in the volatile provinces of southwest Baghdad. Currently MAJ Robinson is conducting training to become a European Foreign Area Officer and has completed Serbian-Croatian language training at the Defense Language Institute. He is currently in Serbia conducting his one year in country training. His decorations and badges include two Bronze Stars, the Meritorious Service Medal, the Army Commendation Medal with V Device, the Combat Action Badge, Airborne and Air Assault Badges.

Major Rick Rouzer, **U.S. Army** of Cumberland, MD enlisted in the US Navy in 1976. He completed a 4-year tour as an Aviation Electrician (Support) in Key West, Florida then transferred to the Navy Reserves where he served as a P-3B

Plane Captain in Patuxent River Naval Air Station from 1980-1988. He received his commission from the Pennsylvania National Guard Military Academy in Fort Indiantown Gap, PA in 1989. He served as a Reserve platoon leader and company executive officer in the 365th Engineer Battalion, New Cumberland, PA., before his acceptance into the Active Guard Reserve (AGR) program in 1995. He served as an assistant battalion S-3 (operations) with the 854th Engineer Combat Battalion (Hvy) for three years and spent the next three in Richmond, VA, as a Facilities Management Specialist in the Engineer division of the 9th Regional Support Command. In 2001 he was board selected for a one year command tour with the 793rd Engineer Detachment (Utilities) on the island of American Samoa. This was followed by a three year tour as the Senior Plans Officer for the 9th Regional Readiness Command, based at Ft. Shafter Flats, Oahu, Hawaii. During this time he was command selected to complete a second command tour and lead the 793rd to Tikrit, Iraq. Following a successful combat tour he was assigned to Washington DC, where he is currently serving in the Army Chief of Staff, Installation Management, Army Reserve Office (ACSIM-ODR) as a Strategic Plans Officer. MAJ Rouzer is happily married with six children and four grandchildren.

1LT Kyle T. Trottier, U.S. Army earned a commission from Texas Christian University in 2005. He is a graduate of the Mounted Maneuver Officers Basic Course, Ranger School, Airborne School, and Northern Warfare School. His awards include the Bronze Star, the Army Achievement Medal (2 OLC), The Iraqi Campaign Medal, Global War on Terrorism Service Medal, Army Service Ribbon, Overseas Service Ribbon, the Combat Action Badge, and the German Armed Forces Proficiency Badge in Gold.

Major Diogo P. F. Tavares is a 1998 graduate of Seton Hall University ROTC, commissioned as an Armor Officer. Major Tavares has served as a platoon leader in Korea, executive officer at Fort Knox, KY Battalion Rear Detachment Commander and as Company Commander in garrison at Fort Stewart, GA and combat in Ramadi, Iraq; including countless staff positions at both the brigade and battalion levels. Currently Major Tavares is serving as a Small Group Leader at the Engineer Captain's Career Course at Fort Leonard Wood, MO. He is a graduate of the Armor Basic Officer Course and Armor Captain's Career Course, as well as the Combined Arms Staff Service School, Airborne and Ranger Schools.

Michael Yon (born 1964) is an American author, independent reporter, and blogger. He has been embedded on numerous occasions with American and British troops in Iraq, most prominently with the 1st Battalion, 24th Infantry Regiment (Deuce Four) of the 25th Infantry Division in Mosul, Iraq, a deployment that ended in September 2005. He continues to blog from Iraqi towns and battlefields.

His writing is marked by fondness and admiration for American service personnel and Iraqis who he sees as engaging bravely in nation-building. It is also marked by candor about what he regards as U.S. and Iraqi failures. Because of this candor, in particular Yon's criticism of U.S. leadership during the early days of the Iraqi insurgency, the U.S. military twice banned Yon from Iraq. Among Yon's targets for criticism are military officials who, in his view, hamper independent reporting from the theater. In particular, Yon has accused LTC Barry A. Johnson of US Central Command of "a subtle but all too real censorship" and "ineptitude in handling the press."

In April, 2008, Yon's book Moment of Truth in Iraq was published by Richard Vigilante Books. The book describes how U.S. counterinsurgency methods are creating what Yon sees as a foundation of success in Iraq. Within two weeks of its release date, Moment of Truth entered into Amazon.com's list of Top 10 bestsellers.

Yon's dispatches have been excerpted by several American newspapers, including the Northwest Guardian, the Boston Herald, The Seattle Times, the Star Tribune, and The Weekly Standard. Although his venture initially relied on reader donations, Yon gained the praise of some well known and respected journalists, including Brian Williams, war correspondent Joe Galloway, and Michael Barone, a writer for US News and World Report. Barone has referred to Yon's work in his column.

Yon is a Special Forces veteran. He was charged with killing a man in a barroom fight, but the charges were subsequently dismissed when it was determined that he had acted in self-defense. His book, Danger Close, details this event and tells the story of his life up to the age of about 20, after he had completed the selection and training process for the Special Forces.

Bruce Willis has stated his intention to produce a movie about Deuce Four's deployment in Iraq, to be largely based on Yon's experiences with the unit.

In 2007, Yon was present in Basra with 2 RIFLES during the British withdrawal from the city, and he subsequently visited England, meeting the Duchess of Cornwall, whom he praised for her unstinting support for her troops.

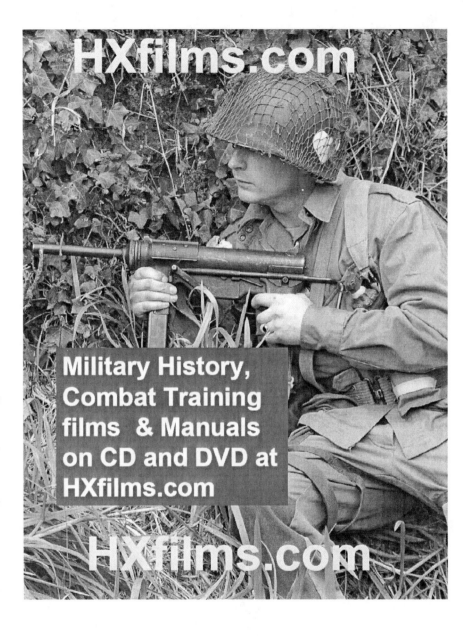